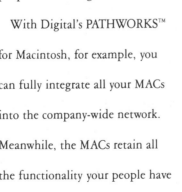

LIVING IN JAPAN

The American Chamber of Commerce in Japan

The American Chamber of Commerce in Japan

President (1993~): Richard J. Johannessen
President (1990-1992): Edmund J. Reilly
Executive Director: William R. Farrell
Chairman, Publications Committee: Paul Hoff
Director of Publications: Carol Simons
Chairperson, *Living in Japan* Book Committee: Linda E. Laddin

Editing, Design, and Production IBI, Inc.

President: Dr. C. Tait Ratcliffe
Managing Director: Thomas R. Zengage
Production Manager: Clyde Newton
Managing Editors: Clare Johnson, Diane Rubinstein, Matthew Clothier, Darrell Hall
Senior Consultant: Sandra Treadwell
Advertising Coordinator: Carolyn Ryan
Printer Liaison: Kazuyuki Shimizu
Designer: Keiko Mitsuhashi
Assistant Designer: Chikako Tomono

Cover Katsunori Hamanishi   # 30056873

Photograph Credits Imperial Household Agency, Chiba Prefectural Government, Hokkaido Prefectural Government, Kanagawa Prefectural Government, Kobe Municipal Government, Osaka Prefectural Government, Saitama Prefectural Government, Chuo Ward (Tokyo), Meguro Ward (Tokyo), Shinjuku Ward (Tokyo), St. Joseph International School, Santa Maria International School, Ira Caplan, Lewis Simons, Nigel Sutcliffe, Clyde Newton, Diane Rubinstein, and others.

©1993 The American Chamber of Commerce in Japan
7th Floor, Fukide Bldg. No.2,
4-1-21, Toranomon, Minato-ku, Tokyo 105, Japan
Tel: (03) 3433-5381   Fax: (03) 3436-1446

Eleventh Edition
Printed in Japan
ISNN: 0913-8102   ISBN: 4-915682-02-1

President's Message

As you open this book, you may well be setting out on the adventure of a lifetime: flying across the vast Pacific to build a new life in a very different environment and culture.

Excited? I bet you are. And I'd guess that you have at least a mild case of the butterflies. I know I did when I first came to Japan, more than 20 years ago. An unfamiliar language and customs, strange foods, tightly packed cities—life here can be overwhelming in the beginning.

Whether you're coming on your own to work or study or you're being transferred to Japan by your employer, before long you'll find you've developed the street smarts of an old hand. And like many of us residents, you may just find that you really enjoy living here.

At the American Chamber of Commerce in Japan (ACCJ) we sincerely hope you are able to thrive and enjoy life in Japan. In fact, let me take that one step further and inform you that we consider your success *vital* to the national interest of the United States of America.

How so? If we are to overcome our much-discussed trade problems with Japan, access to this country will be crucial. And *access* assuredly means much more than a mere absence of tariff barriers.

For example, if we are to learn the ways of the Japanese marketplace and to succeed in it, a growing number of American individuals and families will have to live in this country for extended periods. But if we are to ask our people to make that kind of long-term commitment, cash and career opportunities are only part of the answer. Access to a satisfying lifestyle is thus also imperative.

Having watched Americans come and go from these shores over the years, ACCJ members have learned what really counts: a healthy, happy lifestyle in Japan for the whole family.

And that's what this book is all about. In the following pages, we will introduce you to the community resources, the social activities, the services, and the sources of information that help make life in Japan much more than just bearable.

Read on and I believe you'll find that Americans in Japan are fortunate—at least in the metropolitan centers—to have an extensive network of social services and schools, clubs, and other facilities to ensure their welfare.

That's not to say we've reached perfection—and many lifestyle-related issues await resolution. In some cases, we will rely on our Japanese hosts to make improvements, but in many other instances it will be the volunteer spirit of our community that makes the difference.

Indeed, many of the resources you will find mentioned in this book owe their existence to committed volunteer efforts—some that began decades ago. For many of our international school and health-care facilities, we have to thank 19th-century Christian missionaries. For our community theater, Tokyo International Players, applause should go to the expat drama enthusiasts of the 1890s. And for our crisis hot line in Tokyo, TELL, we are indebted to some very dedicated contemporaries.

These are only a few examples of the "social capital" that underpins our lives here in Japan, and I'm glad to note the spirit that built them remains alive and well, not least among the ACCJ membership. The proof—a fine joint effort by ACCJ volunteers and the experts at IBI—is in your hands.

Although this book has been compiled mainly with Americans in mind, I hope that many new residents from all countries will be able to benefit from the information provided. Let me welcome you all and wish you health, happiness, and prosperity during your time in Japan.

Edmund J. Reilly
President (1990-1992), The American Chamber of Commerce in Japan

Living in Japan

Living in Japan has been in print for more than 30 years, which, in this age of fleeting fads and fashions, qualifies the book as a classic. On the surface, *Living in Japan* may seem to be simply a straightforward, commonsense guide to the opportunities and challenges of moving to and living in a complex and sometimes very foreign country; but it is much more than that.

Living in Japan is the continuation of an ACCJ tradition: each edition of the book builds on the experiences of a new generation of ACCJ members residing in Japan. Among the members of the 1993 *Living in Japan* project team alone, the accumulated Japan experience totals more than 150 years. We have tried to distill the essence of that experience into a practical, easy-to-use handbook that will help you prepare for and make the most of your time in Japan.

By capturing a moment in time and interpreting it for readers, *Living in Japan* also provides a record of the profound changes over the years in the expatriate experience in Japan. A look through the previous 10 editions of *Living in Japan* reveals the many ways in which Japan and the lives of resident expatriates have evolved since the first edition was published in 1961. We hope that we have been as successful as our predecessors in producing a valuable resource for expatriates in Japan.

I would like to take this opportunity to thank the people who gave their time and talents to help create this book: the ACCJ members who reviewed the contents; the guest writers who contributed their prose and their insights; the members of the ACCJ Publications Committee for their support and suggestions; the consular section of the U.S. Embassy for its assistance; and particularly the staff at IBI, Inc., who worked so patiently and thoroughly for so many months.

Charles Binford deserves the credit for launching this project and guiding its initial phases during his two-year tenure as chairman of the Publications Committee. At IBI, Thomas Zengage and Clyde Newton provided the expertise and professionalism required to write and produce this book. Finally, I would like to give my personal thanks to Carol Simons, my committee partner and ACCJ director of publications, for dedicating her considerable editing talents and experience and many hours to this project.

It has been an honor for me to work with all the talented people on the project team. Their work ensures that this edition of *Living in Japan* will continue the tradition of excellence and service established many years ago by the ACCJ members who initiated this publication.

Linda E. Laddin
Chairperson, *Living in Japan* Book Committee

Table of Contents

Featured on the cover of this book is a mezzotint copperplate print entitled *Division–Work No.26* by artist Katsunori Hamanishi. The artist was born in Hokkaido in 1949 and has exhibited worldwide since 1974, receiving numerous awards for his work. He has also been visiting professor at the University of Alberta, Canada. Katsunori Hamanishi is regarded as one of Japan's most promising print artists.

Imagine it moving. The soundtrack is CD-quality Mozart. You've accessed a database half a world away, and it's coming at you in real time. We're talking about your telephone.

NTT is making it happen. By the end of this year, ISDN services will be available to over 90% of Japan's population. Comprehensive VI&P (visual, intelligent and personal) services experiments are underway at our Yokosuka and Musashino R&D Centers. In 1993, they will focus on use of Broadband Integrated Services Digital Networks (B-ISDN).

By the 21st century, our B-ISDN networks will link households throughout Japan. Equipped for high-quality, high capacity digital access to networks around the world, our telephones will be terminals that make access to all forms of information as simple as calling a friend.

And because we're cooperating with other telephone service providers around the world, the friend they call could be you.

NTT

NIPPON TELEGRAPH AND TELEPHONE CORPORATION

1-6 Uchisaiwai-cho 1-chome Chiyoda-ku, Tokyo 100 Japan

It looks like a floral arrangement but it's really a philosophy

Chapter

1

Introduction to Japan

Japan comprises four major islands—Hokkaido, Honshu, Kyushu, and Shikoku—as well as several thousand smaller islands. Its total landmass is 377,812 square kilometers (145,874 square miles), slightly smaller than the state of California. The country's population of 123.6 million is ranked seventh highest in the world after China, India, the United States, Indonesia, Brazil, and Russia. Most of the Japanese islands feature mountain ranges in their interiors, and the larger cities are therefore concentrated in areas close to the sea. Japan has few natural resources and must import almost all its oil and coal. Despite this, and although it is small and densely populated, Japan has become by far the wealthiest nation in Asia and a global economic superpower.

In terms of its economic development, standard of living, trading partners, and political system, Japan is now considered to be part of the West. In many other areas, however, Japan is distinctly Asian. Even though the country may outwardly seem Westernized, it remains part of Asia in terms of its culture, social systems, and daily life.

Although Japan's spoken language does not closely resemble that of Korea or China, the written language is centered on a system of ideograms, or *kanji* (literally, "Chinese characters"), common to both those countries. In addition, the language includes two indigenous syllabaries: *hiragana*, used for phonetic transcription and parts of speech not covered by *kanji*, and *katakana*, used chiefly for transliterating foreign names and words, of which many have become part of daily Japanese.

The Japanese people can be said to adapt well, but the perception that they lack creativity is no more than a myth. At the beginning of the Meiji Era, in the late 1860s, there was a tremendous technology gap between Japan and Europe and the United States. Unable to maintain the state of almost total isolation in which the country had been kept for over two centuries, the government of the time came to believe that Japan would have to imitate the West to survive. By doing so, the country was able to rise as an industrial and military power with remarkable speed. Following the devastation of World War II, Japan found itself in a situation similar to that of the early Meiji Era and spared no effort to imitate and improve upon foreign technology. Its success in these endeavors is recognized and respected throughout the world, and the country has now become a world leader in its own right in the development of advanced technologies.

Japan is a country of paradoxes. On the surface, its bureaucracy does not appear to be a model of efficiency, with an emphasis on paperwork and seemingly endless series of proposals, reviews, and approvals. But the system is effective, formulating coherent policies through consensus, and fully capable of ensuring that the government apparatus functions smoothly in times of political turmoil.

This paradox is reflected in the Japanese company, where employees work considerably longer hours than their Western counterparts while often appearing to be idle or attending unproductive meetings. The success of the Japanese work ethic, however, is rarely disputed.

What are the other reasons behind Japan's extraordinary rise as an economic superpower? One is education. The Japanese people are well educated, with a literacy rate of close to 100%. The education system relies heavily on learning by rote, but the pressure to excel encourages diligence and discipline, other contributors to Japan's success. Also among the country's strengths are superior teamwork and the achievement of consensus through group decision making. Japanese society, indeed, tends to be group-oriented and conformist, with a great emphasis on personal relationships. Other characteristics of Japan's inhabitants that have brought the country prosperity are their perseverance and the prodigious energy that is put into achieving goals.

Although Japan is unquestionably a modern country, certain of its customs have not changed dramatically for centuries. For example, time is still divided into eras of a variable number of years corresponding to the reigns of emperors, the best known of which is perhaps the Meiji Era (1868 to 1912), during which Japan was transformed from an isolated backwater into the leading military power in Asia. This era ended with the death of the Meiji emperor in 1912 and was followed by the Taisho Era (1912 to 1926), during which his son, Emperor Yoshihito, reigned. The Showa Era (1926 to 1989), under Emperor Hirohito, was the longest in the nearly 2,000 years of recorded Japanese history since the early, mythological emperors. The Showa emperor died in 1989 and was succeeded by his son Akihito, marking the start of the current Heisei Era. The year 1993 is thus known as the fifth year of Heisei.

Geography

Japan, as previously stated, consists of four main islands and thousands of smaller islands. The Japanese archipelago extends 2,807 kilometers (1,744 miles) from northeast to southwest, with Japan's southernmost territory at about 25 degrees north and the northern tip of Hokkaido at about 45 degrees north. Hokkaido, Honshu, Kyushu, and Shikoku are the main islands. Honshu includes the Kanto, Chubu, and Kinki (including Kansai) regions, which form the economic and industrial hub of Japan. The twin cities of Kitakyushu and Fukuoka, forming another key industrial zone, lie on Kyushu. Hokkaido, the northernmost main island, is still largely agrarian.

Japan is divided into 43 prefectures, or *ken,* and four areas with equivalent status. The island of Hokkaido, although large, has a relatively low population by Japanese standards and is classified as a region with prefectural status. Tokyo is classified as the capital metropolis, or *to,* consisting of 23 central wards, or *ku,* and 26 outlying cities. Osaka and Kyoto are referred to as metropolitan areas, or *fu,* also consisting of central wards and outlying cities.

Tokyo is situated at 35 degrees north, a similar latitude to that of Santa Barbara, Albuquerque, Memphis, Algiers, Tehran, and Kabul. Okinawa and the other southern Japanese islands are subtropical, with Ishigakijima, one of the Okinawan islands, only about 80 kilometers (50 miles) from the northern coast of Taiwan.

Hokkaido was the last region of Japan to be developed, with full-scale settlement beginning only in the late 19th century. Hokkaido has been far less transformed by industrialization than other regions of Japan and has some of the best agricultural land in the nation.

The city of Wakkanai, on the northern coast of Hokkaido, is only about 48 kilometers (30 miles) from Sakhalin, in the Russian Federation. The southern part of Sakhalin, below the 49th parallel, and the Kuril Islands were Japanese possessions until August 1945, when they were seized by the Soviet Union. Japan recognizes Sakhalin and the islands in the Kuril chain from Urupu northward as Russian territory but claims Kunashiri, Etorofu, and the Habomai and Shikotan archipelagoes, of which control passed from the Soviet

Union to the Russian Federation in 1991, as historical Japanese territories. These sparsely populated but strategically important islands are collectively known as the Northern Territories by Japan, and their return is seen as a precondition for large-scale economic aid to Russia.

The larger Japanese islands all have mountain ranges, with more than 60 active volcanoes and many more dormant ones, such as Mount Fuji, which at 3,776 meters (12,388 feet) is the highest mountain in Japan. Fugendake, a volcano near Shimabara in Nagasaki Prefecture that had been dormant for nearly 200 years, erupted in June 1991, claiming a number of lives and destroying homes and farms.

Japan has become increasingly urban, and the area from Tokyo to Osaka/Kobe is considered more or less a single industrial belt. Japan's cities are often highly built up and may be extremely crowded, but other areas of the generally mountainous countryside are largely unspoiled. There is much beauty in rural Japan, and many of the country's great cultural artifacts, such as its shrines and temples, enjoy perfect natural settings.

Climate

Although there are significant seasonal variations, Japan's climate is generally temperate. Summers are hot and humid, and winters are cool and dry. Temperatures may fluctuate widely from day to day in spring and fall, but April, May, October, and November are generally considered to be the most pleasant months of the year.

Tokyo, which is close to the sea and sheltered by mountain ranges, has mild winters and hot summers. Although Tokyo is situated roughly midway on the Japanese archipelago, in autumn and winter it sometimes has the highest temperatures in the country, excluding Okinawa and other southern islands.

In the Kanto region, which includes Tokyo, the lowest average temperature is approximately 5°C (40°F) and the highest average temperature about 27°C (80°F). In the Kansai and Chubu regions (centered on Osaka/Kobe/Kyoto and Nagoya), temperatures are slightly lower than in Tokyo in winter and slightly higher in summer. Throughout Japan, the hottest month is August, while January and February are usually the coldest months.

Winters tend to be dry in Japan, although there may be a number of rainy days in any month. The Sea of Japan coast, especially the Niigata region and areas further north, frequently has heavy snowfall, but Tokyo may sometimes have no snow at all. When snow does fall, it rarely exceeds a few inches. Kyushu, likewise, has little snowfall, and further south, in Okinawa, winter temperatures usually remain above 12°C (55°F).

All of Japan, with the exception of Hokkaido, experiences two rainy seasons. *Tsuyu,* a mild equivalent of the Southeast Asian monsoon season, begins in early June in most of the country and often lasts until the middle of July. During this period, there are a few sunny days, but usually there will be several days of rain every week, with fairly warm temperatures. There is a second, shorter rainy season from early September to mid-October. This is also referred to as the typhoon season, and in the average year at least four or five typhoons of varying intensity sweep across Japan, with the greatest concentration in September. Typhoons usually travel northwest from their starting points in the Pacific near Guam and the Philippines, taking about a week to reach Japan's shores.

The Kanto region, including Tokyo, is almost never directly hit by typhoons as the surrounding mountain ranges create a protective cordon. However, when typhoons approach within a few hundred miles, heavy rainfall and strong winds are not unusual. Okinawa, Kyushu, southern Honshu, and the Kansai region (Osaka/Kobe/Kyoto) are the areas most frequently hit by typhoons. Suggestions on how to prepare for a typhoon are given in Chapter 6.

A Condensed History

Determining the precise origins of the Japanese people is difficult. Although the overwhelming majority of Japanese resemble such other Mongol peoples as Chinese, Koreans, and Mongolians, there is substantial evidence that southern Asians, perhaps from the Malay region, may also have reached what is now Japan.

Honshu and Kyushu were linked to the Korean Peninsula until the end of the last Ice Age, and Hokkaido was linked to the Eurasian continent through the island of Sakhalin. Archaeological excavations and research have established that the Japanese islands, including what is now the Tokyo area, were inhabited tens of thousands of years ago.

The Ainu, a people with roots in central Asia and possibly Europe, were probably the first settlers. At one time, the Ainu controlled Hokkaido and most of Honshu, but they were gradually driven north by the ancestors of contemporary Yamato Japanese. The few Ainu who remain are concentrated in Hokkaido and have now largely been absorbed into Japanese mainstream society. However, efforts are being made to preserve the Ainu culture and language.

The first Japanese state is said to have emerged at least 2,000 years ago and produced the Shinto religion as well as the first emperors. This early stage of Japan's history is shrouded in legend and speculation, with written records beginning only toward the end of the fifth century when *kanji* ideograms were introduced from China. At this time, Japan also adopted the Chinese calendar, Chinese medicine and astronomy, and the teachings of Confucius. Furthermore, the Chinese form of government was studied, and Buddhism was introduced in the sixth century. It has since peacefully coexisted with Shinto. Commerce between Japan, China, and Korea flourished, and for several hundred years, Chinese coinage was used in Japan.

The first permanent capital was established in Nara in the early eighth century. In 794, the capital was moved to Kyoto, where government and the aristocracy remained for more than 1,000 years. During the years the emperor lived in Kyoto, court officials devoted themselves largely to a life of ceremony and ritual and paid little attention to political or social life in other parts of Japan. At times, an *insei* system prevailed, under which a young, sometimes infant prince would be made the titular emperor, with the previous emperor abdicating his title while assuming true power. In general, however, the emperor and the imperial family rarely played an active role in politics or the rivalries between feudal warlords that characterized this period.

Japan's history is rich with stories of local clans that built their own private armies. One such family, the Taira, took over the reins of government in 1156. In 1192, Yoritomo, head of the Minamoto family, established a military government in Kamakura known as the shogunate. Upon his death, members of his wife's family, the Hojo, carried on ruling until their overthrow in 1333.

The Kamakura Era was to be one of the most interesting periods in Japanese history. The *samurai* were the warriors of the time, loyal only to their overlords, the *daimyo*, who in turn pledged fealty to the *shogun*, or supreme military leader. The nation was militaristic, and the code of *Bushido*—the way of the warrior— embodied the Japanese spirit of chivalry. The *samurai* not only followed their *daimyo* in life but also in death, sometimes committing *seppuku*, or ritual suicide, when the *daimyo* was defeated or died. One of the most celebrated cases—albeit from a later era—is that of the 47 *ronin,* who in 1702, during the Edo Era, followed their feudal leader to death after avenging his dishonor and forced suicide.

Following the overthrow of the Hojo family in 1333 and a brief return to imperial rule, Japan entered the Muromachi Era. Marked by a decline in the authority of the central government and continuous wars between rival clans jockeying for power, this period lasted until 1573.

One of the key events of the era was the arrival of the first Westerners in 1543, when Portuguese traders landed on the island of Tanegashima, off Kagoshima in southern Kyushu. The firearms they brought with them were the first introduction of Western technology into Japan. The Portuguese traders were soon followed by Dutch and English traders as well as Portuguese and Spanish missionaries who converted several tens of thousands of Japanese to Roman Catholicism, mostly in the coastal areas of Kyushu, such as Nagasaki.

In 1603, Tokugawa Ieyasu established himself as *shogun.* Concerned about intrigue and the undue influence of Catholic priests and other missionaries and fearing colonization, the Tokugawa government expelled the Westerners, prohibited Christianity, and persecuted Japanese converts. Ieyasu permitted only restricted trade with the Dutch, Chinese, and Koreans at Deshima, a barren island just off Nagasaki. Thus began the Edo Era, one of the most peaceful in Japanese history and marked by two and a half centuries of almost total isolation.

During the Edo Era, Japanese arts flourished, while advances in European technology managed to creep in through Deshima. Few Japanese, however, had access to European technology or culture, though the Tokugawa government appears to have had at least a rough idea of events transpiring in Asia. Foreigners were not permitted to enter Japan, with the exception of those necessary to maintain the very limited commercial ties at Deshima. Likewise, Japanese were not permitted to leave, and the few who did—generally fishermen who, lost, drifted across the Pacific to the North American continent—were prohibited from returning on pain of death.

In 1853, a U.S. naval officer, Commodore Matthew C. Perry, sailed his fleet of four Black Ships into Uraga Harbor, near present-day Tokyo. This event was the single most important factor in the subsequent opening of Japan to the outside world and the forerunner of trade treaties with the United States, Russia, Great Britain, the Netherlands, and France. The Tokugawa shogunate was not eager to accept Perry's ships nor his demands for the opening of ports, but the superior armament the U.S. ships possessed gave the Japanese authorities little choice.

The Tokugawa shogunate, which had already begun to show signs of decline, disintegrated rapidly after the arrival of the Westerners. The last *shogun,* Yoshinobu, was overthrown in 1868, and power reverted to the direct line of the emperors, in a period known as the Meiji Restoration. The young Meiji emperor, Mutsuhito, established his residence in the *shogun's* former headquarters in Edo, 500 kilometers east of Kyoto, and the new capital was named Tokyo, or "eastern capital." The Meiji Restoration marked the time when the young samurai and members of the nobility began their remarkable work of change and Westernization. The new government's open-door policy, in stark contrast with the isolationism of the Edo Era, paved the way for the development of modern Japan.

A constitutional monarchy was established under the Japanese constitution of 1889. The ensuing modernization of Japan proceeded at a remarkably fast pace, and much emphasis was placed on creating a strong army and navy equipped with the most up-to-date European weaponry. Japan fought and won two wars in this period—the Sino-Japanese War of 1894-1895 and the Russo-Japanese War of 1904-1905. The Russo-Japanese War was especially significant, as Japan was at the outset very much the underdog in its first struggle with a European superpower. A total defeat of the Russian expeditionary forces in Manchuria and Korea was achieved through the perseverance of General Maresuke Nogi, tremendous sacrifices of men and material on land, and the destruction of the Czarist Baltic fleet by a skillful Japanese admiral, Heihachiro Togo.

As a result of these wars, Japan gained Taiwan and Karafuto (the southern part of Sakhalin) and was able to annex Korea in 1910. In 1903, Japan entered into a military alliance with Great Britain and, during World War I, participated on the side of the United States and its allies, occupied German possessions in the Pacific, and was recognized as one of the world's great military powers.

The Meiji emperor died in 1912 and was succeeded by his son, Emperor Yoshihito, and the Taisho Era began. The era was a period of relative liberalism, known as the Taisho Democracy, and of great achievements in the arts. Increasing unrest, however, was characterized by the rise of fanatical nationalist, communist, and anarchist groups. Democratic elections were carried out for the Diet (parliament), with suffrage being reserved for males over 25 years of age.

Emperor Hirohito (known posthumously as the Showa emperor) succeeded to the throne in 1926, beginning the 64 years of the Showa Era. Early in his reign, Japanese military commanders in Manchuria began to exceed the authority they had been granted by the relatively moderate government in Tokyo, resulting in the total takeover of Manchuria and the establishment of a puppet empire, Manchukuo, headed by Pu Yi, the last emperor of China.

In the years that followed, various militarist factions sought to violently usurp the powers of the central government in Tokyo, resulting in the assassination of five prime ministers or former prime ministers during the 1920s and 1930s. Full-scale war with Chiang Kai-Shek's Kuomintang regime in China broke out in 1937, giving rise to trade embargoes and increased tension with the United States. This was eventually to lead to the attack on Pearl Harbor on December 7, 1941.

Japan, by then a member of the Tripartite Alliance with Italy and Germany, was successful in the opening months of the Pacific War. Japanese forces seized Malaya, Singapore, the Netherlands Indies, and the Philippines in addition to vast areas of the southeast Pacific. However, the navy's defeat at the Battle of Midway in June 1942 turned the tide of the war. By the end of 1944, Japan was in a desperate position, running out of fuel and materials and having lost almost all its navy; the government, though, refused to consider surrender.

In August 1945, the war came to an abrupt end with the atomic bombings of Hiroshima and Nagasaki and the Soviet invasion of Manchuria, Sakhalin, and the Kuril Islands. The Showa emperor took the unprecedented step of personally going on the radio to broadcast the news of the end of the war with his memorable words, "We must bear the unbearable." Although fanatical army officers tried to stage a coup d'état to prolong the fight to the last man, the emperor's decision held.

For nearly seven years, Japan was occupied by the Allied Forces, primarily the forces of the United States. Until 1951, the occupation was under the command of General Douglas MacArthur. The United States provided generous assistance to help a devastated

Japan get back on its feet, and the occupation forces disarmed and dissolved the Imperial Japanese army and navy, carried out extensive land reform, and broke up the *zaibatsu,* or industrial conglomerates, that had largely dominated the prewar Japanese economy. In May 1947, a new constitution formulated with the support of the United States came into effect.

During the first two years of the occupation, Japan was virtually destitute. About half of Tokyo had been leveled by bombing, and industrial plants in the major cities had been either destroyed or severely damaged. Food was scarce, and it was only emergency imports from the United States that prevented millions of people from starving. The yen collapsed and became practically worthless, falling from ¥8 to the dollar in September 1945 to about ¥700 per dollar on the black market in 1947. Choice land in Tokyo was very cheap, and people who had invested in real estate then and sold in the 1980s or later easily became millionaires.

Japan's industrial recovery got fully under way after the outbreak of the Korean War in June 1950. The Japanese steel industry bounced back with increased demand. By the time the U.S. occupation was over, food supplies were adequate and the economy was beginning its dramatic recovery.

Japan regained its sovereignty in April 1952, with the promulgation of the peace treaty signed in San Francisco in September 1951. The country renounced its control over Korea, Manchuria, and other nations and areas in Asia that had been taken over. The United States continued to occupy Okinawa and other offshore islands, such as the Ogasawara Islands and Amami-Oshima. The last of these territories, Okinawa, was returned to Japan in 1972.

Japan's recovery from the tremendous damage sustained in World War II was achieved remarkably fast. The standard of living rose rapidly, and by the mid-1950s, it was the highest in Asia. After admission to the United Nations in 1956, Japan secured membership in the Organization for Economic Cooperation and Development (OECD), the Asian Development Bank, and other major international organizations. Japan is now an economic superpower and will, in the future, no doubt assume a more active leadership role in the world community.

When the new constitution came into effect on May 3, 1947, some radical changes were made to establish a democratic form of government:

- The emperor became the symbol of the state. The sovereign

power came to rest with the people instead of with the emperor, who was to preside at state functions and perform other duties but not in any way participate in partisan politics.

• Japan renounced war as a sovereign right of the nation as well as the threat or use of force as a means of settling disputes with other nations. In 1950, toward the end of the occupation, the forerunner of the present Self-Defense Forces was established. The Self-Defense Forces, as their name implies, are intended to be used only for the defense of Japan. Toward this objective, they cooperate with American forces stationed in Japan under a security pact. In 1992, the Japanese Diet passed legislation that permits the Self-Defense Forces to participate in overseas peacekeeping missions mandated by the United Nations, with the exception of armed combat.

• Fundamental human rights were established. The constitution guaranteed universal suffrage for all citizens 20 years of age and over; freedom of speech, assembly, and worship; and freedom of the press as well as other basic human rights.

• The House of Peers was abolished and replaced by a popularly elected Upper House (House of Councilors). The Lower House (House of Representatives) was endowed with preeminence over the Upper House.

• The Cabinet became responsible to the Diet.

Of the five main political parties in Japan today, Jiminto, or the Liberal Democratic Party (LDP), has remained the strongest. Since its establishment in 1955, it has had an outright majority in the more powerful Lower House. Since the party and its conservative predecessors have been in power continuously since 1948, it has largely controlled the political arena during the entire period of Japan's economic growth. The bureaucracy, however, has continued to wield power behind the scenes, and proposed legislation is usually drafted by ministry bureaucrats. A large proportion of LDP Diet members are former civil servants, and several postwar prime ministers have been former senior Finance Ministry bureaucrats.

The major opposition parties are Shakaito, or the Social Democratic Party of Japan (SDPJ); Komeito, or the Clean Government Party, which is the political wing of the Buddhist Sokagakkai religious organization; Minshato, or the Democratic Socialist Party (DSP); Rengo; and Nihon Kyosanto, or the Japan Communist Party (JCP). Rengo, a grouping of moderate, labor union backed politicians, expanded its number of seats dramatically during elections in 1989 and 1990 but suffered a severe setback in balloting for part of the Upper House in the 1992 elections. In these elections, Shin Nihonto, or the New Japan Party, a reformist party established by a former LDP Dietman and prefectural governor, fared remarkably well for a newly organized party, securing four seats.

The SDPJ has been in power only once, for a six-month period in 1947. The opposition parties combined have held a majority in the Upper House since 1989, but the LDP can generally achieve a majority on crucial legislation through cooperation with conservative independents and the increasingly right-leaning Komeito and DSP. Despite a number of major scandals related to bribery and illicit political donations over the years, the LDP's power is unlikely to wane in the foreseeable future.

The Emperor and the Imperial Family

The emperor is the symbol of the state, as stipulated in Article 1 of Japan's constitution. He takes a strictly nonpartisan role and does not have powers related to government but performs a wide range of acts and duties that are defined in the constitution. Thus, he appoints the prime minister, as elected by the Diet, and the chief justice of the Supreme Court, who is nominated by the Cabinet. With the advice and approval of the Cabinet, the emperor performs on behalf of the people such acts as the promulgation of laws and treaties, the convocation of the Diet, the awarding of honors, and the reception of visiting foreign heads of state and government leaders.

Members of the Imperial Family are highly respected by the general public. As part of an unbroken line going back to ancient times, the Imperial Household represents a link with Japan's rich historical and cultural heritage.

The present emperor, Akihito, was born in 1933. He was educated mainly in postwar Japan and as Crown Prince traveled widely both overseas and in Japan. Like his father, the Showa emperor, he is scholarly and especially interested in the sciences. He has striven to bring the Imperial Family closer to the public through increased contact with ordinary citizens during his official appearances. The Empress, who in 1959 became the first commoner to marry an heir to the throne, performs a wide range of official duties and heads several charitable organizations. The Emperor and Empress make state visits together overseas, as often as once a year.

Emperor Akihito's birthday is on December 23. On this day and on the second day of every new year, the palace grounds are open to the public, and thousands of people go to offer their best wishes and get a glimpse of the Emperor and Empress and other members of the Imperial Family, who wave from a glassed-in balcony of the main palace building.

The People

In recent years, the Japanese people have attained a far higher standard of living than at any time in the past. Prewar Japan was not affluent, despite possessing a vast empire stretching from the fringes of the Gobi Desert, in northeastern China, to New Guinea. Whereas the prewar government emphasized the development of heavy industry and armaments, postwar Japan has concentrated on exports, become a leader in advanced technologies, and, in the past 20 years, become a true consumer nation. With the country's new affluence, the Japanese lifestyle has been somewhat modified, and it looks certain to undergo many more changes in the years to come.

Japanese people through the centuries have traditionally lived and worked in groups, individual enterprise not being encouraged. In many areas, however, individuality is becoming more and more apparent. Even the Ministry of Education, usually perceived as being highly conservative, has seen the need for more attention to be paid to the development of individual initiative and creativity in the nation's education system.

Japan has also traditionally been a male-oriented society. Until quite recently, the typical Japanese wife's daily life has been centered on her home and the local community, with much time devoted to the care and education of her children, while the husband's life and most of his social activities have been tied to his work. In this way, the spouses' respective roles in the home and in society have been clearly delineated.

There are, however, definite signs of change. In recent years, women have made significant inroads into the work force, due in part to the fact that the Japanese population is rapidly aging, with the highest life expectancy in the world and one of the lowest birthrates. Almost all Japanese women work before they marry, and many now continue to work after marriage. Although there are still relatively few women in executive or decision-making positions in commerce and fewer still in the civil service, increased expectations among women are resulting in gradual changes in these areas too.

Many traditional perceptions, though, continue to shape the Japanese home. Custom dictates that the Japanese man is deferred to in his household. There is an old Japanese saying that the four things to be feared are "earthquake, thunder, fire, and father." However, in bringing up the children, the wife tends to play a far more important role, especially since the husband is absent most of the day. Total working hours and time spent in work-related recreational activities in Japan are still high compared with other industrialized nations.

The old custom of requiring a bride to live with her husband in the family home is rapidly dying out, as more and more elderly people live independently, away from their children. It has long been said that the Japanese people hold the elderly in high esteem and traditionally feel a great debt to them. In the past, the aged were cared for by their children and grandchildren with love, affection, and respect. No doubt the love, affection, and respect still remain, but—as in many other areas of the world today—extended families are becoming rarer. With the high life expectancy in Japan, more and more aged people are healthy and able to live independently well into their 80s.

By tradition, however, the eldest son and his wife are responsible for looking after the son's parents in their old age, and as a result, in a family with more than one child, the eldest son has often been the last to marry. When the *obaasan* (grandmother) is the most senior person in the household, she truly comes into her own and will be consulted in most matters concerning the home. This tradition is strongest when *obaasan* holds assets in her own name, which she frequently does.

On the other end of the age scale, children are usually treated with a great deal of love and attention. They are indulged, especially in matters of discipline, by parents and grandparents alike, perhaps to compensate for the rigors of school life and the demands that will be made of them at later ages.

Religion

Shinto and Buddhism are the two major religions of Japan. Confucianism, which has now practically disappeared as a system of beliefs (although a temple still remains in the Kanda area of Tokyo), has also had a strong influence on the Japanese mind. The importance of benevolence, propriety, wisdom, and obedience, as emphasized in Confucian philosophy, is a concept that has been carried through from the Edo Era.

Buddhism was introduced into Japan in the sixth century. A tolerant and gentle faith, with high moral and ethical principles and a rich cultural heritage, it spread throughout the country without conflicting with Japan's indigenous religion, Shinto. By A.D. 800, Kyoto had six Buddhist colleges, and the percentage of Japan's population who could read and write had risen substantially. Portuguese travelers in the country in the 16th century estimated that over half the Japanese people were literate—a far higher rate than in Europe at that time. Japanese Buddhism generally falls into the Mahayana branch of Buddhism, the faith prevalent in Korea, China, and other areas of Northern Asia.

Shinto is Japan's oldest belief, with its animist origins dating back over 2,000 years. Like Buddhism, Shinto is not a dogmatic religion demanding exclusive allegiance of its adherents. Because of this, the two faiths have been able to coexist peacefully for more than 1,400 years and have become an essential part of Japan's culture. Shinto and Buddhism are perceived by most people as a part of daily life rather than as intensely held faiths, and the overwhelming majority of the Japanese people observe both religions, each at different times, as called for by social custom.

In Japan, the chief role of Buddhist priests is conducting funerals and memorial services for the dead, which are held at specific intervals over a period of many years. Cemeteries are usually attached to Buddhist temples. There is, of course, far more to Japanese Buddhism than funerals, but most people tend to think of the religion in terms of rites for the dead and the veneration of ancestors.

Shinto, on the other hand, is more closely associated with the living. Many Japanese take their children to Shinto shrines, or *jinja*, soon after birth, and weddings are often Shinto, although Western-style church weddings have become popular recently even among non-Christians. At least two-thirds of the nation's population visit *jinja* at the New Year to pray for health and prosperity. Buddhist weddings and Shinto funerals do also exist but have by now become quite rare.

In the past, governments tended to favor one or other of the major religions. In the Edo Era, Buddhism was favored by the *shogun's* family and thus in ascendancy, while Shinto became the state religion after the restoration of imperial power in the Meiji Era until the end of World War II. The postwar Japanese constitution guarantees complete freedom of worship and mandates a strictly secular state.

Buddhism and Shinto have many offshoots in Japan,

including Sokagakkai and Tenrikyo. These faiths tend to be closely knit, demand strict adherence by believers, and are enthusiastic in recruiting new followers. Sokagakkai, roughly translated as "value-seeking society," is a form of Nichiren Buddhism, although the Nichiren sect has recently excommunicated Sokagakkai as its lay organization as the result of a power struggle. Sokagakkai claims to have roughly 10 million followers, and through its unofficial political wing, Komeito (the Clean Government Party), it has considerable influence.

In addition to the hundreds of major shrines and Buddhist temples throughout Japan, there are innumerable small shrines and Buddhist temples in places where foreign visitors might least expect to find them, on rooftops or wedged between high-rise buildings. Neighbors may cooperate in maintaining a small shrine for their own area. Shrines are usually meticulously kept, and offerings of flowers, fruit, and *sake* are regularly placed there. Many families also keep small *kamidana* (Shinto) and *butsudan* (Buddhist) altars in their homes, the latter of which are used for paying respects to parents, grandparents, and other ancestors who have passed away.

Christianity was introduced into Japan by Saint Francis Xavier, a Spanish Jesuit missionary, in the 16th century and spread rapidly. However, its progress was halted when, in the late 16th century, a Spanish ship was wrecked on the coast of Shikoku and salvaged by the local lord. Angered to see his cargo stolen, the captain threatened to summon the power of the Spanish king, who was then ruler of the Philippines and most of the Americas. Asked how his king had become so powerful, the Spanish captain replied that priests and traders would first establish themselves in a country, to be followed eventually by military contingents. In this way, he insinuated, the Spanish king would take over a country.

Under the Tokugawa government, recognizing this danger, Japan closed itself to both the Spaniards and the Portuguese and ultimately to the English—when their king married a Portuguese princess—and Christianity was forced to go underground to survive. When it was eventually allowed to resurface in 1872, it was discovered that thousands of descendants of the original converts were still practicing their religion in hidden enclaves, mostly in Kyushu.

Today, the number of practicing Japanese Christians is close to 900,000, with slightly more Protestants than Catholics. The activities of Protestant sects date back to 1859, in the form of services for the first foreign residents and clandestine contacts with Japanese people.

Apart from the faiths that have sprung up as offshoots of Buddhism or Shinto, many new religious sects have emerged in postwar Japan, usually under a dominant founding figure. Generally speaking, relations between the various religious sects and faiths have continued to be harmonious, and modern Japan has a high level of religious tolerance.

Words of Welcome

by Robert J. Collins

Japan is a land of mystery and intrigue, skyscrapers and super-highways, tradition and ritual, and computers and high-tech communication.

It is a land of the peaceful tea ceremony and rock gardens and a land of more people than you have ever seen in your life all attempting to enter your subway car.

Japan is the land of *sumo,* an ancient sport that dates back 2,000 years. It is also the land of instant televised replays—employed for the first time anywhere in the world—to determine winners in *sumo.*

In Japan, Western housing is considered relatively inex-pensive at $5,000 per month, while a Japanese "salaryman" might find lunches relatively expensive at over $5 per meal. Japanese think that they know America and Americans, but they wonder why Minneapolis and Indianapolis are not twin cities.

Japanese people are industrious, dedicated, hardworking, and self-sacrificing. However, everyone stops what they are doing in springtime when the cherry trees bloom so that they can be dutifully admired.

Japanese families spend nearly twice as much as American families on leisure activities and entertainment, yet the average working day in Japan is nearly 10 hours.

Americans in Japan include doctors, lawyers, scientists, technicians, military personnel, bankers, secretaries, teachers, businesspeople, fashion models, journalists, students, diplomats, housewives (and househusbands), advisers, practitioners of witch-craft, frauds, and garden-variety weasels. However, if the total number of all residents of Japan were to be expressed as a segment of a 24-hour clock, Americans would represent less than two minutes.

Will you like living in Japan? You will and you will not. As with anything dynamic, complex, and different, there are the normal challenges of adapting to your environment that must be overcome. It is, quite simply, a matter of attitude. Fortunately, the structure for support exists—as you will discover reading this book.

When it comes right down to it, the successful management of your professional and personal life is a function of relationships with other people. Rarely will you find an international situation where those relationships are more respected than they are in Japan. The treasures of Japan are not the silk screens in museums or the poetry and literature in libraries. The treasures are the people.

Add to that the worldwide significance of business decisions made in Japan, and the fact that the international schools are among the best in the world, and you will find that Tokyo is one giant, walk-through restaurant. With an abundant number of facilities and random violence about as common as colliding planets, you are likely to come to appreciate a lifestyle all but forgotten elsewhere. You could, as the philosopher said, find worse.

Welcome to Japan.

Bob Collins, a former president of the Tokyo American Club, has written extensively during his stay in Japan. His first novel was *Murder at the American Club* (published by Tuttle).

Smart thinking.
It's Japanese companies using American know-how to get Japanese products to American customers.

NISSAN

TAKASHI MUROSAWA
Marketing and Sales Department
Latin America and the Caribbean
NISSAN MOTOR CO., LTD.

They're using the same service and know-how companies in the United States have come to depend on over the years.

NEC

SOICHIRO OSAKA
General Affairs Division
NEC CORPORATION

They're using Federal Express.

And like them, you get 72 outbound flights every week from Japan to the U.S., Asia and Europe. Your cargo, like theirs, can be computer-tracked, all the way.

CASIO

TETSUSHI ICHIMORI
International Marketing Headquarters
Timepiece Division
CASIO COMPUTER CO., LTD.

All this means we can deliver absolutely, positively by 10:30a.m. the next morning* to most mainland U.S. cities.

⊕TDK

YUICHI KOSUGI
Logistics Section
Overseas Administrative Dept
Electronic Components & Syst
Sales & Marketing Group
TDK CORPORATION

In fact, the same Federal Express technology you get at home, you get right here.

MADA

MASAMI OKUMURA
Export & Import Section
Overseas Administration Dept.
AMADA CO., LTD.

*USA local time. Some conditions and limitations apply. Call for details.

0120-00320

Toll-free number

FEDERAL EXPRESS

Packages, Document
& Freight Worldwid

Chapter

2

Language and Customs

Japan is a country with a long history and a rich culture. The Japanese language has evolved to reflect this culture and the various levels of social interaction that characterize it. While you will not be expected to be an expert on Japanese customs, any efforts you make to speak the language and follow the rules of etiquette in Japan are likely to be highly appreciated.

This chapter will introduce you to the Japanese language and a few of Japan's customs and give you some tips on avoiding faux pas. When in doubt, a simple *sumimasen* ("please excuse me") or *gomen-nasai* ("I'm sorry") will usually serve to right all but the most grievous errors.

The Japanese Language

Many people find that they can get by in Japan with little knowledge of the language, but most will agree that learning to speak some Japanese adds greatly to the overall experience of living here. Without any Japanese at all, you will certainly encounter a few difficulties; simply asking directions or ordering in a restaurant may be frustrating, especially if you venture outside Tokyo. If you are in Japan for an indefinite period, or if your interests or future plans involve Japan, you may wish to start learning the language as soon as possible.

To some extent, you will need to decide what your priorities are in learning Japanese. Some courses focus on everyday language, some on business Japanese. Some stress speaking, while others emphasize reading and writing. You should have no problem finding a class or combination of classes to suit your particular requirements.

Spoken Japanese is unlike English and most Western languages in the degree to which vocabulary and grammatical forms vary according to levels of politeness; you will find yourself using a style of speech with your friends that is very different from the one you will use in a business meeting.

To add to the complexity, written Japanese comprises three writing systems: *kanji, hiragana,* and *katakana.* Reading a vernacular newspaper or book requires knowledge of all three.

Kanji is the beautiful but sometimes frustrating system of ideograms, or characters, borrowed from China. A serious investment of time and effort is required for *kanji* study; you must be familiar with over 1,500 characters before you can be considered "proficient," although recognizing a few *kanji* will allow you to start reading signs in subways and shops.

Hiragana and *katakana* are phonetic syllabaries, quite easy to learn and use. *Hiragana* is the newest of the systems; it was originally created for the use of women only, and some of Japan's great works of literature were written entirely in this style. *Katakana* was developed for the transcription of Buddhist sutras into Japanese; today, it is used mainly for writing foreign loanwords, of which there are many.

The amount of time and effort you spend on learning Japanese will depend on a number of factors: how long you will be staying in Japan, whether you will continue to be involved with Japan after you leave the country, how much you like learning a foreign language, and, of course, the amount of time you can spare for study.

Once you have resolved to study Japanese, you have a number of ways to go about it. There are hundreds of language schools in Tokyo and other major cities, and they vary in teaching methods and tuition costs; small classes will generally be more expensive than large classes. Private lessons are also available, either at a school or in your home or office. Some companies encourage their employees to learn Japanese by footing the bill for classes. Alternatively, the language—particularly written Japanese—can be mastered through self-study, and many excellent *kanji, hiragana,* and *katakana* textbooks and workbooks are available at foreign-language bookstores throughout Japan.

If you would like to set some tangible goals for yourself, you can take the annual Japanese proficiency tests, the *Nihongo Noryoku Shiken.* Passing each of the four levels will give you an objective assessment of your progress.

Bowing

Bowing is a complex ritual in Japan, with the angle of the bow determined by your relationship with the other person, relative company rank, age, and the circumstances. Foreigners, of course, are not expected to understand all the subtleties of this formalized system. When meeting a Japanese person for the first time, you should bow (but not at an extreme angle), say "*hajimemashite*" ("pleased to meet you"), and if it is a business appointment—and often even if it is not—proceed to exchange business cards.

There is also a possibility that the person to whom you are being introduced will offer to shake hands. This is an automatic reaction of many Japanese when they are introduced to foreigners. Indeed, Japanese people sometimes shake hands with each other, especially if it is a casual situation, not a first meeting, and the other person is close in age. If you are not sure how or whether to bow or whether to opt for the handshake, just follow the example of those around you or ask advice from a Japanese friend or colleague beforehand.

Meishi

Business cards, or *meishi,* are absolutely essential in Japan. Almost everyone in Japan has a *meishi* except children.

Meishi will probably be exchanged whenever you meet someone for the first time, so it is a good idea to have a supply of your cards with you at all times. If you are working for a Japanese or foreign company or organization in Japan, your office will almost certainly prepare *meishi* upon your arrival and provide you with a steady supply. If, however, you are an independent entrepreneur, order your *meishi* as soon as possible. One side of the *meishi* should be printed in Japanese and the other in English.

It is standard practice to exchange *meishi* after being introduced. You should give and receive the *meishi* with both hands; if in a meeting, once you are seated, you should place the *meishi* you have just received on the table and keep it there during the meeting. Do not write on it, at least not in view of the giver. Always retain *meishi*; not only will they help you remember the often bewildering number of unfamiliar names you will encounter, but they will also have addresses and telephone and fax numbers you may need.

Table Etiquette

There is a huge variety of restaurants in Japan, and as in any country, dining manners vary with the quality of the restaurant.

Before and sometimes after your meal, most restaurants will provide an *oshibori* (a wet washcloth) with which to wipe your hands. *Oshibori* are usually warm during the cooler months and chilled during the summer, adding a refreshing and pleasant touch to dining out.

Japanese, Chinese, and Korean food is almost always eaten with *hashi* (the honorific *o* often precedes the word), or chopsticks. If you have difficulty using *hashi,* many restaurants can also provide you with a knife and fork. Etiquette pertaining to the use of *hashi* is simple. Always hold both sticks in the same hand; never pick up food using one stick in each hand. Avoid leaving your *hashi* stuck into your food during the meal, and never pass food from your chopsticks to someone else's, as this mimics a traditional funeral ceremony ritual used in crematoriums and is considered to be in very bad taste.

At a formal buffet or family-style meal, if the dishes are not accompanied by a spoon or *hashi,* turn your own *hashi* around before helping yourself, holding them from the ends you put into your mouth so that only the "clean" ends are used for the serving dish. Once you have finished eating, place the *hashi* neatly across the top of your rice or soup bowl.

Something else to remember is that most Japanese people slurp when eating noodles, and rather than being in bad taste, this is considered a sign of enjoyment and appreciation of the food. Do not hesitate to give it a try.

In Japan, drinking etiquette requires the ritual pouring of beer or *sake.* Ideally, you should not pour your own drinks, and it is polite to raise your glass so that your host can fill it with ease. Make sure your host also has a full glass before the opening *"kanpai,"* or "cheers," and throughout the meal.

Footwear

Shoes, considered dirty, are never worn in Japanese homes (and often not in the homes of foreigners who live in Japan), regardless of whether the floor has a carpet, *tatami* (straw mats), or tiles. In a Japanese home, there is an area just inside the front door, the *genkan,* for removing shoes; having taken them off you will usually be offered slippers.

If you use the toilet, you will find another pair of slippers there for use in that room only; don't forget to change back to the house slippers before leaving the toilet. The traditional Japanese toilet does not have a raised seat like the Western type but is at floor level. About half the toilets in Japan are now the Western type, but the Japanese "squat" type is still prevalent in older buildings, railway stations, and Japanese-style homes. When using this type of toilet, squat down facing the raised end of the rim.

Shoes are worn in offices, except for small offices in apartment buildings or in very old buildings with fragile floors. Japanese restaurants often have *tatami,* and in such establishments you will be expected to remove your shoes before dining.

Tipping

One of the most pleasant surprises for newcomers to Japan is that, with very few exceptions, tipping is not expected. In fact, the rule is "don't tip," as this custom has fortunately never been adopted in Japan.

Salaries of hotel staff, waiters and waitresses, and taxi drivers are considerably higher than in other countries, such as the United States, and consequently people in these positions do not depend on tips for their livelihood and will be surprised or unwilling to accept them.

Certain exceptions to the tipping rule do exist, although few and far between. Staff at some *ryokan* accept gratuities, as will, for instance, the *dekata,* employees of the traditional tea houses who purvey food and drink to most of the better boxes and seats at *sumo.* In the rare instance that you give a gratuity to someone in Japan, your thoughtfulness will be appreciated if you place the money in an envelope, as is customary.

Gift Giving

Gift giving has been an elaborate social ritual in Japan for centuries. Gifts are given to express gratitude for past or continuing favors, in anticipation of future favors or services, to show respect for a superior, or in return for gifts previously received. Japanese companies routinely exchange seasonal gifts with clients and contractors.

There are two traditional seasons for gift giving in Japan: *oseibo,* in December, and *ochugen,* in July. During these periods, department stores and some smaller shops display a wide selection of elaborately wrapped gifts that are usually delivered directly to the recipient. The cost of these gifts ranges from ¥3,000 to ¥10,000 or more, depending on the relationship, either business or personal, in question. The items most commonly sent as *oseibo* and *ochugen* gifts are high-quality foods or beverages—such as ham, canned fruit, coffee, and beer—but nonedible items, such as towels or soap, are not unusual.

If the gift is being sent to a company, rather than to a certain individual in management, it should be consumable in an office environment. Nonalcoholic beverages, coffee, tea, cakes, chocolates, and fruit are ideal. Although cash is never sent as an *oseibo* or *ochugen* gift, department store coupons and book, beer, restaurant, and other vouchers and prepaid cards are widely used as personal gifts.

There are three common types of monetary gifts in Japan. Wedding gifts are always in the form of money and are presented in decorated envelopes called *shugi bukuro.* Crisp, new bank notes should be used if possible. The average wedding gift is ¥30,000, but the amount varies between ¥10,000 and ¥60,000 or more, depending on your relationship with the bride or groom. Never give ¥40,000, as the word for four in Japanese, *shi,* also means death.

Money is also used for *koden,* or condolence gifts. It is placed in a funeral money envelope, or *bushugi bukuro,* which is similar in appearance to the *shugi bukuro* used for weddings but has a black border. If the deceased was Christian, a slightly different *bushugi bukuro* with a cross in its design should be used. You may present the *bushugi bukuro* at either the wake or at the funeral itself; there will be a reception desk where you can offer your condolence gift and sign the register. If you plan to attend both, present the condolence money at the wake.

Shugi bukuro and *bushugi bukuro* are available at stationery shops and convenience stores. Use a felt Japanese-style calligraphy pen to write your name and the amount on the envelope. (You can ask a Japanese friend or colleague to help you.)

In return for monetary gifts, wedding guests usually receive a bag of gifts, such as tableware or towels, at the reception or when they leave. For funerals, similarly, it is customary for the bereaved to send gifts to those who offered condolence money, generally after the 49-day Buddhist mourning period.

The third type of monetary gift is *otoshidama.* This is a gift given to children, from kindergarten to high-school age, on New Year's Day or shortly thereafter and need only be given to relatives (including relatives by marriage). Money or gift coupons are placed in a decorated envelope, with the amount varying according to the age of the child.

If you are visiting a Japanese friend's home for the first time, after a long interval, or at a festive season, you should take a small gift, such as wine or sweets.

Doctors and nurses at hospitals are often given gifts by patients or the families of patients. These gifts are usually foods or beverages—for example, whiskey or wine—rather than cash. If you employ domestic help, such as part-time maids or gardeners, who are paid hourly wages and receive no bonuses, it is a good idea to give them gifts during the *oseibo* or *ochugen* seasons. Vouchers, coupons, prepaid cards, or cash would be appropriate.

In Japan, it is not customary to open presents when they are offered but rather to take them home unopened or to open them once the guests have departed. Hence, if you are given a gift, do not open it unless you are asked to do so. Likewise, if you give gifts, do not expect the recipients to open them in front of you.

Weddings

Japanese weddings, or *kekkonshiki,* are often expensive, lavish affairs held at hotels or special wedding halls. The cost of the average wedding, where the reception is attended by several hundred people, is about ¥7 million, including the cost of the honeymoon. By tradition, the parents of the bride and groom split the wedding expenses equally.

The wedding ceremony itself takes place earlier in the day, often with just relatives and close friends present. Traditional wedding ceremonies are Shinto, but in the last decade, Christian ceremonies have become popular and are considered quite fashionable.

Although some variations have appeared in recent years, most Japanese-style wedding receptions tend to follow a similar pattern. The *nakodo,* or go-between (almost every couple selects a go-between for the wedding, even if, as in most cases, the marriage has not been arranged), makes a speech, followed by speeches by friends, supervisors from the office, and colleagues. Finally, the go-between proposes a toast, and the wedding party gets under way with more speeches. Very large weddings have a buffet-style meal, while for smaller receptions there is usually a sit-down dinner. The average length of the party is about two and a half hours, during which time the couple may change their attire two or three times, from traditional Japanese wedding dress to Western-style tuxedo or gown.

Male guests at a wedding are expected to wear dark suits, white shirts, and white ties. Women may wear either a *kimono* or Western-style formal attire.

Funerals

In Japan, funerals are usually held between two and four days after a death. On the night before the funeral, an *otsuya*, or wake, is held. There may be two wakes if the funeral is several days after the death.

Appropriate attire for men at wakes and funerals is a dark suit, white shirt, and black tie. In fact, the suit and shirt worn to a funeral may be the same as those worn to a wedding, with the only difference in dress being a black instead of a white tie. Women wear a black dress or black *kimono*. Pearls may be worn, but any other jewelry should be minimal.

Japanese wakes can be somewhat similar to Irish wakes: after the Buddhist priest has finished conducting the service, friends and relatives will eat and drink while reminiscing about the deceased.

The actual funeral takes place the next day, usually around noon, and is divided into two parts: the *ososhiki*, or funeral service, conducted by a priest or priests, and the *kokubetsushiki*, or farewell ceremony, which includes speeches by friends and relatives. The whole service takes about two hours.

In the case of a company executive, former executive, or other dignitary, there are invariably two and sometimes even three funerals. The first funeral, known as the *hiso*, or private funeral (often private in name only), is followed by the *shaso* (company funeral) or *honso* (formal funeral), usually held at a large funeral hall.

You may be invited to an *isshuki, sanshuki,* or *nanashuki,* memorial ceremonies held to commemorate the first, third, or seventh anniversary, respectively, of a death. Dark attire is worn at these occasions too.

A new experience lies waiting.

Around each corner it's waiting.
Something new to see or do.
A new taste to savor.
Warmly surrounded in hospitality
that comes from the heart.
And where American Express is always welcome.

Don't leave home without it.®

Chapter

3

Office and Home Life

Corporate Life

Before World War II, the Japanese economy had been largely controlled by the *zaibatsu,* or industrial conglomerates that held virtual monopolies on business. These emerged in the Meiji Era when Japan began its age of industrialization, continued to expand during the Taisho and early Showa years, and played an essential part in sustaining Imperial Japan's war machine.

During the occupation, the *zaibatsu* were compelled to dissolve, and free enterprise was encouraged. Although the *zaibatsu* were broken into smaller corporate units, many of the companies spawned by this process maintained ties with other segments of the former conglomerates. Indeed, a great number of present-day Japan's *keiretsu,* or large corporate groups, trace their history back to the *zaibatsu,* and many companies within these groups maintain close ties, including cross-shareholding and mutual personnel transfers.

Vital links between major industries and banks also exist. A high-ranking director of a major company may also be an influential member, or even the chairman, of the board of directors of a major bank. It is not uncommon for the board member who doffs his industry cap and dons his banking cap to recommend financial assistance to his own company. A company that appears to be in financial trouble will often be bailed out or have a merger arranged by its principal bank. The motivation for such actions stems from the system of extensive cross-shareholding among the major Japanese corporations; however, there are those who doubt the long-term viability of this system.

If you are interested in learning more about the structure of modern-day business in Japan, a number of excellent books on the subject are available at the larger bookstores stocking English-language publications, such as Maruzen and Kinokuniya.

The "Salaryman"

Among the best-known representatives of corporate Japan is the Japanese "salaryman." A hardworking, lifetime company employee, the average salaryman has played a large part in bringing about the "Japanese miracle."

The relationship between large Japanese companies and their employees differs substantially from the corresponding relationship in Western companies. Japanese companies select their employees on the basis of examinations given to high-school and college students, during their senior year. The student goes to work for the company immediately upon graduation. Although the personnel department may consider the new employee's career aspirations, the final decision regarding job allocation lies with the company; in Japan, you apply for the opportunity to work for a given company rather than for a specific position. Likewise, subsequent transfers and reassignments are at the discretion of management.

Until recently, it was extremely unlikely that a salaryman would leave the company to accept a better offer, and another large company would be very hesitant about hiring a mid-career worker. In recent years, however, switching jobs and executive recruitment have become increasingly common in Japan, although the majority of workers still work for the same company throughout their career. The predominant "lifetime employment system" allows Japanese companies to invest heavily in the training and education of their staff. The salaryman thus dedicates himself wholly to his company. In return, he enjoys many valuable fringe benefits, for example, low-rent company housing and paid transportation costs and medical care. Unless a flagrant violation of company rules is committed, an employee will never be fired, and rarely will a worker be dismissed for inefficiency or prolonged illness.

Nearly all large companies own lodges in resort areas where employees and their families can enjoy moderately priced vacations. The company may also maintain a store where employees can buy furniture, clothing, electric appliances, TVs, and other goods at discount prices. Lunches are often subsidized, and if needed, an interest-free loan can usually be obtained from the company.

Retirement is generally at 60 or 62 years of age, and an employee will receive separation pay of over one month's salary for every year worked with the company. With the lifespan of the Japanese already the longest in the world—and continuing to increase—the retirement age is likely to rise to 65 and perhaps

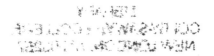

even 70 years of age. In the past, retirees have had little hope of finding a new employer, but today the employee retiring at the age of 62 may continue to work on a part-time basis, perhaps even with his "former" company or one of its subsidiaries. This long and usually beneficial relationship between the Japanese salaryman and his company remains one of the cornerstones of modern Japanese society. It will be interesting to see if and how this relationship changes as Japan becomes more leisure-oriented.

The "OL"

More than 65% of adult Japanese women are employed. Until the late 1980s, the traditional employment pattern for Japanese women was to enter the work force after graduating from high school, junior college, or university, work for several years, and then leave.

A large proportion of Japanese women become "OLs" (office ladies). Almost all Japanese companies, even smaller firms, employ OLs. They usually handle secretarial or clerical work, such as making copies, typing, and organizing material for their supervisors.

As this kind of position affords little opportunity for career advancement, most OLs have, until recently, resigned after getting married, often to men working in the same company. Japanese women tend to marry in their mid-to-late 20s. Many devote themselves full-time to keeping house and raising children, usually returning to work, perhaps in a part-time sales position, in their late 30s or early 40s, after their children have entered high school.

This pattern, however, has begun to change. Now, nearly 50% of married women work outside the home, and approximately 40% of these married women have children. Although the perception most Japanese men have of the role of women in the workplace has changed only marginally in the past decade or so, a labor shortage, the declining birthrate, and an aging work force are likely to result in an improvement in career prospects for Japanese women. The rush to marry by a given age, say 26 or 27, is less apparent today, and more and more Japanese women are choosing to remain single into their 30s. At least a fourth of the women in Japan are still single on their 30th birthday.

In the early 1980s, the Diet enacted an equal employment law that supposedly prohibited sexual discrimination in hiring and mandated equal compensation. The law, however, had no teeth—no punishment for offenders was stipulated—but the government did put pressure on larger corporations to follow the spirit of the law, and this has led to many companies opening management positions to women. Some companies are also guaranteeing women who resign because of childbirth the right to return to their former jobs at the same salary levels as soon as they are able to begin working again. Thus, women who have recently graduated from college can opt for either an OL position or a career that may lead to management. However, many Japanese women who have chosen to pursue a career have complained that their male colleagues expect them not only to fulfill management responsibilities but also to perform clerical tasks.

Perhaps the most affluent Japanese working women are middle-aged OLs. These women elect to remain single or postpone getting married and remain in clerical positions for their entire career. Their salaries and fringe benefits increase with seniority, and as they work less overtime than men, they enjoy a relatively comfortable lifestyle.

The advance of office automation will eventually reduce the need for OLs, while a declining and aging population will simultaneously open more doors for women in management and other professional positions. Therefore, assuming women's junior colleges and other educational institutions begin to train women to perform more challenging roles in the workplace, it is quite probable that the future holds much better career opportunities for Japanese women.

Business Attire

The standard attire for male Japanese company employees (and government officials), from the youngest recruit to the president, tends to be a sober suit, usually gray, blue, or beige. Shirts are almost invariably white. Neckties, while traditionally conservative, are the one part of the business wardrobe where the modern salaryman can express his individuality. During the summer months, most men wear short-sleeved shirts, although jackets are worn for formal meetings.

Some companies, including all Japanese banks, require female office workers and clerks to wear a uniform. While the majority of companies have no uniform, women tend to dress conservatively in short- or long-sleeved blouses and suits.

The Japanese Home

Some foreigners are puzzled by the fact that they are never invited to a Japanese home. Actually, the Japanese rarely entertain in their homes as Americans do, largely due to the lack of space. There is no reason to feel slighted, and unless you are on particularly good terms with a Japanese friend, you may never visit a home. It is simply not customary. However, if you want to visit a typical Japanese household, this can be arranged by JNTO Tourist Information Centers (TICs, see directory for telephone numbers). Details regarding such visits are published in the *Tour Companion.* You can also get a feel for the traditional Japanese home by staying in a Japanese-style inn, or *ryokan,* while traveling in Japan.

Few Japanese living in urban areas can afford to own a house because of the shortage of space and the high cost of land. Even the homes of those who can afford to pay the usually prohibitively expensive real estate prices tend to be small and crowded and have very little extra room for the large number of domestic gadgets and modern conveniences. The ideals of simplicity and elegance that underpin traditional Japanese thinking about the home are often incompatible with the realities of modern life. Nonetheless, the ideals remain.

In the late 1980s, the exorbitant price of land in large Japanese cities soared still higher, a consequence of what was termed the "bubble economy." Many people became millionaires almost overnight simply by owning small plots of land in the cities. The price of condominiums in and around Tokyo rose well out of the reach of the average Japanese office worker, even within the framework of a 20- or 25-year mortgage. Rents also rose. However, in 1991, the bubble burst, land prices dropped marginally, and the government declared its intention of bringing the cost of a home down to a level equivalent to five years' wages for the average male company employee.

These developments are good news for the prospective Japanese homeowner and may indicate housing is becoming more affordable in Japan. Although recently there has been much construction of new, Western-style apartments and houses, there are still many houses that reflect traditional construction and design.

The traditional Japanese home has thick *tatami* (straw mats) covering the floor. In eastern Japan, *tatami* measure approximately 90 by 180 centimeters and are about 6.5 centimeters thick (western Japan has a different standard size). A room's size is designated by the number of *tatami* it equals, and you will often hear Japanese refer to six-mat rooms, eight-mat rooms, and so on.

Rooms are separated by sliding screens called *fusuma.* These are made of heavy paper stretched over wooden frames and are decorated with traditional or modern designs. In a Japanese home, doors usually slide, and houses often have three or four sliding glass doors across the entrance. For protection from wind and rain, there are sliding wooden or metal doors called *amado,* which can be closed to cover the outer glass doors.

Inside the glass doors, there may be a *roka,* a corridor about 90 centimeters wide. The inside boundary of the *roka* is lined with *shoji,* sliding panels covered with a special, thick paper that lets in light.

In the living room of most Japanese houses, there is a *tokonoma,* a small alcove that is reserved for objets d'art, *ikebana* (flower arrangements), and a *kakemono* (a long, narrow scroll). *Kakemono* are often beautiful works of art and are justly treasured.

Home heating and cooling systems vary with the style and age of a house. In modern concrete buildings, central heating and air-conditioning units are now extremely common. In traditional houses, however, central heating is rare. With their sliding doors and relatively thin walls, traditional Japanese homes tend to be drafty, and heating them can be difficult. Even in wealthy households, heating is usually supplied by kerosene, propane gas, or electric heaters in each room and by the *kotatsu.*

The *kotatsu* occupies the pride of place in the middle of the main *tatami* room, and, in a sense, it represents the center of the home itself. The *kotatsu* is a table about 45 centimeters high, under which, in a traditional Japanese house, there is a deep hole in the floor. In the winter, hot coals glow at the bottom of the *kotatsu* and a heavy quilt is draped over the table. The family gathers around this table, sitting on floor cushions, called *zabuton,* huddling under the quilt, and dangling stockinged feet into the *kotatsu* area. These pits are not a feature of most modern homes, and nowadays many people have electric *kotatsu,* which work on a similar principle except that the warmth is provided by an electric heating unit affixed to the underside of a movable table. In either case, when cold hands and feet are tucked under the quilt, warmth seeps through the body. Sharing a meal or simply relaxing around the *kotatsu* is the Japanese equivalent to the family gathering in front of the fireplace.

Before the evening meal or before retiring, the family will bathe. Traditionally, Japanese people do not bathe in the morning, although nowadays showers in the morning or during the day are common. The classical *furo* (often referred to in its honorific form as *ofuro*), or bathtub, is deep and made of wood, but modern homes will usually have a ceramic or plastic tub. Water is heated by an attached burner, and you will find that most Japanese like their baths extremely hot. In a Japanese bath, you wash and rinse off thoroughly outside the *furo* before getting in it, because the water is not usually changed after each person bathes. Whether you bathe in a private home or at a Japanese inn, follow the same procedure—make sure you are completely clean before getting in the tub, and never use soap once inside it.

In traditional homes, when it is time for bed, the table is removed from the main room, transforming it into the master bedroom, or in some cases, the only bedroom. Quilt-like mats, called *futon,* are spread out on the *tatami* for sleeping. Pillows are a little firmer than most Americans are used to, and there will always be one or more quilts to curl up under in the colder months.

Housing standards have improved in recent years, in terms of both space per family and the quality of household equipment. Refrigerators, microwaves, color TVs, videocassette recorders, stereos, personal computers, washing machines, and other appliances are found in almost all homes. Also, Western-style furniture—such as beds, chairs, and kitchen tables—is increasingly being used by many younger couples, even though it makes less efficient use of the limited space available.

Despite the high cost of land, the next few years may see further improvement in the quality of living space. Government agencies are constructing thousands of rental apartments in suburban housing developments. However, the waiting lists for these housing units are long, and tenants must be selected by lottery. Many upmarket apartments (known in Japanese by the English word "mansion") are purchased as condominiums.

In addition, many large Japanese companies provide their staff, especially young, single employees, with affordable housing. In spite of these positive factors, the scarcity of affordable housing in urban areas is likely to remain a problem in Japan for the foreseeable future.

Accommodating the Past
by Jean Pearce

People often ask, "What is Japan really like?" There is no answer, any more than you can explain the real America. The whole is made up of too many parts.

Still, there are areas that readily lead to generalizations, and one is this: Japan is a country of rapid change, and what we see today will likely be gone tomorrow. So while our memories weave images of picturesque streets, brown wooden houses, and miniscule gardens, our eyes report sweeping patterns created by overhead expressways and clusters of skyscrapers so automated, so high-tech, that they are known as "intelligent buildings."

However, can anyone maintain an accurate, up-to-date image of such a city? Buildings are destroyed, new ones are built, and, a few years later, they are once again recycled. This can be a shock to those who want their memories intact, convinced that whatever went before must somehow be superior to what has replaced it.

There is much to say for change. Traditionalists may speak sentimentally of the past, but they want that past recreated with TVs, air conditioners, and central heating—and five minutes from the subway. It is easy to forget that convenience is the usual companion of modernization, that measurement of time was once based on how long it took to walk to the next village.

Yet, within the massive changes, reminders of the past are retained. Let me give you an example: an old community bathhouse, a relic of days when the bath was the place for meeting friends and discussing the day's happenings.

This remarkable bathhouse was in Ikebukuro, a section of Tokyo that is a bridge between the countryside and the city. There was, of course, the bath, but people came mainly for the sociability. After bathing, people gathered together in the lounge. Here anyone could sing a song or do a dance while sharing favorite foods brought from home and passing along neighborhood gossip.

A few years ago, the old bathhouse was replaced by a modern spa with a water-jet massage, scientifically blended mineral water, and a selection of health products.

Now it, too, is gone. Instead, there is a hotel for businessmen. Don't look for luxuries; it's a place to eat and sleep before going back to work the next day.

Oh yes, and to relax. Even though each room has its own molded plastic unit bath, today's guests, in a way, continue the old tradition. They, too, look to the communal bath for relaxation after a stressful day. Only now, the bath is a sauna, a modern update of Japan's neighborhood *sento*.

Perhaps that is the answer to the question, "What is Japan really like?" For me, the wonder of Japan is how it constantly keeps changing while at the same time staying the same.

Jean Pearce, a longtime resident of Tokyo, has written the column "Getting things done" in the *Japan Times* since the early 1960s and is the author of several books containing valuable information and insights for foreign residents in Japan.

4,900 Times A Day, To Over 300 Cities In 34 Countries. And You Thought You Had A Busy Schedule.

If you're always on the go, why not fly an airline
that can help you get there more easily.
With 20 flights a week between Japan and the United States,
Delta Air Lines gives you convenient connections to
one of the most extensive route systems on earth.
Not to mention, of course, the warmest, most personal service in the sky.
For reservations, see your Travel Agent. Or call Delta Air Lines.
With so many flights to so many places, chances are
you won't have to rearrange your busy schedule to meet ours.

DELTA AIR LINES
We Love To Fly And It Shows.

Information & Reservations: TOKYO (03) 5275-7000   Call toll free #0120-333742
when calling from areas excluding TOKYO (03)

Chapter

4

Entering Japan

You will have no difficulty entering Japan if you follow the immigration rules and carefully prepare all the required documents. Japanese officials place great emphasis on proper documentation. Double-check that all your traveling and immigration papers are in order; if they are not, you will probably have to make another trip to the immigration office to supply the missing documents.

How immigration rules are applied may vary from case to case, but immigration procedures must be followed. As in all countries, politeness and patience are essential in dealing with government officials. Show them respect and they will reciprocate and do their best to handle the matters at hand.

The information in this chapter applies to U.S. citizens. Some regulations differ depending on citizenship, so citizens of other countries should consult the Japanese Embassy or consulate nearest them for information.

Visas

Visa applications should be made with the presentation of the appropriate visa application form, your passport, other documents required depending on what type of visa you are applying for, and two passport-sized photographs to the Japanese Embassy or nearest consulate. The Japanese Embassy in the United States is in Washington, D.C., and it has consulates in New York, Atlanta, San Francisco, Los Angeles, Chicago, Seattle, Honolulu, Kansas City, Houston, Anchorage, New Orleans, Portland, and Agana, in Guam. You can also apply for a visa by writing to the Japanese Embassy or the consulate nearest you if you live far away from the locations listed above and cannot appear in person.

The type of visa you apply for will depend on the purpose of your visit to Japan. You should note that spouses who wish to work in Japan must apply for a special work permit.

Expatriates are now finding it easier to be issued a visa for Japan. In 1990, the Japanese government revised its visa categories. Changes were made to simplify the visa application and renewal processes for eligible residents, such as businesspeople and other skilled workers and their families.

Japan prohibits the entry of unskilled workers, although some local business sectors have strongly urged the government to reconsider this policy in light of the labor shortage in Japan and the reluctance of young Japanese to engage in work involving the so-called three Ks, namely, work that is *kitsui* (demanding), *kiken* (dangerous), and *kitanai* (dirty). In the late 1980s and early 1990s, there was a large influx of illegal unskilled workers from various third-world countries with which Japan had mutual visa exemption arrangements for tourists. Japan has since suspended visa-free travel with the nations in question; however, in 1992, over 250,000 foreigners illegally remained beyond their visa expiration date.

Status of Residence and Period of Stay

The following visa categories are in use:

Status of Residence	Period of Stay
Category 1 (Activities limited to those specified below)	
Diplomat	Duration of mission
Government Official	Duration of mission
Professor	3 years, 1 year, or 6 months
Artist	3 years, 1 year, or 6 months
Religious Activities	3 years, 1 year, or 6 months
Journalist	3 years, 1 year, or 6 months
Category 2 (Business activities limited to those specified below)	
Investor/Business Manager	3 years, 1 year, or 6 months
Legal/Accounting Services	3 years, 1 year, or 6 months
Medical Services	1 year or 6 months
Researcher	1 year or 6 months
Instructor	1 year or 6 months
Engineer	1 year or 6 months
Specialist in Humanities/ International Services	1 year or 6 months
Intracompany Transferee	1 year or 6 months
Entertainer	1 year or 3 months
Skilled Laborers	1 year or 6 months

Category 3 (Cannot work)

Cultural Activities	1 year or 6 months
Temporary Visitor	90 days or 15 days
College Student	1 year or 6 months

Category 4 (Cannot work without special permission)

Precollege Student	1 year, 6 months, or 3 months
Trainee	1 year, 6 months, or 3 months
Dependent	3 years, 1 year, 6 months, or 3 months

Category 5 (No restriction on activities)

Designated Activities	3 years, 1 year, 6 months, or 3 months
Permanent Resident	Indefinite
Spouse or Child of Japanese National	3 years, 1 year, or 6 months
Spouse or Child of Permanent Resident	3 years, 1 year, or 6 months
Long-Term Resident	3 years

Visa Exemption

Under a mutual visa exemption arrangement, U.S. citizens are eligible to enter Japan without a visa for a period not exceeding 90 days. This is especially useful for tourists or relatives of expatriates stationed in Japan. However, anyone intending to work in Japan must obtain a proper working visa. The visa exemption period can be extended for a second three-month period, but changing to another status is not possible without first leaving Japan. Japan also has visa exemption arrangements with most European nations, New Zealand, Canada, Mexico, and several countries in Central America, South America, Africa, and Asia. In addition, Japan has mutual working holiday arrangements with Australia, New Zealand, and Canada. Nationals of these countries can enter and work in Japan for a period of six months or one year, and applicants must usually be between the ages of 18 and 30.

Commercial Visa

To obtain a commercial visa, two copies of a letter from the company for which you will work in Japan must be submitted. The letter should state the purpose and length of your stay and should guarantee your living expenses and return passage. If the company you will be employed with is not licensed to do business in Japan, additional material explaining the firm's business activities may have to be supplied.

Health Requirements

Japan has relaxed inoculation requirements during recent years, as have many other developed countries. Although it may not be required, vaccination against smallpox is recommended as a minimum, and you may want to be inoculated against other illnesses depending on your travel plans both before and during your stay in Japan. Persons coming from areas of epidemic or endemic diseases must be inoculated against typhus, cholera, yellow fever, and smallpox. If you have not received inoculations against these diseases, your entry into Japan may be delayed. When you apply for your visa to enter Japan, ask the relevant authority for an International Certificate of Vaccination card or obtain one from your local Department of Health. For further information concerning inoculations, you should contact either the nearest representative of the United States Health Service; the Division of Foreign Quarantine, Department of Health, Education, and Welfare, Washington, D.C.; or the Japanese Embassy or the nearest consulate in the United States.

Immigration

If you have the proper documentation, immigration procedures after disembarking at an international airport in Japan should proceed smoothly. The process is not very different from that in other countries. An immigration officer will briefly inspect your passport, and he or she will understand enough English to spare you any inconvenience.

On entering Japan, you must present a valid passport, visa (if required), and a completed Embarkation/Disembarkation Card (this card is usually provided by the airline or your travel agent). With certain visas, you may also be required to provide a copy of your visa application, including supporting documents. This requirement rarely applies; nevertheless, consult with Japanese Embassy or consular officials before leaving.

The immigration inspector endorses any certificate for approval to enter Japan by attaching one copy of the Embarkation/ Disembarkation Card to the passport. The period of stay stamped into your passport by the immigration officer legally overrides any prior recommendation written by an embassy or consular official.

If all requirements are met, there are usually few, if any, problems in going through immigration. However, entry will not be permitted even if all requirements are met in the event that the applicant falls into any of the following categories: a person to whom the Antiepidemic Law applies, a person who is mentally troubled, beggars and vagrants who are likely to become public charges, ex-convicts who have served a sentence exceeding one year, anyone with a previous narcotics conviction, prostitutes, possessors of firearms or explosives, people deported within a recent period of time, people who are determined to be likely to work illegally, terrorists, and other undesirables.

Customs Clearance
Accompanied Baggage
If you are arriving by air, no written declaration is required for accompanied personal baggage and effects that are to be cleared through customs at the time and at the port of arrival; if all requirements are met, you should meet with little trouble at this time. If you are arriving by sea, however, a declaration must be made in writing, covering both accompanied and unaccompanied baggage.

Unaccompanied Baggage
The improper handling of unaccompanied baggage has been the cause of many a headache, so please note the following carefully. Form C-5360 or Form C-5360-2 (in English), entitled Declaration of Accompanied Personal Effects and Unaccompanied Articles, must be filled out in duplicate and verified and stamped by customs at the time and at the port of entry for articles arriving in Japan separately. These forms are available on the airplane or in the baggage claim area.

Although customs does all it can to see that you receive a Declaration of Accompanied Personal Effects and Unaccompanied Articles form, it is ultimately your responsibility to ensure that you obtain one. Be sure to keep it for the retrieval of your goods—this cannot be emphasized enough. Furthermore, these articles must reach Japan within six months of your arrival. Everything that is not accompanied by you at your time of entry must be described and listed on the declaration form. If you are not sure how many boxes, crates, or packages you will have, estimate the value of your shipment on the high side and identify these items as household effects.

Remember too, that new, unused appliances are subject to duty; used appliances are not. For example, if your air conditioner arrives in the factory crate in the original packing with instructions for operation all neatly enclosed, you may very well be charged duty. Be sure to use an appliance before it is shipped.

If your automobile is to be shipped, it can be included on Form C-5360 or Form C-5360-2. Pets must also be included on these forms (see below for further information). Japanese customs will not levy any duty on such products as personal computers, word processors, typewriters, and their peripherals and software, as these items are considered to have educational value. On the other hand, duty on new shoes and other leather products is high. For goods purchased by mail order from overseas, the 3% Japanese consumption tax is sometimes imposed.

Personal Effects

Personal effects that are not for sale are free of duty with the appropriate declaration form. When coming to Japan you may also bring in duty free three bottles of liquor, two ounces of perfume, and two new watches (of which neither may exceed ¥30,000 in value). Tobacco products in the amount of 400 cigarettes, 100 cigars, 500 grams (approximately 17 ounces) of smoking tobacco, or any combination of these totaling no more than 500 grams may also pass duty free.

Pets

If you are bringing your pets to Japan, they should be declared "ordinary" items upon entry with you, or, if unaccompanied, on Form C-5360 or Form C-5360-2.

Japanese regulations concerning the importation of pets, especially dogs, are quite explicit and rigidly enforced. In the case of dogs, for instance, you must have proof that your dog has been inoculated against rabies at least 30 days and not more than 60 days prior to entry into Japan, and you must have a veterinarian's certificate endorsed by the Inspector-in-Charge, Bureau of Animal Husbandry, Department of Agriculture, or equivalent in the country of prior residence. In the United States, these inspectors are located in the capitals of each state, with the exception of Maryland and Delaware, which are both served by the Baltimore office. Endorsement should be requested from the inspector-in-charge of the state in which the certificate of health is issued.

When dogs are imported from the United States, they are quarantined for 14 days or more, usually at Tokyo's international airport at Narita. Owners will find that the facilities are clean and modern and the dogs are cared for adequately. As in other instances, do not expect to circumvent established procedures.

In the case of cats, the Japanese government requires an endorsed certificate of good health signed by a licensed veterinarian. While there is no federal agency specifically charged with endorsing these certificates, your state's Bureau of Animal Husbandry may be able to provide such an endorsement.

Living and Raw Products

The importation of many plants and plant products is prohibited. Most fresh fruit falls in this category, but oranges, lemons, grapefruit, and melons may be brought directly from the mainland United States (although not via Hawaii), and pineapples, coconuts, unripe bananas, and papayas may be brought from Hawaii, provided you furnish a Plant Quarantine Certificate. Flower bulbs are subject to a one-year quarantine.

The prohibitions and restrictions are so varied that it would be advisable for anyone considering the importation of living or raw products to write to the Ministry of Agriculture, Forestry and Fisheries in Tokyo for a table of prohibited plants. This table, too detailed to duplicate here, is available in English and readily obtainable.

Currency

There is no restriction on the amount of money that may be brought into Japan, although in some circumstances there may be income tax considerations. U.S. currency, letters of credit, traveler's checks, and other financial instruments denominated in U.S. dollars are allowed, as are those of third countries. Likewise, Japanese citizens and foreigners in Japan may purchase foreign currency.

Foreign currency, with the exception of certain soft currencies, may be readily exchanged for yen at authorized banks and money changers, such as travel agencies and hotels. Passports are sometimes requested by these institutions for identification purposes.

Prohibited Items

The importation of firearms of any kind is prohibited (possession of such items in Japan is a felony), as is bringing in narcotics, illegal stimulants, and magazines or other media considered pornographic.

Alien Registration

In general, any foreigner who intends to spend at least three consecutive months in Japan must report to local authorities to be issued a Certificate of Alien Registration. Your alien registration card, which is about the same size as a driver's license, is as important in Japan as your passport. Persons 16 years of age and older are required to carry their cards with them at all times. If you have arrived within 90 days and have not yet obtained this certificate, you must carry your passport. If identification is required for any purpose, the alien registration card is always accepted. All arrangements for acquiring this card and subsequent reporting of any changes in your status must be handled directly by you with the office of the ward, town, or city where you reside.

The following is a summary of the requirements and procedures for alien registration:

• Within 90 days after your arrival, but preferably immediately after you arrive, you and each person in your family 16 years of age or older must appear in person at the office of the ward, town, or city where you reside with your passport and two 4-by-3-centimeter photographs taken within the last six months. These items should be submitted with a completed Certificate of Alien Registration application form. You will be fingerprinted if your approved length of stay in Japan is one year or more (see the end of this section). Children under 16 years of age must also obtain a Certificate of Alien Registration, but the application may be made by a parent.

• Changes in your passport number, its issue date, your address in your home state, the householder's name, and your relationship to the householder should be reported as soon as possible to the office issuing your Certificate of Alien Registration. However, changes in your Japanese address, visa status, authorized period of stay, nationality, name, and profession or occupation and the name of your employer or your company's location must be reported within 14 days.

• Your Certificate of Alien Registration is valid for five years. The expiration date will appear on the front side of the card. Application for renewal must be made not more than 30 days prior to the date of expiration. If your passport or your authorized period of stay expires, you will not be able to renew your Certificate of Alien Registration. Children under 16 years of age are not required to renew their certificate until they reach 16.

• When you leave Japan temporarily and have a single or multiple reentry permit (see following pages), you will retain your Certificate of Alien Registration. When you return to Japan with your reentry permit, you should have your Certificate of Alien Registration with you.

Fingerprints are now taken only once, upon initial application. From 1993, permanent residents will be exempt from fingerprinting (this does not apply to the majority of Americans in Japan, who are on one-year or three-year visas). The Japanese government initially considered total abolition of the fingerprinting requirement, but the National Police Agency exerted strong pressure to maintain the system for identification purposes. It is possible that eventually fingerprinting and perhaps even the need to carry alien registration cards will disappear, but until the law is amended, existing regulations must be adhered to.

Departure and Reentry

Any foreigner who wishes to leave Japan temporarily—regardless of reasons and duration of stay—will need to obtain a reentry permit. There are two types of reentry permit: single and multiple. Application can be made at the nearest regional immigration office (refer to the end of this chapter) by presenting your passport and Certificate of Alien Registration in person; you can also apply on behalf of your spouse and immediate family. (Reentry permits may also be obtained, in an emergency, from immigration authorities at the airport before your departure. It should be emphasized, however, that this is strictly an emergency option, which may involve you writing a letter of apology explaining why you failed to obtain your permit in the normal way.)

The cost is ¥3,000 for a single reentry permit and ¥6,000 for a multiple one. Payment is made by purchasing a revenue stamp, which is available at the immigration office. If you need a multiple reentry permit, you may have to submit a letter addressed to the director of the regional immigration office explaining why a multiple reentry permit is necessary; for instance, because frequent travel is required by your business.

When you leave Japan you will be required to present your passport, Certificate of Alien Registration, and boarding pass to an immigration inspector. If you depart with either type of reentry permit, you will also be required to present a completed Embarkation/Disembarkation Card, which is available from your travel agency, the airline counter, or an immigration checkpoint.

Where to leave your troubles when you fly JAL.

It's a big, busy, competitive world out there, especially for business travelers. And at every stop on your schedule you have to be your best. On Japan Airlines you can escape the hassles for a while. You can experience some peace and quiet, and enjoy a friendliness and warmth that is a hallmark of JAL's experienced flight attendants. Yes, business life on the road can be tough. But at least in JAL's world of comfort, you can leave your troubles behind.

Japan Airlines

A WORLD OF COMFORT.

If you have a reentry permit you will be allowed to retain your Certificate of Alien Registration, which you must show to immigration officials upon your return to Japan. If you have not obtained a reentry permit, you will be required to surrender your alien registration card upon departure and go through the process of obtaining another when you return to Japan.

Visa Extension

Before the period of stay authorized by your visa expires, you must go to your regional immigration office to apply for an extension if you wish to stay in Japan.

You will need to bring your passport, your Certificate of Alien Registration, and a letter from your sponsor guaranteeing continued support. You may also be asked for copies of your work contract, withholding tax receipts, or documents explaining your company's activities. The application requires a ¥4,000 revenue stamp.

You will ordinarily receive a reply on the same day at the immigration office (80% of all requests are handled this way), but in some cases you may have to wait two to four weeks for a reply. If a reply cannot be granted on the spot, the immigration officer will stamp your passport with a notice that you have applied for a visa extension. If, in the meantime, your original period of stay expires, you need not worry.

Permanent Residence

You may apply for permanent residence status in Japan if you meet the following conditions:

• You have lived in Japan for a number of years. There is no definite minimum residence requirement; in principle, however, five years is considered the absolute minimum except for former Japanese citizens, spouses or children of Japanese or those who have permanent residence, or persons who have made a notable contribution to Japan.

• You have sufficient income or assets or the ability to make an independent living (not required for spouses or children of Japanese or those who have permanent residence).

• You are in good health.

• You have conducted yourself well (not required for spouses or children of Japanese or those who have permanent residence).

•When you are granted permanent residence status, your passport will be stamped by an immigration official granting you the stamp Permission of Permanent Residence, or *eiju kyoka*. The revenue stamp charge is ¥8,000.

Newborn Babies

The following procedures apply for babies born to foreign parents. If one parent is Japanese, different requirements exist; the Japanese parent should check the appropriate procedures. For further information, refer to Chapter 15.

•U.S. Embassy. Babies born in Japan to American parents must be registered at the U.S. Embassy or the nearest consulate.

•Immigration Office. Parents of a newborn child should take their passports, alien registration cards, the newborn child's passport, and a copy of the Japanese birth certificate to the nearest Japanese immigration office within 30 days after the baby's birth. The child's Japanese birth certificate will be issued by the office of the ward, town, or city where you reside. A picture of the baby is not required by the immigration office. The baby will only be granted a single reentry permit (whether the parents hold multiple reentry permits or not), and remember to obtain this in advance if the baby is to be taken out of Japan.

•Ward/Town/City Office. The parents should register their baby at the office of the ward, town, or city where they reside within 60 days after birth. A picture of the baby is not required. The parents' passports and alien registration cards, along with two completed copies of an Application for Alien Registration, provided at the office, should be presented.

Location of Immigration Bureaus

In the Tokyo area, there are two main immigration offices: the central office in Otemachi, in downtown Tokyo, and a branch office at the Tokyo City Air Terminal, in Hakozaki. The Otemachi office handles all documentation relating to visas and issues reentry permits. The Hakozaki office, however, only processes reentry permits and straightforward visa extensions. For residents of Kanagawa Prefecture, there is an office in Yokohama.

Offices are open Monday through Friday, from 9:00 A.M. to 12:00 A.M. and from 1:00 P.M. to 5:00 P.M.

Tokyo Regional Immigration Bureau
2nd & 3rd Floors, Otemachi Godo Chosho,
1-3-1, Otemachi, Chiyoda-ku, Tokyo 100
Tel: (03) 3213-8111

Hakozaki Immigration Branch Office
Tokyo City Air Terminal Building,
42-1, Nihonbashi Hakozakicho,
Chuo-ku, Tokyo 103
Tel: (03) 3664-3046

Tokyo Haneda Branch Office
Tokyo International Airport, Ota-ku, Tokyo 144
Tel: (03) 3747-0102

Yokohama Immigration Bureau
37-9, Yamashita-cho, Naka-ku, Yokohama 231
Tel: (045) 681-6801

Major immigration offices elsewhere in Japan are at the following locations:

Fukuoka Immigration Office
1-22, Okihama-cho, Hakata-ku, Fukuoka 812

Hiroshima Immigration Office
6-30, Kami-Hachobori, Naka-ku, Hiroshima 730

Kobe Immigration Office
Kaigan-dori, Chuo-ku, Kobe 650

Nagoya Immigration Office
4-3-1, Sannomaru, Naka-ku, Nagoya 460

Narita Branch Office
New Tokyo International Airport, Narita, Chiba 286-11

Osaka Immigration Office
2-1-17, Tanimachi, Chuo-ku, Osaka 540

Sapporo Immigration Office
12, Odori Nishi, Chuo-ku, Sapporo, Hokkaido 060

Sendai Immigration Office
1-3-20,. Gorin, Miyagino-ku, Sendai, Miyagi 983

Takamatsu Immigration Office
1-1, Marunouchi, Takamatsu, Kagawa 760

Chapter

5

What to Bring and What to Buy

When making a move to Japan, you should plan carefully what to take with you. Certain items, such as personal documents, you will need to have with you, but as for appliances and furniture and furnishings, whether to ship your own belongings or lease or buy in Japan is up to you, your family, and your company. You will have to weigh such factors as the availability and cost of similar articles in Japan, the risk of loss or damage in transportation, and sentimental attachment.

Personal Documents

When you are packing for your move, you will need to decide which personal papers to store at home and which to bring with you. Documents that you may need in Japan include:

•College or university degrees or an original copy of your academic transcripts certified by the relevant institution of graduation;

•Résumé;

•Children's school transcripts;

•A number of photographs of yourself and individual family members, in both black-and-white and color and in several sizes, including passport size—you will need these for a variety of purposes, so it is worthwhile having some photographs taken;

•Your family's birth certificates;

•Driver's license—if this does not show the date of issue, you will also need a statement from the appropriate authority stating in which year your license was originally issued;

•Previous year's tax records;

•Insurance policies;

•Medical and dental records; and

•Medical and optical prescriptions.

Electric Goods

Electricity for home use in Tokyo and the rest of eastern Japan is a 50-cycle, 100-volt alternating current. In the Kansai area and the other parts of western Japan, the current is 60 cycles (the same as in the United States) and 100 volts. Such electric appliances as irons and toasters from the United States will work but at a slightly reduced efficiency, as will kitchen appliances with motors, which will run slower at 50 cycles. You will probably want to leave your microwave or electric stove at home. Most families use gas ranges for cooking, as gas is relatively cheap compared with electricity, and in recent years, microwaves have become more common.

If you are bringing an appliance from a European country or certain other countries operating on 200-to-240-volt currents, you will need a step-up transformer to use it on Japan's 100-volt current. These transformers are readily available in Japan. Sockets are also different, and you will need adaptors.

Household Appliances

Most upmarket apartment complexes and rental homes are furnished with automatic washing machines and dryers; in the case of the former, units are installed either in the apartment itself or in a central laundry situated in the basement or on the roof of the apartment complex. Laundromats, or *koin randori,* are found in most urban areas, and some share facilities with or are adjacent to *sento* (public bathhouses).

Stoves and refrigerators in Japan are generally smaller than those in the United States; however, *gyomuyo* (large business-use) models may be available. These larger units, the prices of which are often substantially marked down at retail outlets, may prove to be ideal for families. Landlords will sometimes agree to furnish Western-style appliances where they have not already been installed, but this must be negotiated before the rental contract is signed; with company-provided housing, these appliances are often already installed.

Many Western-style apartments also come equipped with gas or electric air conditioner/heaters; central heating is still rather rare. If your house or apartment is not provided with one, these units can be purchased at quite reasonable prices and can be installed in almost any newer building. Most of them have a humidifier function, which is a great relief during the dry winter months. Separate humidifier units made and sold in Japan are efficient but expensive.

Audiovisual Equipment

AM radios from the United States can be used in Japan without any problems, but the FM band in Japan is different from the U.S. FM band, so you will need to use an adaptor, which is obtainable here, with your FM tuner.

Extensive adjustment is necessary to use a U.S. TV in Japan. Reversal of this adjustment to permit you to use your TV again in the States may be difficult, so it is probably wiser to buy or lease a Japanese TV after you arrive. You can easily obtain a TV with or without the capacity to receive satellite broadcasts and with or without a built-in tuner—decide in advance which type you need. While many apartment buildings are already equipped with a cable hookup or a satellite dish, this is less common in private houses. You might choose to buy an indoor satellite antenna, eliminating the need to ask the landlord for permission and the expense of installing a cable hookup or an outside dish. Reception through cable or an outdoor satellite dish is the best.

U.S. VCRs follow the same NTSC standard as Japanese models, and U.S. videotapes can be used in Japanese VCRs. The PAL video format used in Europe and Australia, however, is incompatible with the majority of Japanese models. Multisystem televisions and VCRs that handle both formats are now readily available but are more expensive than standard models.

If your CD player or analog record player does not have a cycle-adjustment system built in, you will need to get it adjusted if you are moving to Tokyo; the adjustments are not necessary if you move to the Kansai region. This process varies depending on the model and can be as simple as changing a ¥50 pulley or somewhat more complicated. Most tape recorders and cassette tape recorders are designed to operate on either 50 or 60 cycles, in which case no adjustment is needed.

In fact, much of the audiovisual equipment sold in Japan nowadays is compatible with both systems, either automatically or by a switch at the back of the unit, so that it is quite easy to find products that you can take back and use at home after your time in Japan is over. If you decide to buy here, spend a day in the Akihabara district of Tokyo to check out the possibilities and the prices. You may want to look in particular at the duty-free shops, as most of the goods will be compatible in other countries and English-language instruction manuals are nearly always provided. Despite the duty-free status of the merchandise, however, as a permanent or temporary resident you will still have to pay the consumption tax at these stores.

When buying electric appliances in Japan, it is worth remembering to ask for manuals in English. If these are not available from the retailer, make sure before you buy the product that they can be obtained from the manufacturer.

Another option is to buy used household appliances or other items from other foreigners who have come to the end of their stay in Japan and are ridding themselves of extra baggage before their move. These so-called *sayonara* sales are announced in English-language newspapers and periodicals and are well worth investigating, as the sellers are usually anxious to part with articles that may be just what you need.

Furniture and Furnishings

Unless money is no object and you have some special attachment to certain pieces of furniture or furnishings from home, it is hardly worth the trouble and expense to bring them over. Western-style furniture can be found fairly easily in Japan. Most department stores carry some European and U.S. imports, although prices are high. There are also well-designed Japanese lines available; however, the dimensions of Japanese-made furniture are generally smaller than what you may be used to. For larger Western-style beds, try contacting one of the American bed companies operating in Japan, such as the Simmons Co. Used furniture as well as used appliances can often be purchased from departing foreigners.

If you are here for a relatively short stay, or if the length of your stay is not yet determined, you may want to inquire at any of the several companies, such as Tokyo Lease, and department stores, such as Isetan, that offer foreign-made furniture, furnishings, and other items for lease.

Lamps and drapes and other soft furnishings are readily available in Japan, but the selection is limited and these items are expensive. If possible, have windows measured and bring drapes from home or do this upon arrival and then place an order back home.

It is a good idea to bring a supply of bed and bathroom linen in sizes you prefer; locally produced towels tend to be smaller than those commonly found in the United States, and imported linen can be expensive.

Tokyu Hands, a chain store with six outlets in Tokyo and its surrounding areas, is a good place to buy adaptors, light bulbs, storage items, modular build-it-yourself furniture, and various other household and hardware goods—everything you need to make yourself feel more at home.

Clothing

For both teenagers and adults, it is advisable to bring appropriate attire for each of Japan's four seasons. The climate is mild in both the Kanto and Kansai regions and in Kyushu. Coats are recommended for winter, but they need not be of the heavy types common in the northern United States and Canada. Summers are hot and humid, and clothing should be light.

Until relatively recently, the limited availability of larger sizes for all types of clothing was a major problem. Although the average height of Japanese people has increased substantially over the past 20 years, and clothing and shoes for men of average build up to about 180 centimeters (5 feet 10 inches) are readily available, sleeve and trouser lengths may be a problem.

Japanese women are generally smaller than Western women, and clothes are cut accordingly. Trouser and sleeve lengths are usually short, dresses short-waisted, and bust lines small even for moderately endowed Western figures. Some department stores carry larger sizes, but these have the same problems. Many Western designer brands are available here, but most are made under license in Japan and are not imported, so sizes are Japanese. Even some imported European clothes displaying standard European sizes have been cut for a Japanese body and not for a Westerner. Women should also bring a supply of underwear and hosiery, as Japanese sizes may not be comfortable.

Large shoe sizes used to be almost impossible to find in Japan; however, men's shoes up to 28 centimeters (U.S. size 9) are now easy to obtain, and the largest readily available women's size is 24.5 centimeters (U.S. size 7). Although shoe stores are abundant and selections wide in Japan's metropolitan areas, some Western women find shoe buying in Japan difficult if not impossible. Bring a lot of shoes with you, particularly shoes suitable for walking.

A wide selection of well-made clothing and shoes for babies and children is available in Japan; however, prices are usually high. The range of maternity clothes available is limited and tends to be designed for young women, generally in a pinafore style. Fashionable maternity clothes may be difficult to find.

Most people dress conservatively for work. Men usually wear sober gray, blue, or beige suits and white or pale shirts. For women, the style in Japan is somewhat dressier than in most Western countries, with tailored suits and smart accessories. Attire worn at social functions in the business and diplomatic communities tends to be more formal than in most U.S. and European cities.

First-class dressmakers and tailors are available in Japan, but, unlike in Hong Kong or Bangkok, the prices they charge are relatively high. Off-the-rack suits and dresses are reasonably priced. For black-tie events, rental agencies for tuxedos in sizes suitable for Westerners are available; women can rent long or short evening dresses for such occasions from these agencies too.

Medicines, Cosmetics, and Toiletries

Life in your first months in Japan will be much easier if you bring an ample supply of your favorite toiletries and cosmetics and any necessary medications.

You may not want to give your children unfamiliar brands of over-the-counter (OTC) medicine. To decide which types of medication to bring, go through the contents of your medicine cabinet at home and buy at least one of each item. (It should be noted, however, that many OTC medications in the United States, for example, Sudafed and Vick's Nasal Inhaler, are illegal in Japan.) Japanese medicines, both OTC and prescription, are low in dosage compared with Western products.

A wide range of both Japanese and foreign cosmetics are available in Japan, albeit at higher prices than you will have been accustomed to. Although you should have no trouble finding the cosmetics you need here, you may want to bring a supply of your favorite items with you. The same is true if you dye your hair, have a perm, or have a favorite shampoo, since some Japanese hair treatment products do not necessarily suit Western hair types.

Certain items, such as deodorant, talcum powder, and body lotion, may be hard to find in Japan, at least of the type and in the selection that you are used to. Japanese people tend to use body sprays rather than antiperspirants, if anything, so you are advised to bring what you need from home.

If you wear contact lenses, you should be aware that the cold sterilization process for lenses has not yet been approved in Japan. If this is the process you use to sterilize your lenses, bring the necessary solutions with you; if you intend to change to heat sterilization, consult with your optometrist first, as there are sometimes difficulties in changing from one process to the other with the same set of lenses. Wearers of glasses or contact lenses should bring a backup pair in case of loss or damage. Keep in mind that frames for glasses are very expensive in Japan.

The American Pharmacy in Tokyo's Yurakucho district sells U.S. OTC medications and a range of foreign toiletries, cosmetics, and other goods, such as household items, which may be hard to find elsewhere.

Pets

It is relatively easy to bring your pet into Japan; see Chapter 4 for details on customs clearance and quarantine requirements. But before coming to Japan, if possible, you should check whether you will have any problems keeping your pet in your new residence. Many apartment buildings and some houses do not allow pets of any kind, although in many cases this rule is not strictly enforced. Also, keep in mind that you may encounter even more rigorous quarantine restrictions with your pet when you leave Japan or send it back ahead of you, particularly when entering such countries as Australia and the United Kingdom. Chapter 21 gives details on customs clearance requirements for entering the United States.

Kennels and other facilities for animals are available in Japan, and with some assistance, you should be able to find a qualified English-speaking veterinarian.

Dogs must be registered at a local ward or municipal office, and registration must be renewed every year in April. When registering your dog, you receive a notice of registration for the next year and a registration tag. All dogs must be registered within 30 days after becoming three months old and vaccinated against rabies. Vaccinations are mandatory every year and are administered between April and June at a fee of ¥2,540, plus ¥480 for a tag that must be attached to your dog's collar at all times. The local authorities must be notified if your dog dies or disappears or if you change your address.

If you do bring a dog to Japan or acquire one here, be sure to keep it on a leash when walking and take one or two plastic bags with you to clean up any mess. This is not only common practice in Japanese cities, it is the law.

What good is an insurance broker if you can't get insurance?

Insurance underwriters have become highly selective about insuring risks. In fact, some kinds of coverage just aren't available today.

In this climate, the right broker can help you a lot more than you might think. For example, the way your insurance risks are presented can be the key to getting acceptance by an insurer. And the right program design can help you obtain maximum coverage.

But if you still can't get all the insurance you need, the right broker can give you other options, such as self-insurance. Or pooling your risks with other companies in a captive insurance company. We manage more "captives" than any other broker.

In today's market, you need a good insurance broker more than ever. And nobody knows better than the clients of Johnson & Higgins.

JOHNSON & HIGGINS

A Partner In UNISON

Consulting on a lot more than insurance.

Tokyo Office: DF Bldg., 10th Floor
2-2-8 Minami Aoyama, Minato-ku, Tokyo 107
Phone: 3478-1291
Fax: 3478-1228
Osaka Office: 10th Floor, Fudo Kensetsu Bldg.
2-16, Hirano-machi 4-chome
Phone: (06) 202-2435
Facsimile: (06) 202-2437
RISK AND INSURANCE MANAGEMENT SERVICES.
HUMAN RESOURCES AND ACTUARIAL CONSULTING.
PROPERTY LOSS CONTROL ENGINEERING.

*Tokyo's famous Ginza draws
thousands of shoppers and
strollers on Sundays.*

The Emperor and Empress host garden parties in the grounds of the Akasaka Palace, in Tokyo, in spring and autumn. (Courtesy of the Imperial Household Agency)

Tokyo's Shinjuku Gyoen is especially popular in spring for its magnificent cherry blossoms.

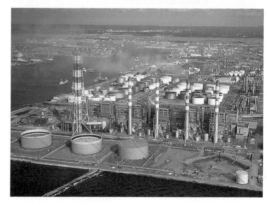

Industrial complexes line Tokyo Bay.

At many Japanese weddings,
the bride and groom wear both
Western clothes and Japanese
kimono for different parts
of the proceedings.

The Imperial Palace moat and its embankment and watchtowers were built in the 16th century by the shogunate.

Many of the prewar Gothic-style bank buildings—seen in this view from the Yaesu exit of Tokyo Station in the 1960s—have now been replaced by modern glass-and-steel structures.

Elaborate armor of this type was used by warriors until the Edo Era.

Suitengu, a shrine in downtown Tokyo, houses a deity worshipped by women seeking a safe childbirth. The deity is also said to have powers related to safety in the water and success in the entertainment world.

The Emperor and Empress greet the public at an ippansanga (a function at which the public can extend their best wishes to the Imperial Family). Ippansanga are held on December 23, for the Emperor's birthday, and on January 2, for the New Year. (Courtesy of the Imperial Household Agency)

Sweet potatoes are among the many treats for sale at this festival in Meguro, Tokyo.

Garbage from several dumps, such as this one in Tokyo Bay, is used for creating reclaimed land.

The Nihonbashi Bridge was initially built in 1603 and was subsequently designated the starting point of all roads in Japan. The current bridge—shown here in the early 1960s—was built in 1911 but is now obscured by an elevated expressway.

In the past, rice planting was done by hand. Today, farmers throughout Japan use state-of-the-art machinery to plant and harvest rice.

On weekends, some major streets in Tokyo are closed to traffic; this one is in the center of Ginza. Wako department store, the old building with the clocktower, has been a symbol of Ginza for more than 60 years.

Many of the major American fast-food chains have branches in Japan, but this outlet is one of a competing chain operated by a Japanese company.

An aerial view of the Shinjuku subcenter; the tallest building is part of the Tokyo Metropolitan Government complex.

The presentation of traditional Japanese delicacies combines color and shape to dramatic effect.

Many American foods have found a place in daily life in Japan.

Having finished his bento (boxed lunch), this tired Tokyo salaryman has hung his jacket on the branch of a pine tree and is enjoying a few minutes of sleep.

*Though hardly elegant,
restaurants like this typical
Tokyo eatery offer a great
variety of dishes and also serve
alcoholic beverages. There are
thousands of these establishments
scattered throughout Japan, with
the largest concentration in areas
close to railway stations.*

Only KDD can take you all over the world. Wherever they are, you can be there, too.

001
INTERNATIONAL DIRECT DIALING (IDD)

All you have to do is dial in the following sequence:

001 → **country code** → **area code** → **telephone number**

For the U.S.A. [1], N.Y. [212] 123-4567

001 → **1** → **212** → **123 − 4567**

Charges: 6-second units
Economy (20% discount) and Discount (40% discount) rates are applied during the hours shown in the table below.

■ **Standard Rates** are shown in **green.**　■ **Economy Rates** are shown in **red.**　■ **Discount Rates** are shown in **blue.**

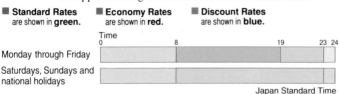

Time
0　　　　　8　　　　　19　　23　24

Monday through Friday

Saturdays, Sundays and national holidays

Japan Standard Time

Dial Coupon 001
⟨Discount service available from home

- KDD's "Dial Coupon 001" monthly discount service offers you an unlimited number of IDD calls during the economy-rate hours with an economical fixed charge, for a specified total monthly duration.
- You can sign up for a "Dial Coupon 001" service duration of 30, 60, or 90 minutes. For instance, if you were to make 3-minute calls twenty times a month to the U.S.A., you would save over 20% compared to IDD calls at the economy-rate hours.
- You can make a contract to over any of 50 areas throughout the world, including the U.S.A., Korea, the U.K. and Germany.

0051
OPERATOR-ASSISTED CALLS

First dial **0051** to contact the KDD operator.

■ **Charges:** Basic charge (first three minutes) plus each additional minute.

- Station-to-station and person-to-person calls are available only through KDD.

- Collect calls and credit card calls may be placed through the KDD operator.

0039
HOME COUNTRY DIRECT

■ With this service you can contact the operator in your home country.

Just dial **0039** followed by the three-digit code for your country.

For the U.S.A. (mainland): 0039-111,121,131

- **Charges** for collect or credit card calls are paid in your home country– no payments have to be made in Japan.

- When calling from special Home Country Direct telephones located in airports, hotels and other locations, just press a single button.

These calls can be made from your home, office or hotel room, as well as from green public phones with a gold plate.

If you have any questions regarding KDD's telephone services:

Call 0057 (toll-free)

 **KDD**

Chapter

6

Settling In

Orientation Services

The experience of finding yourself in a foreign country, surrounded by unfamiliar sounds and customs, can lead to a rather overwhelming sense of isolation. In Japan, there is a wide range of groups and services that can help you settle in by introducing you to the community around you.

Most Americans are no doubt familiar with the "Welcome Wagon" or similar services that greet newcomers to many communities. In the Greater Tokyo/Yokohama area, there is a similar service, sponsored by local business, known as Welcome Furoshiki (named after the square cloth used for wrapping and carrying packages, boxed lunches, and gifts). If you contact Welcome Furoshiki, an English-speaking representative will call on you with an assortment of helpful household items, lists of essential services and telephone numbers, and useful advice on settling into your new life in Japan.

Tokyo General Agency (TGA), Oak Associates, and Tokyo Orientations are among the several organizations that help people acquire the knowledge and skills they need to live comfortably in Japan. Programs range from orientation sessions and consultations by telephone to clubs, which for a moderate fee introduce members to traditional culture through social activities and newsletters.

Hot Lines and Help Lines

The most complete guide to community services, groups, organizations, and survival information for any English-speaking person in Japan is the Tokyo English Life Line (TELL) *International Community Calendar*. Looking through this list of names and telephone numbers, you will be able to fully appreciate the range of support services available: the Foreign Resident's Advisory Center, TELL, Japan Helpline, and Japan Hotline, to name just a few. The latter two are particularly helpful if you have general questions and do not know where to start finding the answers.

Accommodation

In addition to the following information, ACCJ Monograph No.1 *Finding a Home in Tokyo* will be helpful in finding accommodation in Tokyo.

Hotels

Japan's hotels, especially in Tokyo and other major cities, compare favorably with first-rate hotels in the United States and Europe in terms of service and comfort, although rooms are generally smaller. The number of hotel rooms available in Japan's major cities has expanded greatly over the past 20 to 30 years, but at times demand for rooms in good hotels may outstrip availability when international conventions are held or during traditional sight-seeing seasons—such as Golden Week in May—and school and university examination seasons, when students from rural areas spend days or even weeks in hotels in preparation for critical tests.

Rates at practically all Japan's better hotels are high compared with U.S. prices. At a good hotel, a standard room for two persons with a private bath will cost a minimum of ¥15,000 to ¥20,000 a day. Although tipping is not required at hotels in Japan, a 10% service charge is placed on the total room and restaurant charges. A special local consumption tax of 3% is imposed on hotel bills exceeding ¥15,000 including the service charge, in addition to the regular 3% consumption tax.

In Tokyo and other cities, a wide range of Western-style business hotels are also available. Rates are between ¥6,000 and ¥12,000 a night.

Meal prices vary substantially in hotels. Generally speaking, breakfast ranges from ¥1,500 to ¥3,000, lunch will be about ¥2,000, and dinner at least ¥5,000. These prices represent the minimum amounts you can expect to pay and do not include tax or service charges. Although hotel bars can be inexpensive, charges for lounges offering entertainment are generally high in hotels.

Businesspeople and their families may sometimes have to stay in a hotel for a few weeks or even months in the process of finding suitable living quarters; if this is your case, remember that some hotels are more suited to family living than others. Making reservations well in advance is always advisable, especially in the tourist seasons of April, May, and October and the school and university entrance examination season in February. Also, as many hotels offer both Western-style and Japanese-style rooms, it is wise to specify which you prefer.

Serviced Apartments

A temporary apartment may better suit your lifestyle if you do not wish to move into permanent accommodation immediately or if you are unable to do so. Although the range of serviced apartments available is not very large, some real estate agents are able to provide this type of temporary housing. People staying in Japan for only a few months and those likely to have a lengthy search for suitable living quarters will find that a serviced apartment in an "apartment hotel" may be much less costly than a hotel room or a regular apartment. Serviced apartments offer newly arrived residents complete privacy and safety as well as adequate living space.

Serviced apartments are fully furnished and have TV sets, washing machines and dryers, and everything you will need for cooking except the food. Limited maid service includes vacuuming and the weekly changing of bed linen and towels.

Prices range from ¥300,000 a month for a one-room apartment (about 25 square meters, or 270 square feet) to ¥700,000 a month for a three-bedroom apartment (about 93 square meters, or 1,000 square feet). Most apartment hotels require tenants to have a corporate or a Japanese personal guarantor, and the rent is inclusive of all utility, maintenance, and security charges.

Other Rental Housing

In the early 1990s, with the bursting of the "bubble economy," real estate values in Tokyo fell for the first time in well over a decade, and by 1992, there was a glut in both housing and office space in Tokyo. This, however, does not imply that you can expect to find housing bargains in Tokyo or the other major cities. Real estate values soared to unbelievably high levels in the late 1980s, and although land prices have fallen, rents have remained more or less static.

Rental of a Western-style house or apartment of a size you have been accustomed to overseas will be prohibitively expensive in Tokyo. For a family with two children, finding adequate housing in a central location for less than ¥600,000 a month might be difficult. This is a minimum, and rents of up to ¥1.5 million per month for large houses or apartments are not unusual. Rents will be cheaper in areas further away from the center of Tokyo and in areas less popular with foreign residents. For example, a reasonable-sized family apartment in a suburb can be found for ¥300,000 or less. Rents for Japanese-style houses and apartments are also significantly cheaper, and you might be able to find a three-room apartment for ¥150,000 a month.

Apartments will often be described in terms of "LDK," which stands for a combined living/dining/kitchen room; thus, a 1LDK apartment will have one room in addition to a combined living/dining/kitchen room, a 2LDK apartment will have two additional rooms, and so on. Apartments may have small veranda gardens or larger communal gardens at ground level. Individual houses in central Tokyo often have no real garden to speak of, and the rare home with a large garden is likely to command a very high rental fee.

Upon signing a rental contract, you will usually have to pay a large lump sum. This may comprise the following: an advance payment of rent, which varies in amount but three months' to one year's rent is often requested; a one-time, non-interest-bearing deposit, or *shikikin,* which may range from two to six months' rent; a monetary gift to the landlord, or *reikin,* of one month's to two months' rent (this is not applicable to housing over ¥500,000 per month or most housing for expatriates); and a real estate agent's fee, equivalent to one month's rent. Both *shikikin* and *reikin* are negotiable; the real estate agent's fee is not. Traditionally, *shikikin* is refunded, minus fees for damages, but *reikin* is kept by the landlord. The refund of money on departure is occasionally a source of friction between Japanese landlords and foreign tenants. Some landlords may not make any refund even if the premises are vacated in fine condition, and there is usually very little the tenant can do in such cases.

Once you have moved in, rent is usually paid on a monthly basis, in cash or by bank transfer. Utilities are paid for separately, in addition to the rent. Utility rates for a Western-style house will increase monthly operating costs approximately ¥60,000 to ¥90,000. Air-conditioning and heating may add another ¥40,000 a month to these costs.

In Japan, available housing is advertised through real estate agents, and "For Rent" signs are sometimes posted on buildings. It is best to use the services of a reputable real estate agency, many of which now have English-speaking sales personnel. It is also a good idea to visit more than one agency, as cross-listings are not used in Japan. As in any country, you should state your requirements clearly and ask the real estate agent to show you any premises that match them. Proximity to work, schools, and public transportation and parking facilities are factors that you will want to consider when making your decision. When you find a suitable house or apartment, you should put down a deposit (usually minimal) as soon as possible; if you do not, the apartment may be rented to someone else in as little as a day.

Make sure you are aware of the terms of the contract before signing—such as the minimum rental period and when the rent is likely to be raised—and, if possible, make efforts to develop a good relationship with your landlord. This is common procedure in Japan and can help minimize any future difficulties you might have. Often the landlord will become a valuable help during your stay in Japan. Wallpaper and floor coverings are usually changed when a property is vacated, and you should check that all appliances provided are in good working order and that all necessary repairs are made before you move in. It is also worth agreeing in advance with your landlord or the real estate agent on who is to pay for future repairs.

Notifying the Authorities

When you move into a new neighborhood, you should advise the authorities at your local *koban,* or police box. They will want to know your home and work addresses, telephone numbers, the number of people in your family, and other details that they consider relevant.

They will also want to explain the procedures to be followed in the event of a crime; they will often leave you with their *meishi* and a warm welcome to the neighborhood. Whether you have registered at the *koban* or not, the police might pay you a visit soon after you move in as part of their routine procedure.

It is also a good idea to register with your embassy in Japan. This is usually a simple matter of telephoning the embassy and saying you wish to register; you will be sent a form or card to fill in and return. In the event of a major earthquake, for example, it is important that the embassy be able to quickly contact you.

Utilities

Gas and electricity meters are checked once a month and a service inspection card showing how much has been used will be left in your mailbox. The monthly bill will be sent to you shortly after the inspection, unless you have arranged for the automatic payment of your bills. The water meter is checked once every three months, and a bill for both water and sewage is sent every two months.

Utility bills can be paid at post offices, most Japanese banks, or branches of Citibank, the Bank of America, and some other foreign banks. You can also arrange for the automatic payment of bills from a Japanese bank or post office account— ask for the form for *jido barai.*

Refuse Disposal

Household refuse must be divided into burnable and nonburnable waste. Burnable waste, or *moeru gomi,* includes food scraps, disposable diapers, wastepaper, paper packaging, and clothing. Nonburnable waste, or *moenai gomi,* includes bottles, cans, light bulbs, and anything else made of glass, metal, plastic, styrofoam, rubber, or leather. Recycling efforts are becoming more widespread, and in some areas you may have to separate bottles and cans too.

Used batteries can be returned to stores for disposal. Spray cans should be pierced to avoid the danger of explosion, and glass, pottery, fluorescent lamps, and other breakables should be packed in thick paper and marked "glass" (*garasu*) or "dangerous item" (*kikenbutsu*) in Japanese to avoid injuries to the garbage collectors.

Burnable waste is generally collected twice or three times a week, while one collection day each week is set aside for nonburnable waste. Refuse must be placed in the specially designated pickup areas and should not be put out before the morning of collection. Ask your landlord or a neighbor for the location and time of the pickup.

Tokyo residents and residents of most urban areas can make use of a private paper collection and recycling service (*chirigami kokan*), which exchanges old newspapers and magazines for toilet paper or tissues. A van will come round regularly for collection; again, to find out when, you might ask your landlord or a neighbor.

The city sanitation department makes two collections a month of bulky waste (*sodai gomi*), such as furniture or electric appliances (which must have any PCB removed first and will not be accepted without a PCB removal seal). You will have to pay a modest fee of ¥1,000 upward for the collection of bulky waste, depending on size and weight. The sanitation department also handles the disposal of dead animals weighing 25 kilograms (55 pounds) or less; the ¥2,500 fee includes collection and cremation.

Gases, fireworks and other explosives, oil products, tires, and pianos are among items that cannot be collected as either refuse or bulky waste. The sanitation department at your local ward office can refer you to a junkyard (*ponkotsuya*) that can scrap or recycle these items.

Disposing of cars and other vehicles is becoming increasingly difficult in Japan. Some people abandon their old cars and motorcycles under highways and bridges, in back streets, or in the garages of buildings slated for demolition. There are two legitimate methods of disposal: if you are a buying a new car, the dealer will be glad to arrange for the disposal of the old vehicle free of charge; if this is not the case, contact a junkyard, which will accept the vehicle for a fee of between ¥20,000 and ¥30,000 and arrange pickup if the vehicle is no longer roadworthy.

Telephone Services

Some houses and apartments will already have a telephone line installed when you move in; in other cases, you will need to buy or rent a line. You can buy a telephone line by applying at the nearest Nippon Telegraph and Telephone Corporation (NTT) office with documents certifying your name and address and paying ¥75,000. A cheaper alternative is to buy a line from someone who is moving or leaving Japan; these lines are often advertised in the English-language newspapers and magazines. In such cases, it is easier if both parties go to the NTT office that covers either the seller's or the buyer's address.

Telephone lines can be rented from various companies or brokers, most of whom do not speak English. Although the initial outlay when you rent a line is small, a significant disadvantage is that international calls cannot be made or received on a rented line.

Companies that offer international telephone services are KDD (001), IDC (0061), and ITJ (0041). KDD has the most extensive coverage and is the only company through which you can make operator-assisted calls, by using access code 0051; however, both IDC and ITJ are cheaper to use than KDD. If you are calling the United States, you also have the option of using the Sprint (0039-131), AT&T (0039-111), or MCI (0039-121) access codes.

Domestic calls are charged on the basis of distance, the duration of the call, and the time of day, starting at ¥10 for a local three-minute call. Both domestic and international telephone bills are monthly, and like utility bills, can be paid at post offices and banks or by automatic transfer.

There are several types of public pay phones in use, in a range of colors. The ones that you are most likely to come across will be green, green with a gold front panel, or pink. Pink phones only take coins, while green phones and most other phones will take ¥10 and ¥100 coins or telephone cards, with the gold-fronted variety providing international service. More telephones providing international service are being installed (green, yellow, and blue telephones), and you should soon be able to place international calls from nearly 90% of all public telephones. Telephone cards can be purchased from convenience stores, vending machines, tobacconists, and station kiosks.

Several English-language telephone directories, such as *City Source* and the *Japan Yellow Pages,* are available from foreign bookstores or may be obtained free of charge from JNTO Tourist Information Centers (TICs).

Postal Services

Mail service in Japan is generally prompt, and it is known for its safety; the loss or theft of mail is rare. Local post offices go to considerable trouble to deliver incorrectly or illegibly addressed mail. To assist the delivery of mail and other types of goods, it is advisable to have a nameplate with your name in both *katakana* and English by your front door or on your mailbox.

Post offices in Japan provide not only mail services but also banking and domestic and international remittance services as well as life insurance. The larger post offices sell a range of convenient products apart from stamps (*kitte*), for example, aerograms (*kokushokan*), prestamped postcards (*hagaki,* which can be exchanged for new ones if you make a mistake), special envelopes for sending cash safely through the mail (*genkin kakitome*), revenue stamps (*shunyu inshi,* not valid for postage) for use on official documents and contracts, and boxes and bags of various sizes that can be used for mailing parcels and packets.

If you are a philatelist or would like to purchase Japanese stamps as a gift, visit the Tokyo Central Post Office, in front of Tokyo Station, which has a large collector's corner. About 200 different commemorative stamps (*kinen kitte*) or definitive stamps are usually available, in addition to attractive gift packs with text in English. Unlike issues in some nations, Japanese stamps remain valid permanently, and most yen-denominated postage stamps issued in this century are legally usable.

To find a post office, look for a red "T" with a double bar on top, the symbol of post offices throughout Japan. Major post offices are usually open from 9:00 A.M. to 8:00 P.M. on weekdays and from 9:00 A.M. to 3:00 P.M. or even 5:00 P.M. on Saturdays, with the larger post offices open from 9:00 A.M. to 12:00 P.M. on Sundays too.

Major post offices stock a small book in English called *How to Use the Post Office,* which provides valuable information on services and prices. For example, you can save on the postage of small, light items by sending them as small packets rather than as ordinary parcels. Another useful tip: printed matter, such as

Christmas cards, can be sent at reduced rates if it is left unsealed and your written message does not exceed five words, not including your name.

It is much cheaper to send overseas Christmas mail by surface mail (*funabin*, which will take approximately three to four weeks to the United States) or by surface airlifted mail (SAL, or *sarubin*, taking two or three weeks), rather than by airmail (*kokubin*). Packages will require customs tags, and you must declare the actual cost of the article. Items costing less than a few hundred dollars are usually exempt from U.S. duties. Only the larger post offices can handle foreign express or registered mail or accept parcels.

If you are going away, you can arrange to have your mail held at one of the larger post offices for up to 30 days; however, this does not apply to parcels and registered mail, which will be returned to the sender if not claimed within a limited time. Also, if you change address in Japan, you can have your mail redirected to your new address for a period of one year (delivery may actually continue for up to two years), at no expense. To use this service, ask any post office for a change of address notification card (*tenkyo todoke*). Simply fill in your old and new addresses on the card and mail it to the post office closest to your previous address.

International Air Express Services

Several companies, including Federal Express, DHL, Nippon Express, and UPS Yamato, offer international air express services. These services are available for items ranging from documents to large packages weighing up to about 30 kilograms (66 pounds). The time required for delivery to the United States varies between one and three days, and rates will be between ¥5,000 and ¥12,000 for a one-kilogram (2.2-pound) package.

English-Language Publications
Books

A good selection of English-language books is available at large bookstores and hotel bookshops. Among the most well-known bookstores in Tokyo stocking foreign books are Jena in Ginza, Maruzen in Nihonbashi, Kinokuniya in Shinjuku and Shibuya, and Biblos in Takadanobaba. The Bookworm, in Tama, is the largest used book/book exchange shop in Tokyo.

All residents are eligible to register at and use any of the public libraries run by local governments in Japan. Some of these libraries, particularly those in areas where there are many English-speaking people, have a number of English-language books for loan. U.S. residents can use the library facilities at any of the American Cultural Centers (the libraries themselves are open to everyone) operated by the U.S. Information Service. Members of the Tokyo American Club and the Foreign Correspondents' Club of Japan may use their libraries; the British Council and some embassies also have library facilities. The National Diet Library has the largest collection of books and newspapers in Japan. Anyone aged 20 or over is welcome to use the Diet Library; however, books cannot be taken off the premises.

Newspapers

There are four general English-language daily newspapers published in Tokyo. The morning papers are the *Japan Times,* the *Mainichi Daily News,* and the *Daily Yomiuri,* while the *Asahi Evening News* appears in the afternoon. All provide wire service reports, reprints of features and syndicated columns from foreign publications, translations from the Japanese press, and articles by English-speaking staff writers to keep you up-to-date with events in Japan and around the world. These newspapers can be delivered anywhere in Japan and are sold at most station newsstands in major cities.

Other newspapers that may be of interest are the *Asian Wall Street Journal,* the *International Herald Tribune,* and the *Nikkei Weekly.* Also, some newspapers published abroad are available at bookstores stocking foreign books and at major hotels.

Periodicals

Weekly publications available include the international editions of *Time* and *Newsweek.* The *Weekly Review* from the Sunday edition of the *New York Times* is available by subscription. The *Japan Times Weekly* carries many interesting articles not found elsewhere.

Tokyo Journal, Tokyo Time Out, and *Tokyo Today* are monthly magazines in English that have complete listings of movies, concerts, and theater performances. A number of other English-language periodicals are available; most of these address special interest topics and can be bought at bookstores or hotel bookshops. Prices are considerably higher than back home, so if you have a favorite magazine you want to receive regularly, it is best to continue subscribing in your home country.

Free Publications

The biweekly *Tokyo Weekender,* distributed at selected locations—such as hotels, bookstores, supermarkets, and other shops serving the foreign community—carries good movie listings and classified advertisements as well as articles of general interest. *Tokyo City Guide* is also available at a number of different locations and includes valuable features on forthcoming festivals and other sightseeing attractions. *City Life News* is a monthly publication that is available at a number of hotels and shops. These publications can also be subscribed to, for a fee, if you wish to have them delivered to your home.

Television

There are seven nonsubscription television channels in Tokyo: NHK channels 1 and 3, both government-owned, NTV (Channel 4), TBS (Channel 6), Fuji (Channel 8), TV Asahi (Channel 10), and TV Tokyo (Channel 12). Some programs are broadcast in a bilingual format that allows viewers, at the touch of a button, to watch foreign television programs or movies in the original language. Some stations also provide simultaneous English translations of news and sports programs. Programs in this bilingual format or with simultaneous translations represent about 10% of all television broadcasts. Your TV must be equipped with a bilingual function to receive these broadcasts, but this is standard in most new models sold in Japan.

Three satellite channels in Tokyo are available by subscription, all operated by the government-owned station, NHK. To receive them, you will need a special tuner; you can get a separate unit for this, although some new TVs have a built-in component for receiving two of the three channels. You will also need to have a satellite dish installed if your house or apartment complex does not already have one. Satellite channels offer extensive live coverage of sports and run more recent movies (many of them in English) than the regular television channels.

A number of cable television stations are available in the greater Tokyo area, offering a variety of sports, entertainment, and news broadcasts. The cost is quite high unless you already have a cable hookup in your house or apartment block. There are subscription, tuner rental, and installation fees as well as a monthly charge and special fees for some channels.

NHK charges compulsory fees for any household that has a TV set (the law stipulates that anyone using a TV set must pay fees to NHK, but there is no penalty for those who fail to pay), and there is an additional charge if you receive satellite broadcasts. An NHK collector will call regularly to collect payment, starting shortly after you move in. If he or she has called more than once or twice and you have not been home, don't be surprised if the next call is around 7:30 A.M. or 9:00 P.M.

Radio

There are many radio stations throughout Japan offering a variety of programs in Japanese. J-Wave, a music station on the 81.3 FM wavelength, broadcasts in a mixture of Japanese and English. The U.S. Armed Forces radio station, the Far East Network (FEN), broadcasts 24 hours a day entirely in English on the 810 AM wavelength and features comprehensive news programs daily as well as five-minute news bulletins every hour.

Natural Disasters

Japan, situated in a seismically active region, experiences thousands of earthquakes every year, although the vast majority of these are too small to be felt by humans. Japan is also in the path of typhoons originating in the western Pacific, most of which reach the country's shores during the summer months. Both the national government and local governments have done much in the postwar era to lessen the impact of natural disasters.

Building standards in Japan, especially in earthquake-prone areas, are among the strictest in the world, and Japanese construction technologies are highly advanced. However, buildings and other structures are only earthquake-resistant to a point, and preparedness on the part of the public is therefore essential in keeping casualties and damage to minimum in the unlikely event of a major disaster. As a foreigner in Japan, especially if you have children, you should take the minimum precautions of registering with your embassy—as mentioned earlier in this chapter—and preparing an emergency kit, the contents of which are described in the following sections. Once you have done this, you can put it out of your mind and concentrate on enjoying your stay in Japan.

Typhoons

Typhoons may occur any time from June to October but are most frequent in September. Typhoons can bring heavy rain for several days, sometimes resulting in floods and landslides and fierce winds that pose a threat to shipping and may damage unsound structures on land. Typhoons very rarely strike the Tokyo area directly, thanks to the mountain ranges that shield the Kanto region, and no typhoon has wrought major damage in Tokyo for decades, although there are often strong winds and heavy rain. Okinawa, Kyushu, the Kansai and Tohoku regions, and occasionally even Hokkaido, however, are sometimes in the direct path of typhoons, and precautions should be taken, especially in areas close to rivers and wherever there is a danger of landslides. Past experience has shown that taking simple precautions during the typhoon season, including in Tokyo, can reduce damage to property significantly and prevent unnecessary personal injury.

Warnings and information on typhoon conditions and high winds that may affect your area are issued on the radio and television and in the newspapers. If a typhoon is approaching, the following precautions should be taken:

•Bring indoors all freestanding objects, such as garbage cans, lawn furniture, flowerpots, children's toys—anything that could blow away and cause damage or become damaged.

•Tell children not to stray far from home and keep them indoors during high winds.

•Check emergency lighting equipment, such as flashlights and candles, and keep these things close at hand. Make sure you have extra batteries for flashlights, radios, and other items and matches for candles.

•Fill all available containers with water (including your bathtub) in case the supply is interrupted. If at any time it should become necessary to use water that is not known to be potable, it should be treated with iodine tablets or boiled for 20 minutes before use.

•To avoid the danger of injury caused by broken windows, draw all curtains, blinds, or shutters. Where there are none, fix a cloth to the window to catch broken glass.

•If a typhoon is very close, it is advisable not to use elevators, as power outages may occur.

•Avoid unnecessary trips outdoors if winds are very strong. If there is heavy rain for a protracted period, avoid areas close to riverbanks.

Earthquakes

Thousands of small earthquakes are recorded every year in Japan, but most of them are too weak to be noticed. Often, minor earthquakes can be mistaken for vibration from a passing truck. However, medium-sized to major earthquakes do occur in Japan, and these are the type that require thoughtful, calm action.

Although the Kansai region has rarely had major earthquakes, the Kanto region, encompassing Tokyo and Yokohama, has had a large earthquake about once every 70 to 90 years. The most recent earthquakes in the capital area were recorded in 1855 and 1923. The Great Kanto Earthquake of September 1, 1923, with its epicenter in Sagami Bay, west of the Izu Peninsula, measured 7.9 on the Richter Scale and was the most disastrous earthquake ever to strike Japan in terms of casualties and damage. Approximately 2,000 people were killed by the tremor itself, and the ensuing fires, which destroyed half of Tokyo, claimed over 100,000 lives. A key factor in averting a similar catastrophe in the future is preparedness, especially the prompt evacuation of areas threatened by tidal waves and immediate efforts to prevent fires from breaking out.

Major earthquakes may be predictable hours or possibly days in advance. If a reliable prediction is made that an earthquake is imminent, the prime minister will immediately issue a disaster warning to alert residents and disaster prevention authorities in all areas likely to be affected.

The official alert will be in the form of sirens (three 45-second blasts at 15-second intervals) sounded over the speakers of disaster prevention wireless systems and from police patrol cars and fire stations.

Certain steps must be taken if such a warning is issued. There is no need to rush to an evacuation site. You should remain calm and refrain, if possible, from using fire, telephones, and cars. Infants and invalids should be placed in a safe area, and furniture should be secured to prevent it from falling. The accessibility of fire extinguishers, drinking water, food, and emergency supplies should be ascertained. An earthquake kit should be assembled if one is not already prepared; suggestions are given at the end of this chapter.

After the alert is sounded, gas (which you should refrain from using) and electricity supplies will continue. City and government offices will continue to function normally, and supermarkets and departments stores will remain open but concentrate on the supply of food and daily necessities. Public transportation will continue to operate, at reduced speed. All kindergartens and elementary schools will expect parents or other adult family members to collect children, while junior and senior high-school students will go home in groups.

The Tokyo Metropolitan Government has emergency plans that would be implemented in the event of a major earthquake. A system of neighborhood associations and groups provides a network through which instructions will be relayed to Tokyo residents by the authorities during an emergency. Japanese radio and television and FEN (the U.S. military's Far East Network radio station on the 810 AM wavelength) will carry information bulletins as well.

There are designated *hinanbasho,* or refuge areas (usually in parks or open spaces), across Tokyo to be used if evacuation of any section of the city becomes necessary. Maps are displayed on street corners throughout the city showing designated refuge areas for the particular section. You are advised to check the location of the refuge areas closest to your home and office and learn the quickest way to get there.

Of course, a major earthquake can occur without any warning. Tokyo is susceptible to *chokkagata* (earthquakes of which the epicenter is directly underneath the city), which are believed to be virtually impossible to predict. Fortunately, most of Japan's modern office buildings, apartment blocks, and houses have been built to withstand all but the very strongest earthquakes.

You can best prepare yourself for dealing with an earthquake if you take a few necessary precautions and know how to act during and after a tremor. Keep the following in mind:

•Ascertain where the nearest refuge areas are to each location where you and your family members might reasonably be at the time of an earthquake, such as the home, office, and school. Acquaint yourself with emergency plans and guidance and discuss them with your family. Knowing that each member of the family knows what to do will be reassuring for everyone should there be a period of separation when communication may be impossible.

•Always keep the following supplies readily available: a pocket radio, food and drinking water for at least two or three days, warm clothing in the winter or light clothing in the summer, sturdy shoes, blankets, and a first-aid kit. Important documents, such as passports, and a supply of cash should also be kept in an easily accessible place.

•Since fires following earthquakes often cause more injuries, fatalities, and property damage than the quake itself, be ready to extinguish all pilot lights, burners, furnaces, or other flames quickly in the event of an emergency. Have fire-extinguishing equipment available and make sure you know how to use it.

•Find out about the organizations or groups in your neighborhood that are familiar with emergency procedures. If this is difficult because of the language barrier, you should be able to obtain such information from your workplace, the local ward office, or the *koban* (police box) in your neighborhood. Even if nobody in the area speaks English, it will be advantageous if such organizations or groups are aware of your presence in the neighborhood. By following their lead during an emergency, you can be certain that you are complying with the instructions of the authorities designed to ensure your physical safety even if you are not able to understand them.

The following are excerpts of the guidelines and information regarding earthquakes issued by the Tokyo Metropolitan Government. You should make sure you and all members of your family are familiar with them.

What to Do in the Event of an Earthquake

1. Turn off the gas in your house or apartment, including stoves and other cooking appliances. If small fires break out, stay calm and extinguish them immediately.

2. Seek shelter under a door frame, table, or desk to protect yourself from falling objects.

3. If you are indoors, stay there. Going outside increases the chance of injury from falling objects. If you are outside, immediately seek shelter or proceed to an open area.

4. Open a door to the outside as an emergency exit. Door frames can jam during an earthquake and trap you indoors.

5. Keep away from narrow alleys, concrete-block walls, and embankments.

6. If you are evacuating a crowded area, such as a department store, theater, or stadium, remain calm and listen carefully for instructions from the attendant in charge.

7. If you are driving, immediately stop your car on the left-hand side of the street and turn off the engine. Driving will be banned in all restricted areas.

8. Proceed to designated refuge areas as soon as the earthquake is over. Walk, do not run.

9. Do not panic over rumors you hear from people around you. Listen carefully to a radio or TV for information and instructions. In the event of a major earthquake, NHK will broadcast information and instructions in English for foreign residents on all its television and radio networks. On your TV, tune to Channel 1 or to NHK Satellite TV channels 1 or 2 (bilingual service). On your radio, tune to NHK on the 594 AM wavelength or to FEN (the Far East Network) on 810 AM.

Suggested Earthquake Kits

Master Kit

- Medical supplies: alcohol, vaseline, burn ointment, eye drops, band-aids, cotton, gauze, scissors, and tweezers.
- Food: instant rice and/or potatoes and quick-energy foods.
- Other: toothbrush and paste, soap, candles, watch, pen and paper, and money.

Individual Kit

Several weeks' supply of any prescription medicine for chronic illnesses, helmet and gas mask, photocopy of the title page of your passport, money, soap, toothbrush and paste, watch, pen and paper, and maps of Tokyo and your ward.

Japan Meteorological Agency Seismic Intensity Scale

0	Not felt.
1	Slight. Felt by some.
2	Weak. Felt by most.
3	Rather strong. Slight shaking of houses.
4	Strong. Strong shaking of houses.
5	Very strong. Cracks in the walls.
6	Disastrous. Danger of falling objects, landslides.
7	Major disaster.

Two or Three Things I Know about Living in a Japanese Neighborhood

by Bruce Leigh

It didn't take me long after arriving in Japan to begin noticing that things were just a little bit different here than they'd been back in good old Omaha. Right off the bat I had the distinct impression that nearly everyone around me was speaking a foreign language, quite possibly Japanese, which, as it turned out, was absolutely correct and only goes to prove that, even in times of great emotional disorientation, one is still capable of making rational observations.

Then I went and complicated things by moving into a Japanese neighborhood. Not that I had much choice in the matter. By all accounts, Japan is a nation composed of a vast number of Japanese neighborhoods, and little else. You might think that moving into a Japanese neighborhood would be fairly straightforward, but there's virtually nothing you can do straightforwardly in Japan. Things are naturally oblique here, and neighborhoods are no exception.

In Japan there exists what we can call the "group thing," whereby everyone is part of a group or groups, or subgroups within groups, and no one is ever alone. The neighborhood is an important group unit, and moving into one requires taking on the obligation to actively share in the concerns, responsibilities, and activities of that group, thereby helping to generate a sense of harmony and well-being, till death or a company transfer do us part.

Basically, I'd only been looking for a place to stay, and there I was feeling like I was getting married. Not that the harmonizing and well-being stuff wasn't appealing, it's just that even as you attempt to harmonize and well-be, there's no guarantee that any of your neighbors are going to speak to you for the first six months or so. And it's not because they dislike you or believe that, because you're a foreigner, you must be a dangerous lunatic. It's simply because you're an unknown quantity, thereby unpredictable, and hence a source of some stress that everyone wishes would just vanish as soon as possible.

You might, for example, notice your neighbors constantly dashing off to the nearest shrine to pray, or having new locks installed, or buying Akita attack dogs and displaying them prominently in the front garden. Don't take it personally. It's just a temporary breakdown in the flow of the neighborhood continuum.

Take me as a case in point of what not to do. I made the mistake of shouting shortly after moving into my Japanese neighborhood. I just felt like it—didn't regard it as any big deal. Where I come from shouting is a sign of good health. My neighbors didn't see it that way. People in Japan just don't do that sort of thing. Perhaps the entire group unit could, on occasion, shout in unison, possibly to commemorate some special event, but for individuals it's a definite no-no. After my shouting spree, I was shunned for about a year, and I am still referred to as the foreign shouter.

Finally, one of the old women in the neighborhood took me aside and confided in me. "Next time you get angry and feel like shouting," she said, "take the *futons* outside and beat them with a stick instead." Good advice, I think. And welcome to the neighborhood.

Bruce Leigh is a longtime resident of Japan and a regular contributor to the *Japan Times*.

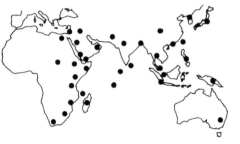

NO MATTER

where you do business, Air Express International gets your shipment there. We're a leading global air freight forwarder with offices in 110 countries. That allows us to offer quality service, competitive pricing and on-time reliability.

WHERE YOU SHIP

is your business, how it gets there is ours. We do more than handle cargo; we deliver innovative transportation, distribution and logistic management services tailored to your company's needs. Think of us as your single source.

IT'S AN AEI

network that makes us second to none. Our LOGIS® Information System instantly links you to 110 countries and 24 world airlines. From tracing and tracking to rating and routing, LOGIS means reliable delivery, better control and improved savings. When you're shipping to or from the land of the rising sun, call the rising star. AEI.

WORLD.

MAEI
Maruzen Air Express International
2-13, Akasaka 6-chome, Minato-ku, Tokyo 107 Japan
Tel: (03) 3585-6531 Fax: (03) 3582-3041

Calling your Uncle has never been easier.

To reach the U.S. with Sprint Express, just dial 0039-131 or 0066-55-877.

No matter who you're trying to reach back in the states, Sprint Express makes it easy. With just one phone call, you can reach Sprint's English-speaking operators in the U.S., who will connect your call. And you don't even have to be a Sprint customer to use Sprint Express. You can bill the call to your Sprint FŌNCARD,℠ to your U.S. local calling card, or collect to the U.S.

To get a FŌNCARD, call 81-3-3794-6601 or write to: Sprint Japan Inc.

    Attn: FŌNCARD Manager
    Nissan Fudosan Building
21-13 Himonya 4-Chome Meguro-Ku
    Tokyo, 152 Japan

For your trips outside of Japan, be sure to use the Sprint Express access numbers below. For additional access numbers call 1-800-877-1992. They make calling your American relations easier than ever.

*Hong Kong	800-1877
*Korea	009-16
*Korea (military phones)	550-FONE
Australia	0014-881-877
*U.K.	0800-89-0877

Chapter

7

Everyday Life

From a practical aspect, many foreign residents find Japan an extremely accommodating, convenient place to live once they have settled in. The quality of the services, in particular, is among the highest in the world. In major cities, public transport is safe, plentiful, and nearly always on time. Taxis can be hailed almost anywhere. A wide range of goods, both Japanese and foreign, can be found in the many stores, which are usually open until at least 7:00 P.M., including on Sundays. If you need to transmit a fax, get film developed, pay your bills, or send an urgent parcel, the local 24-hour convenience store can do all this for you and sell you a hot meal too.

On the down side, some aspects of everyday life will no doubt leave you wringing your hands, at least at the beginning of your stay. Japan's shortage of space makes streets crowded—Americans accustomed to jumping into the car and driving to a nearby mall may have to adapt to a different style of shopping, for example—and the packed commuter trains are notorious.

With a little careful planning, however, you should be able to work out a system for getting around, shopping, and other activities that best suits your needs. There are many consumer and other services available specially for the foreign community; some of these you will find detailed in the free publications mentioned in Chapter 6 and in TELL's *International Community Calendar*.

Perhaps the most worrying aspect of everyday life in Japan to newcomers is the high cost of living, well publicized abroad. Some surveys rate Tokyo's cost of living the highest in the world. Indeed, food and many basic household goods are several times more expensive in Japan than in the United States. One of the factors keeping prices high is an extremely complex distribution system with layers of middlemen; as a consequence, even Japanese consumer goods, such as cameras and computers, may be cheaper in the United States than they are in Japan. Of a typical family's necessary expenditures, only education-related costs (for public schools) are lower in Japan than in the United States or Europe, and rental payments are the largest single expense for the majority of Japanese who do not own their own home.

However, many bargains are available in Japan, and not only to the dedicated shopper. Cheap, delicious food can be bought in restaurants as well as ready-cooked from small shops and supermarkets. Cut-price consumer goods of all kinds can be found in various locations throughout large cities, and whole districts may concentrate on selling one category of goods at discounted prices.

In Tokyo, the most famous of these specialized areas is Akihabara, which is well known even outside Japan for its hundreds of electronics shops offering consumer electronic products at between 20% and 40% below suggested retail prices. Some of the lesser-known stores in the district have state-of-the-art electronics unavailable anywhere else. Okachimachi, near Ueno, has bargain shops selling everything from food and drink to clothing. Office furniture can be found in the street between Higashi-Nihonbashi and Asakusabashi, and Asakusabashi offers Christmas and other decorations at low prices. The area near Kanda specializes in cut-price sporting goods, and nearby Jimbocho is filled with secondhand bookstores. Discount camera shops can be found in Shinjuku and Ikebukuro.

Most of these districts with reasonably priced goods are in Shitamachi, which was Tokyo's downtown area until the 19th century and is now slightly to the east of the city center. In districts where there are a lot of expatriates, such as Minato-ku and Shibuya-ku, prices tend to be high. End-of-season sales in department stores, listed in English-language dailies and magazines, also offer an opportunity to buy goods at cheaper prices.

Stores, Purchases, and Deliveries

There are many interesting, delightful items to choose from in Japan's stores, and simply browsing is quite acceptable. In fact, if you want to purchase an item, you need to attract the attention of the sales assistant by saying "*sumimasen*"; otherwise you will probably be left alone to browse at your leisure.

You can be assured of courteous treatment in almost all stores, and there is often an English-speaking clerk in the large department stores. However, nowhere will you find anyone inclined to hurry; your purchases will be handled with the utmost care and neatly wrapped and bagged. Paying for an item and having it wrapped, regardless of how much it costs, may take as much as 10 minutes. Recently, some department stores have offered to provide "abbreviated wrapping" in response to environmental concerns.

Any purchase, especially large, bulky, or heavy items, can be delivered to your house by most department stores, neighborhood stores, and supermarkets. For a purchase of over ¥5,000, there may be no delivery charge. Take your personal *meishi* with you to show the sales assistant if you are unable to write your address in Japanese.

Until the mid-1980s, credit cards were relatively rare in Japan. Although there has recently been a credit card issuing boom, many purchases are still made with cash. Charge accounts may be opened at most department stores and certain supermarkets, and some of these establishments have started issuing their own credit cards. Nevertheless, you will probably find yourself paying with cash more often than you may have been accustomed to at home.

There is a centuries-old custom in Japan of selling and purchasing goods in odd-numbered lots—the even numbers are considered unlucky. Ten is acceptable since it is a multiple of five; four is avoided because the Japanese word for four, *shi,* also means death. Thus, tableware is sold in sets of five.

Major department stores—such as Hankyu, Isetan, Keio, Marui, Matsuya, Matsuzakaya, Mitsukoshi, Odakyu, Seibu, Sogo, Takashimaya, and Tokyu—can be found in all Japan's big cities and in some of the larger towns. In Tokyo, the department stores are concentrated in such urban centers as Ginza, Nihonbashi, Shibuya, Shinjuku, Ikebukuro, Ueno, and Asakusa. They are open six days a week and closed on one weekday, which varies from store to store (see listing on next page). Most are open on weekends and national holidays, with the exception of New Year's Day. Business hours are usually from 10:00 A.M. to 7:00 P.M., except in the traditional gift-giving seasons of *ochugen* (in July) and *oseibo* (in December), when many stores open daily for a month and may close at 8:00 P.M.

The following is a list of the larger department stores in Tokyo and Yokohama, with their closing days and telephone numbers.

Tokyo

Daimaru, Tokyo Station (Wed.)	(03) 3212-8011
Hankyu, Yurakucho (Thur.)	(03) 3575-2233
Isetan, Shinjuku (Wed.)	(03) 3352-1111
Foreign Customer Service	(03) 3225-2514
Keio, Shinjuku (Thur.)	(03) 3342-2111
Marui, Shibuya (Wed.)	(03) 3464-0101
Marui, Shinjuku (Wed.)	(03) 3354-0101
Matsuya, Ginza (Tue.)	(03) 3567-1211
Matsuzakaya, Ginza (Wed.)	(03) 3572-1111
Matsuzakaya, Ueno (Wed.)	(03) 3832-1111
Mitsukoshi, Ginza (Mon.)	(03) 3562-1111
Mitsukoshi, Nihonbashi (Mon.)	(03) 3241-3311
Odakyu, Shinjuku (Tue.)	(03) 3342-1111
Printemps, Ginza (Wed.)	(03) 3567-0077
Seibu, Ikebukuro (Tue.)	(03) 3981-0111
Seibu, Shibuya (Wed.)	(03) 3462-0111
Foreign Customer Liaison Office	(03) 3462-3848
Seibu, Yurakucho (Wed.)	(03) 3286-0111
Foreign Customer Liaison Office	(03) 3286-5482
Sogo, Yurakucho (Tue.)	(03) 3284-6711
Takashimaya, Nihonbashi (Wed.)	(03) 3211-4111
Tobu, Ikebukuro (Wed.)	(03) 3981-2211
Tokyu, Shibuya (Tue.)	(03) 3477-3111
Tokyu Hands, Ikebukuro (2nd & 3rd Wed.)	(03) 3980-6111
Tokyu Hands, Shibuya (2nd & 3rd Wed.)	(03) 5489-5111
Wako, Ginza (Sun.)	(03) 3562-2111

Yokohama

Matsuzakaya (Wed.)	(045) 261-2121
Mitsukoshi (Mon.)	(045) 312-1111
Sogo (Tue.)	(045) 465-2111
Takashimaya (Wed.)	(045) 311-1251

Small local stores are shut one day a week, some closing on Sundays and some on weekdays, and have variable closing hours, although most are open until at least 7:00 P.M.

In the past several years, convenience stores—such as Seven-Eleven, Lawson, and FamilyMart—have sprung up all over Tokyo and other large cities and their suburbs. These stores, open 24 hours a day year-round, are small general shops that also sell ready-cooked foods. Although selection is limited and you will not usually find foreign goods, a wide range of items is available, and many services are also provided; you can make photocopies, send faxes or parcels, pay utility bills, get film developed, order gifts, and buy movie and concert tickets.

Shopping for Food

The selection and prices of food in Japan vary widely according to the type and location of stores. Food shopping need not be expensive if you avoid the main uptown department store areas; local shops, supermarkets, and stalls sell food at reasonable prices.

Many neighborhoods have small stores specializing in fish, meat, fruit, vegetables, bread and cakes, *tofu,* or rice. Also, in most neighborhoods, you will notice a vendor of produce—such as vegetables or fish—selling from his van and advertising his presence with a loudspeaker or a bell.

Large neighborhoods have supermarkets that offer a selection of domestic and imported products. They are usually conveniently situated and prices are moderate. After visiting one of these supermarkets, you may be tempted to try some of the many Japanese foods on offer, especially when you realize how much less expensive they are than certain Western-style foods.

In Tokyo and other major cities, some supermarkets— such as the National Azabu Supermarket in Tokyo, Kinokuniya, and Meidi-ya—cater specially to the foreign community. Although these supermarkets can be more expensive than the ordinary variety, they carry a number of products and brands that you will be familiar with. If you do a lot of Western-style cooking, you can supplement your general shopping with special items from these stores. Signs are usually in English, English-speaking staff will be on hand, and most stores offer home delivery service and parking facilities.

In nearly every department store, you will notice a tempting aroma coming from the basement floors. Follow your nose and you will find an amazing display of foods; countless bins, counters, and showcases offer a huge variety of delicacies. In department stores in more cosmopolitan areas, you will also find numerous imported foods and wines. In the local department stores, the basement floor resembles a crowded market with stalls selling a wide range of products from all around the country.

Many foreigners, particularly if they speak no Japanese, find the enormous variety of new, unfamiliar foods bewildering. A little homework with a good, illustrated English-language Japanese cookbook can help you find your way around the supermarket shelves; books are also available that can help you identify in Japanese the products that you need to buy. Of course, staple products, both Japanese and Western, are easily found in most supermarkets. For the adventurous, there is a seemingly unlimited supply of exciting new items to try.

Japan is a paradise for the fish lover. Fish is plentiful and generally of very high quality, and you will find a broad range of both familiar and unfamiliar varieties. *Ebi,* or shrimp, are unsurpassed in size and flavor, and oysters, mussels, and scallops are delicious and fairly inexpensive in season. An early-morning visit to the Tsukiji fish market in Tokyo can result in an economical and delicious catch for your home refrigerator.

Meat is also offered in many varieties and sold by the 100 grams (3.5 ounces), not by the kilogram. Prices for beef tend to be high, although they have come down somewhat in recent years with the easing of import restrictions. U.S.-style cuts are often available in the larger supermarkets but are not likely to be found in small neighborhood butcher shops. Domestic beef, including Kobe and Matsuzaka beef, is expensive and has a relatively high fat content. Whole chickens are smaller and fattier than U.S. varieties, but delicious chicken is available at reasonable prices in many cuts as well as minced. Many different cuts of pork can also be found, and like chicken, pork is reasonably priced. Eggs are usually sold in packages of 10, and free-range eggs are becoming increasingly common.

Fresh pasteurized milk is widely available in Japan, although prices will be above those in the United States. As a higher temperature is used in pasteurization, the milk has a slightly different taste and will keep longer (one to three weeks) before spoiling. Low-fat and nonfat varieties can also be bought in many stores. Ordinary cream and whipping cream are sold everywhere, and sour cream is available at larger supermarkets. The cost of butter and cheese is relatively high. Imported cheeses are expensive, and local cheeses, many of them processed, are rather bland. Yogurt can be found in plain, sweetened, and fruit-flavored varieties.

A wide range of high-quality fruit and vegetables is available. Japanese oranges, called *mikan,* are available from fall to spring. Another favorite is *nashi,* with the consistency of an apple but a combination of pear and apple flavors. Locally grown strawberries, available in winter, are worth waiting for. Kiwifruit, bananas, and pineapples are all popular and very cheap when in season, but you might be surprised at the price of apples, which are almost considered a delicacy. Prices of out-of-season or imported fruit are high, and you should avoid specialty fruit shops and specialty fruit sections of department stores as they can be horrendously expensive, although the fruit sold is ideal for gifts to valued friends or business contacts.

There is also a large selection of vegetables, many of which will be new to you. The ones you recognize—such as cucumbers, bell peppers, and eggplant—may be smaller than at home; carrots, however, may be larger.

Japanese-brand frozen vegetables, fruit, seafood, and meat are available in many varieties. Canned goods are plentiful, and, increasingly, manufacturers are labeling their food products in English, so shopping is becoming easier.

Beer, spirits, and wines can be bought at liquor stores, department stores, and some convenience stores. Japanese beer and *sake* (rice wine, although the word in Japanese also refers to all alcoholic drink) come in a huge range of types and prices, and domestic whiskey is widely available. Imported alcohol is much more expensive than in the United States. A limited range of table wines is distributed mainly through supermarkets and department stores that cater to foreigners; however, there are also a number of smaller distributors and wine clubs where a wider variety of wines can be found.

Catalog Shopping

For added convenience, you can buy a wide range of items through either local or overseas catalogs. Clothing, books, baby goods, furniture, and toys can all be purchased through overseas catalogs. While prices are not always cheaper than in stores, catalog shopping can guarantee sizes and brands with which you are familiar. A number of outlets in Japan specialize in distributing a wide variety of food items—including fresh vegetables, health food, and dairy products—by catalog. Although you may have to buy some items in bulk, prices can be cheaper than at the international supermarkets. The Foreign Buyer's Club (East Court Two Suite #307, 1-14, Koyocho Naka, Higashi Nada-ku, Kobe 658 Tel: (078) 857-9001, Fax: (078) 222-3206) can import almost any item from the United States. This nonprofit organization, started by a foreign couple, has a catalog of about 40,000 items. There are a few other organizations offering similar services.

Other Services

Dry cleaning facilities are readily available, but you might need to shop around to find really high-quality service. Prices and the speed of service vary depending on the area, and some dry cleaners offer a convenient twice-weekly home pickup and delivery service.

Shoe repair shops are less widespread but can usually be found in department stores or shopping malls at major train stations. The most common of these is the Mister Minute chain.

As Western hair can be quite different from Japanese hair and often requires different cutting, styling, and coloring techniques, for hairdressing it will be worth your while to go to one of the many Western-trained, English-speaking stylists that can be found in Tokyo and the Kansai region. Outside the major cities, there are a limited number of hairdressers who speak English and even fewer who have had experience in a Western salon. As mentioned in Chapter 5, if you use hair color or if you would like to have a special type of perm, it is safest to bring the necessary solutions with you.

Domestic Assistance

Many foreign families in Japan find it convenient to have domestic help. For those in the work force, the normal working day can be very long, and work commitments may carry over into the weekend. For those who do not benefit from the ready-made structure and network of contacts that a job provides, developing friendships and participating in various community activities can also be time-consuming.

The amount of assistance you will need will depend on the number of people in your family, their ages, the size of your accommodation, and the amount of effort everyone in your family is willing to contribute to housekeeping. Depending on the number of days that you need help, you may decide to use a domestic agency or a part-time or full-time individual. If you require assistance for only half a day per week, you may find that it is safer, if more expensive, to use an agency. Most individual help prefer to work for a full day at one place because of the time and cost involved in traveling between locations, and they may well give up a half-day position when they are offered a full-day one. If you would like full-time assistance, and you can offer appropriate accommodation, it is possible to have someone live in.

If you need someone for three or more days a week and you are unable to hire a Japanese person, then you can sponsor someone from another country who is already in Japan. This is a relatively simple, if time-consuming, process. The various advisory services listed in TELL's *International Community Calendar* will be able to tell you how to go about this.

It is quite difficult to find a Japanese person who will work as a domestic. Most of the people working in this capacity at present are women from the Philippines or Thailand who speak English but not necessarily Japanese. Most people find suitable staff by word of mouth or by advertising on community service notice boards, such as those at the Tokyo American Club or the National Azabu Supermarket.

Although most staff will speak good English, it is important to remember that it will be their second language. This, in combination with cultural differences, means that there is potential for misunderstanding. It is important to confirm that instructions have been understood and that expectations on both sides are perfectly clear.

Domestic agency rates are higher than individual wages, which are about ¥10,000 for an eight-hour day and ¥6,000 for half a day. A full-time, live-in person working six days a week will charge about ¥180,000 per month, with room and board provided. In addition, the sponsor is usually required to pay a return airfare home once a year if the person is from another country, give between one month's and three months' salary as an annual bonus, provide four weeks' paid vacation each year, and pay extra for any evening baby-sitting.

Child Care

Japan has a range of child-care options, including baby-sitting services and public and private day care. If you have domestic help, that person may also be able to take responsibility for some baby-sitting. It is extremely difficult to hire a nanny in Japan, as there are no training courses for this type of work and the concept is almost unheard of. People who come to Japan thinking that they will work as a nanny very quickly discover that they can earn much more working in a private preschool or teaching English.

There are a number of baby-sitting agencies available in the Greater Tokyo area. Charges vary; generally, there is a joining fee to use the service and an hourly fee for a minimum number of hours each time you use the service, and sometimes there is also an annual fee. Certain agencies use only experienced sitters or older Japanese women. Staff at some agencies and some sitters may not speak English, and many sitters will not do any domestic work while they are baby-sitting. Details of the major agencies are provided in *Japan for Kids: The Ultimate Guide for Parents and Their Children* (by Diane Wiltshire Kanagawa and Jeanne Huey Erickson).

Public day-care centers, run by the local ward, town, or city office, provide convenient and economical services for families in which both parents work or in which one parent is disabled. Further information and registration forms can be obtained from your ward, town, or city office. Local governments also license private day-care centers; applications should be made to these centers directly. At both types of centers, hours are generally from 8:30 A.M. to 5:00 P.M., and staff will probably not speak English.

Chapter 12 provides information on nursery schools in Japan. There are also day-care centers that may accept children on a casual basis. Some of these centers are situated in the major hotels in Tokyo or in department stores. The Tokyo American Club also provides casual child care to members at reasonable rates.

Tokyo — One of the World's Fashion Capitals

by Chris Cook

Welcome to Japan!

And welcome to Tokyo, which, alongside Paris, London, Milan, and New York, is regarded as one of the fashion capitals of the world. It is home to over 10 million people, among them such top designers as Hanae Mori, Issey Miyake, Rei Kawakubo, and Yohji Yamamoto.

One of the first things that you will probably notice—besides the utility poles, which often sprout from the middle of sidewalks, or the fact that bike brakes always emit a horrendous squeal—is that, both on a business and social level, Japanese people dress very well.

Although the world economy—including Japan's—is in a recession, you would not believe that when strolling the busy streets of Tokyo.

Women, especially, have a penchant for quality items—brand name goods and designer label clothes—and few young or middle-aged Japanese women are without a Louis Vuitton or Chanel handbag.

The same holds true for men, except that they are not quite so concerned about coordinating their look—unless you check out some of the young trendsetters in Roppongi's discos.

The Japanese "salaryman," unfortunately, is the antithesis of fashion. He looks like he was cast from the same mold as everyone else, wearing a blue or gray off-the-rack polyester suit, a white shirt, polished black shoes, and, in the briefest nod to individualism, a necktie of a different pattern than that being worn by the businessman next to him.

That is basically as far as "fashion" goes for salarymen working for one of the big conglomerates in Otemachi or Nihonbashi.

One of the problems of buying clothes here is that there is so much available.

"Where do I begin to look?" you may ask.

That, of course, depends on what you are looking for and where you shop.

The department stores in Ginza, Shinjuku, Shibuya, and Ikebukuro have the advantage of featuring a lot of designers under one roof, but these places tend to be crowded, especially on weekends.

European—most notably Italian and French—styles are the best-sellers in these stores; however, at every turn there are Japanese designs.

In Shibuya, which tends to have a more youthful bent, less well-known designers from England and the United States can be found in a trendy store called Seed.

The capital's fashion center is undoubtedly the Aoyama/Harajuku area, easily accessible from Harajuku Station between Shibuya and Shinjuku stations on the Yamanote Line. This district has a lot of boutiques selling famous name brands from all over the world.

Ultracrowded Takeshita-dori, which arguably has more bodies per square meter than a Ginza sidewalk on the weekend, has clothes for children and teenagers at relatively reasonable prices.

Omotesando, Tokyo's answer to a Parisian boulevard, is a fun place to stroll down on weekends, just gazing in shop windows, savoring the cosmopolitan atmosphere from a sidewalk café, or marveling at the latest fashions.

With so many different designers and varieties of merchandise, which change with every passing season, Japan is a fashion slave's paradise.

Young Japanese have been quick to take Western fashion to their hearts, and for many there is no stopping. The fact that the economy is ailing is immaterial. The only thing that is on their minds is when the new clothes will appear in the boutiques.

Chris Cook is a fashion writer for the *Japan Times* and for *Studio Collections,* in Australia.

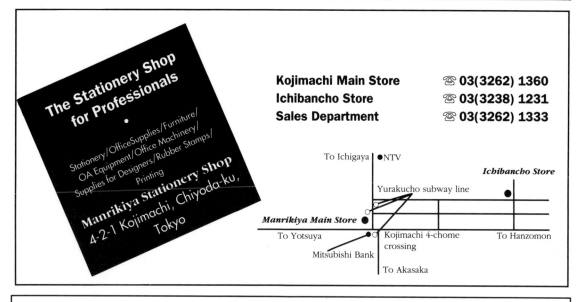

THE ENTENTE
ROKKO ISLAND CITY, KOBE, JAPAN

The Entente is fully functioning and ready for occupancy.

THE QUALITY THAT YOU EXPECT IN A PRIVATE ESTATE RESIDENCE IS YOURS.....

The staff of The Entente would like to welcome you to Japan. This new luxury residence creates a unique environment so individuals and families of the international business and professional community can maintain their lifestyles comfortably in this unfamiliar country. The hospitable staff, with its decades of experience in solving the problems of international people, guarantees that your adjustment will happen swiftly and smoothly.

Your lifestyle, business, educational, and recreational needs will be taken care of by our staff and facilities. Residents will have access to a daycare, a physical fitness facility and a business center for their convenience. Two grocery stores, a shopping center, a bank and a post office are located on the lower floors of this micro city. One bedroom to five bedroom units can accommodate any family. Libraries and classrooms located in the Rokko Intercenter of this complex will provide educational opportunities for you and your children.

Our aim is to make you feel at home. But first, we would like to say： Welcome! Come join us at The Entente.

NORTH TOWER (3-5 BEDROOM)···79 UNITS

SOUTH WING (1-3 BEDROOM)···84 UNITS

ALL AMERICAN MODERN APPLIANCES IN KITCHEN AND LAUNDRY ROOM

EXECUTIVE BUSINESS CENTER
- ● BUSINESS BOOTHS & CONFERENCE ROOMS RENTAL
- ● BILINGUAL SECRETARIAL SERVICES (Word Processing, Dictation), etc.
- ● TRANSLATION/INTERPRETATION SERVICES
- ● INTERNATIONAL FAX, COURIER, PRINTING SERVICES, etc.

- ● INFORMATION SERVICE ON TRANSPORTATION, SHOPPING, EMERGENCY CARE, etc.
- ● CHILD CARE FACILITIES
- ● SATELLITE AND CABLE T.V. & RADIO
- ● FULLY EQUIPPED HEALTH CLUB, SWIMMING POOL, 2 SQUASH COURTS, GYM, WORK-OUT STUDIO, 2 TENNIS COURTS
- ● SHOPPING MALL ON THE GRAND FLOOR

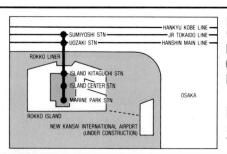

For further information
(Japanese business hours are from 9:30 am to 5:30 pm**)**

DOMESTIC CALL	0120 / 050955	(Toll Free)
OVERSEAS CALL	078/858/0810	
FACSIMILE	078/858/0805	

MAEDA REAL ESTATE
5-15, KOYO-CHO NAKA, HIGASHINADA-KU, KOBE 658
THE ENTENTE Representative Information Center

Nothing compares with
the great taste of real Florida orange juice.

The finest Florida Oranges,
soft squeezed so the juice is never bitter.
That's the secret to the delicious, fresh taste
that's made Tropicana America's favorite juice.
Now, enjoy that great Tropicana taste right here in Japan.

Distributed by **KIRIN-TROPICANA INC.**

The Moment That Refreshes.

Chapter

8

Food

Japanese Cuisine

Japanese cuisine is unique, and the vast number of restaurants in Japan offer a variety of exciting culinary experiences. Types of restaurants range from hushed *kappo* (top-class cuisine) establishments specializing in *kaiseki-ryori* (beautifully presented, multicourse seafood dinners) at the top of the scale to friendly and informal *sushi* bars and boisterous neighborhood *izakaya* eating and drinking places.

Some dishes, such as *tempura, yakitori, sukiyaki,* and *shabu-shabu,* are appreciated by almost everyone, Japanese and foreigners alike. For other delicacies, the taste may need to be acquired. Of course, some people never come to like Japanese food, and a few never even try. The best advice, though, is to give the local fare a chance; you may be pleasantly surprised.

Perhaps one of the best-known Japanese dishes around the world is *sukiyaki.* It can be found almost anywhere, but it is an expensive dish by Japanese standards. Thin slices of beef, chunks of *tofu,* and many vegetables—leeks, onions, burdock, mushrooms, bamboo shoots, and bean sprouts—are cooked in a broth of soy sauce, *sake* or *mirin* (sweet cooking *sake*), sugar, and bonito broth in a skillet-like pan over a charcoal or gas burner at the table. Each mouthful is supposed to be dipped in beaten raw egg, but this is optional. Properly prepared *sukiyaki* is delicious, but there are many poor substitutes in inexpensive restaurants, at which pork may be used in place of beef. *Shabu-shabu* is similar to *sukiyaki,* the main difference being that the meat, which is usually of a somewhat higher quality than that used for *sukiyaki,* and vegetables are cooked in boiling water instead of a broth and then dipped in a sauce.

Tempura, another perennial favorite, usually consists of large shrimp, pieces of white fish, and various vegetables individually dipped in batter and deep-fried in *tempura* oil, which is made from sesame seeds. Each piece is dipped in a special mixture of thin soy sauce and grated radish.

With succulent shrimp, juicy vegetables, and a crisp batter, *tempura* makes for a delightful dinner; however, it can be rather expensive unless you buy it in a small neighborhood restaurant.

Yakitori is a favorite with both Japanese and foreigners. It consists of small pieces of chicken on a short skewer grilled over charcoal. These are either salted or dipped in a Japanese-style barbecue sauce and served.

Certain kinds of food are very popular with students and workers as they are tasty, filling, healthy, and inexpensive. These include *soba,* buckwheat noodles that are delicious hot or cold; *donburi,* a bowl of rice topped with meat, fish, or vegetables; and *oden,* a combination of foods, including pressed fish, cut into geometric shapes and cooked in a special fish stock seasoned with soy sauce. *Ramen,* Chinese noodles, is another cheap and tasty dish; if you are very hungry, you can back the noodles up with a plate of *gyoza,* juicy fried or boiled dumplings, usually containing minced pork and garlic.

Depending entirely on whom you speak to, *sashimi* is either the pièce de résistance of Japanese cuisine or simply not fit for human consumption. *Sashimi* is raw fish deftly filleted into small, tender slices and attractively arranged on finely shredded *daikon* (Japanese radish), usually with a bit of cucumber, carrot, or seaweed to add to the appearance of the dish. A certain type of *sashimi,* called *tataki,* is lightly braised. The fish is dipped in a mixture of soy sauce and *wasabi* (Japanese horseradish) and eaten.

Many foreign visitors may be under the impression that *sushi* means raw fish. In fact, the term refers to the specially prepared vinegared rice that is usually molded into small oblongs and topped with raw fish or shellfish. *Norimaki,* another form of *sushi,* is cylindrical; the center contains a piece of raw fish or cucumber, surrounded by rice and wrapped in a strip of dried *nori,* a type of seaweed.

Chanko-nabe, a delicious stew of vegetables, *tofu,* and fish or meat, is especially popular during the winter months. It has been the staple dish of *rikishi,* the men of professional *sumo,* since the beginning of the century, and most *chanko* restaurants are operated by former *rikishi,* who prepare the ingredients that are cooked in a pot at your table. The ingredients vary according to the season, and there are many possibilities. You can choose from courses that contain vegetables, *tofu,* fish, chicken, pork, and beef in various combinations. *Chanko-nabe* is tasty, substantial, and often surprisingly cheap.

There are more exotic dishes to be tried if you have a sense of adventure and a hearty appetite. One of the many unusual and delightful treats you can experience is *unagi,* or eel. It is broiled, covered with a sweet, delicious sauce, and usually served in a lacquered box on a bed of rice.

At some point during your stay, you are sure to be asked by a Japanese acquaintance, "Can you eat *natto?*" *Natto,* or fermented soybeans, has a powerful odor and a distinctive taste. It is only popular in Tokyo and other parts of Kanto, and many people elsewhere in the country despise it. If you manage to acquire a taste for *natto,* you will gain a measure of respect in the eyes of Tokyoites; natives of the Kansai region will assume you are insane.

Another food that may be set before you as a kind of challenge is *basashi. Sashimi* is not restricted to fish; this variety consists of horsemeat. The flesh is sliced into small pieces and served chilled.

There are other types of Japanese food that may require some courage on the part of first-time tasters. *Fugu,* or puffer, a white fish, is said to make the best *sashimi* and is also served cooked in a broth. This fish, however, has a poisonous liver and ovaries, and an improperly prepared meal can result in death. Today, chefs preparing *fugu* must be specially licensed, and cases of poisoning have become rare.

These are a few examples of the kind of popular delicacies you may wish to try. Japan's cuisine is enormously varied, and you will undoubtedly be able to find any number of dishes that suit your palate.

Dining Out

Tokyo has tens of thousands of restaurants serving food from all over the world. The variety of cuisines is staggering at first—Chinese, Korean, Philippine, Vietnamese, Cambodian, Indonesian, Thai, Indian, Arab, Greek, Czech, Spanish, Italian, French, German, Swiss, English, American, Brazilian, and, of course, Japanese, to name just a few. Hygiene with regard to food preparation is excellent in Japan. You may eat or drink almost anything, anywhere, without hesitation.

One of the first things you will notice is that restaurants in Japan often display more-or-less realistic plastic or wax replicas of menu items in a glass display case near the entrance. Even if you speak no Japanese at all, you can order the dish that strikes your fancy by pointing to it in the window display. This type of display service is occasionally seen in other countries but to a far lesser extent than in Japan. In restaurants that have no displays, menus are often illustrated with photographs.

Tokyo is known as one of the world's most expensive cities, but dining out need not be prohibitively expensive. Of course, a considerable amount of lavish entertaining is done on company expense accounts, and little attention is paid to price or value received at restaurants catering to this type of trade. There are, however, many restaurants where an excellent meal can be enjoyed for a very reasonable price; in fact, dining out can prove cheaper than buying ingredients and cooking at home.

If you eat out, there are several things that you should keep in mind. Restaurants and other establishments tend to close early. In more expensive restaurants there may be a service charge, usually 10%, added to the bill, and there is no custom of tipping in Japan. A 3% special local consumption tax is added to all meals over ¥7,500 per person. This is in addition to the regular 3% consumption tax. Because the service charge is not a tip, it is included in the total to which these taxes are applied.

Some kinds of Japanese eating establishments have already been mentioned; the *kappo* restaurant, the *sushi* bar, and the *izakaya* all have points that recommend them to the seeker of sustenance. For an intriguing taste of Japanese culture and cuisine, *kaiseki* is difficult to surpass. *Kimono*-clad waitresses place before you a seemingly endless series of small dishes that are startling in their visual beauty and in the subtle variety of aromas and flavors. *Sushi* bars are less formal and give you the opportunity to pick and choose your favorites from the display case on top of the counter. *Izakaya* offer a rowdy and relaxed atmosphere; orders for fried fish, *yakitori,* and *sashimi* are shouted across the room, and beer and *sake* flow freely.

In addition to these, you will find a variety of other enjoyable and unusual eating places, including *kaiten-zushi* diners, where you snatch the plates of *sushi* that catch your eye as they pass by you on a conveyor belt; your bill is tallied at the end according to the number of plates you have stacked before you. Small bar-cum-restaurants specializing in *yakitori* are also interesting; you may not have known so much of a chicken was edible. In these places, you can order the little chicken kabobs by the part: heart, liver, skin, intestine, and so on.

There are thousands of small, family-owned restaurants, and these usually confine their fare to one or two kinds of food. One common dish is *tonkatsu,* breaded pork cutlets that are served with a bowl of rice, a mound of cabbage, and a thick, sweet sauce. Similar places might specialize in *tempura, unagi,* or *soba.*

As previously mentioned, your options when it comes to dining out in Tokyo are by no means limited to Japanese food. Japanese people love Chinese food, and there are many outstanding authentic Chinese restaurants in Tokyo; in fact, many gourmets say the best Chinese food in the world can be found in Tokyo. These restaurants are especially good for large groups, as diners are served at a round table with a huge rotating lazy Susan in the center. Quite a few of the best Chinese restaurants are located in Yokohama's famous Chinatown, just half an hour by train from central Tokyo.

The quality of Korean food in Japan is also very good. The most popular kinds of Korean food are *yakiniku,* or barbecued meat, usually beef, and *kimuchi,* the spicy pickled vegetables that are a staple in Korea. These are delicious and generally inexpensive.

When dining out with business guests or with your family, you may find yourself electing to visit one of the many well-known hotels. You will find that hotels in Japan are much more than merely places where travelers rest for the night. Top-notch Chinese, Korean, Italian, and French restaurants can be found in major hotels, and you will undoubtedly be invited to receptions and functions held in hotel banquet rooms.

Many Americans occasionally develop a craving for a taste of home, and this is easily satisfied. A number of American family restaurants, including Tony Roma's, Red Lobster, Denny's, Anna Miller's, and Sizzler, have franchises here, and outlets of American fast-food chains, such as Kentucky Fried Chicken, McDonald's, Wendy's, Shakey's, Dunkin' Donuts, and Mister Donut, can be found everywhere. Hamburgers and french fries are also sold at several of the larger Japanese chains, while others specialize in fast-food variations of *sushi, donburi,* or curry.

Before the fast-food boom, the quickest and most convenient way to enjoy a meal in Japan was to pick up a *bento,* a boxed lunch or dinner, and these are still a favorite choice for busy office workers. The meals are served in a wooden, plastic, or lacquered box and come with chopsticks and soy sauce or other seasonings. They are very popular on long-distance trains, and many stations are renowned for their own unique *bento,* which usually contain local delicacies. *Bento* are sold at kiosks along the platforms and from serving carts on the trains. Department stores even hold *bento* fairs, where you can go and sample specialties from all over Japan.

Another widespread practice in Japan is that of *demae,* or meal delivery. As in the United States, there are a number of pizza delivery chains, but even if you suddenly feel the need for a bowl of hot *ramen,* a tray of *sushi,* or a simple *bento,* it's as easy as picking up the telephone. Many kinds of restaurants have a *demae* menu, and your meal can be whisked by bicycle or scooter to your home or office, usually at no extra charge.

Dining Out in Tokyo

by Clint Hall

Tokyo's restaurant scene is so rich and vast that it beggars description. So let's start small, with a fish just right for a beggar— or a gourmet. Consider the sardine. The *Larousse Gastronomique,* France's great food encyclopedia, lists 11 sardine dishes.

"Only 11! Those poor Frenchmen," scoffs Eijiro Akabashi, a 50-year-old Tokyo chef.

Akabashi has devoted his life to slicing, frying, boiling, baking, grilling, pickling, and steaming sardines. He loves sardines. He eats them every day. He cooks them in a thousand ways. After a lifetime of sardine cooking, Akabashi looks a bit like a sardine. Even his wife agrees that he smells like one.

Akabashi scoops live sardines from a glass tank in his Tokyo restaurant, then transforms the flopping fish into raw, grilled, or pickled delicacies.

For starters, there's *nutta* (vinegared sardines) accompanied by *miso* and seaweed. Mix the three ingredients together in a serving bowl, order a bottle of *sake,* and a memorable meal commences.

Watch Akabashi slice the next course and deliver it quivering on a plate. After the strips of *sashimi* are eaten, the head and bones disappear and then return deep-fried as crunchy as potato chips.

Two sardines are blanketed with *tempura* batter, quickly deep-fried in oil, and served with bell pepper and eggplant.

And so it goes. Seven or so sardine courses are usually enough for me. But you might want to stick around for all one thousand. Course after course of sardines.

True, even at their Akabashi best, sardines are minor poetry. But that's the point. If one obscure Tokyo restaurateur creates a thousand pleasures serving only small, despised "trash" fish, imagine what a multitude of delicious miracles the city's host of equally dedicated chefs perform with more noble ingredients. Imagine what these culinary geniuses can do with, say, pampered Kobe beef or sweet Hokkaido crab.

Imagine. In restaurant-mad, food-obsessed Tokyo, the varieties of gastronomical pleasures approach the infinite. Probably no city in the world houses anywhere near as many dining spots. The last time we checked with the bureaucrats at city hall, who were just then returning from a late lunch, there were exactly 150,594 registered eating places.

It's safe to say that at least one out of 40—or 4,000 or so—of these food establishments is something extra special, something far above sardine class. Each boasts a chef at least as dedicated and as talented as Akabashi. And each uses superb ingredients, too.

These extra-special eating places also include a delectable variety of Asian and European dining places. Tokyo is now a world-class restaurant town—a magnet for accomplished foreign chefs.

So let's say you dine in a different one of these extra-special Tokyo restaurants every day. That's more than 10 years of fine dining—without ever having to eat a sardine.

Clint Hall is the author of the recently published restaurant guidebook *Tokyo Dining Out* (published by The Japan Times) and a regular restaurant columnist for the *Japan Times*. A native Californian, Hill works for the Headquarters, United States Forces, Japan, as chief of the labor branch.

STANDING BEHIND EVERY BMW IS A BMW TEAM STANDING BY YOU

BMW cars are designed for performance and reliability—and so are authorized BMW dealerships.

That's why you can confidently turn to us for professional advice on every aspect of BMW. Our mission is to help you select the BMW model most suited to your needs, then help you maintain the value of your BMW for as long as you own your car.

And to make the decision to own a BMW even easier to make, we offer innovative loan and lease programs. Which means, when yo add in high retained value, your BMW ma well be less expensive to own, in the long rur than many a far less satisfying car.

If you'd like to know more, or reserve test drive, please call us at the number belov

BMW Japan

Chapter

9

Getting Around

Unlike the United States, Japan is very much a public transportation oriented society. The average Japanese family has a car, occasionally two, but many private vehicles are used only on weekends. Traffic congestion is usually heavy in the urban areas of Tokyo, Osaka, and other major cities and is manageable only because the public relies largely on the extensive railway system for commuting. Considering the tremendous number of people who commute daily in Japan, the transportation systems are amazingly efficient.

Finding Your Destination

Destinations in Japan may be difficult to find with only an address, since most streets do not have names and the numbering system for buildings is not necessarily consecutive.

As in the West, addresses are written according to a hierarchy of districts; contrary to the usual Western style, however, in Japan these are arranged in order from largest to smallest. The largest are the prefectures, or *ken*, and four special areas that are considered equivalent to the prefectures: Tokyo, Kyoto, Osaka, and Hokkaido. The central districts of Tokyo and other larger urban areas are subdivided into wards, or *ku*, while those of suburban and rural areas are designated as cities, or *shi*. Within the *ku* or *shi* are general districts, which are further divided into numbered *chome*, smaller areas comprising several city blocks. At the next level, the block inside the *chome* and the number of the building on that block are specified. Finally, the name of the building and the room or floor number may be provided. The system, once you learn it, is very logical.

When written in English, the order is usually reversed to conform to the Western style. For example, a typical residential address in Tokyo might be:

Apt. 204, Homat Welcome,	(apartment number and building name)
5-13-21, Moto Azabu,	(*chome* 5, block 13, building 21, in the Moto Azabu district)
Minato-ku,	(Minato Ward)
Tokyo 106	(postal code 106)

There are several maps of Tokyo and Japan in English available at shops selling English-language publications; however, the only complete map of every ward in Tokyo that also clearly marks every district, every *chome,* and every block is the *Tokyo Metropolitan Atlas* (published by Shobunsha). *Tokyo: A Bilingual Atlas* (Kodansha) is also a good reference, not as detailed but ideal if you are walking.

Names of districts, and sometimes *chome* numbers as well, are often displayed overhead along main roads; *chome* and block numbers are generally prominently posted along each street on metal plates attached to light poles, buildings, or fences. Once you find the right block, you simply walk around the block until you find the correct house or building number.

Some foreign residents have a map locating their house, in both Japanese and English, printed on the reverse side of their personal *meishi*. Others have a separate map that can easily be photocopied and mailed or faxed to guests. In the early days of your stay in Japan, it is a good idea to keep a map with you at all times and make sure that your children do the same.

Foreigners quickly learn what the Japanese already know: if you need to go to a specific address, get the directions, and a map of the area if at all possible, written out in advance. Even if you are always armed with the address written in both Japanese and English, the telephone number of your destination, and a map of the area, you are sure to get lost more than once. Don't let this upset you; it happens to everyone, foreigner and Japanese alike.

Public Transportation
Subway and JR Lines

Generally, the fastest and easiest way to travel around Japanese cities is by rail. Trains run from about 5:00 A.M. to just past midnight. Railways in Japan are safe at all hours, and the graffiti and general decrepitude of some mass transit systems in the United States and Europe are conspicuously absent.

The subway lines are extensive and are constantly being expanded. The newer lines employ state-of-the-art technologies and are highly earthquake resistant. Most of the subway cars, and some of the stations, are now fully air-conditioned, including those on Tokyo's Ginza Line, Asia's first subway, opened in 1927. In Tokyo, there are 12 subway lines run by two separate authorities: the Teito Rapid Transit Authority, which operates eight lines, and the Metropolitan Transit Bureau, operating the four Toei lines. Ordinary tickets for each system are distinct and nontransferable, but transfer tickets are available from some special machines. The various lines are color-coded, so it is relatively easy to find your way around if you have a subway map.

Urban areas are served by railway lines run by a number of private companies, including those in the JR Group of companies formed by the privatization of the Japanese National Railways (JNR) in 1987. In Tokyo, many of the most important lines, including the vital Yamanote loop line, are operated by East Japan Railway Company (JR East).

Some station names are shared by stops on subway and the various railway lines; however, at some locations these stations are physically separate. The passage between such stations is usually well marked but may take some time to negotiate.

Ordinary tickets are sold through station ticket machines. There are a number of different types of machines, some of which sell transfer tickets and some of which sell more than one kind. As many stations have several lines passing through them, it is necessary to check and be sure that the machine into which you are putting your money will give you a ticket for the line or lines you want to take.

Maps are provided above the machines; to find out the amount of the ticket you need to purchase, simply locate your destination and the price will be indicated on the map. The station names are not often shown in English, so buying a ticket sometimes involves a quick *kanji* lesson. If in doubt, buy the cheapest ticket; the ticket collector at your destination will tell you the difference to pay. The *Tokyo Transit Book,* an inexpensive pocket-sized guide to the rail system, is well worth carrying at all times. It is available at bookstores selling English-language publications.

Apart from the ordinary tickets available at all stations, there are a number of "convenience" tickets for frequent users. These include commuter passes, student passes, *kaisu-ken* (sets of 11 tickets), Orange Cards, iO Cards, and Metro Cards. More information about these tickets is available in the book *Living for Less in Tokyo and Liking It!*.

Buses

Although not as well known as the subway system, the bus system in Tokyo provides a practical alternative and services a number of destinations not on the train routes, especially in the outlying areas. Buses are plentiful but are often crowded at rush hour and sometimes not punctual due to unpredictable traffic conditions. Bus lines are operated both by local government agencies and by private companies. They may be a little difficult for newcomers to use, as their routes and destinations are generally written in *kanji* characters only.

In central Tokyo, most buses have a fixed fare of ¥180 that is paid as you board the bus by dropping the exact change into the box next to the driver; if you do not have correct amount, there is also a change machine that will accept coins and ¥1,000 notes. Transfer tickets are not available. On some buses, the fare is different according to the distance traveled; in this case, you must take a ticket when you board the bus. The ticket will be marked with a number, and a lighted board at the front of the bus displays the fare for each number; you pay on the way out. On all buses, each stop is announced through speakers; when you hear yours, simply press one of the buttons located by the windows or on the ceiling of the bus.

One convenient bus route in Tokyo is the No.88, which goes from Shibuya Station along Aoyama-dori, near Kinokuniya, down Roppongi-dori to Roppongi Station, down Gaien Higashi-dori, close to the entrance to the Tokyo American Club, and on to Tokyo Tower, which is just across the street from the Tokyo Medical and Surgical Clinic. Another convenient route is the No.1 from Shibuya Station, which travels along Roppongi-dori, past the Ark Mori Building in Akasaka, and then on to Shimbashi Station.

Taxis

Taxis are generally easy to get, either at a taxi stand, usually located at stations or in front of major hotels, or by flagging one down in the street. Vacant taxis have a red light at the passenger side of the front window; a green light means "taken." The left rear door is usually opened and closed automatically by the driver, so do not stand too close to it and do not shut it after you get out.

When giving directions to the driver, it is useful to know a few words of Japanese or at least the name of a major building or station close to your destination. It is better still to have a map in Japanese. Sometimes the driver will stop in the vicinity of your destination and expect you to get out there rather than spend the extra time trying to find the exact location.

If you are traveling with young children, do not let them put their feet on the back seat unless you have first taken off their shoes; strollers can often go in the trunk or in the front seat, next to the driver.

There are numerous fleets as well as privately owned taxis, and both have the same fare system. For a medium-sized car in Tokyo, the fare is ¥600 for the first two kilometers, ¥90 for each additional 347 meters, and ¥90 per minute if the taxi is waiting or traveling at less than 10 kilometers per hour. In other cities, the fare is slightly lower. From 11:00 P.M. to 5:00 A.M. there is a 30% surcharge. At your destination, pay the fare shown on the meter; it is not usual to tip the driver. If you travel on an expressway, an extra ¥600 is charged that is not shown on the meter.

Taxis can be difficult to hail in bad weather or late at night, particularly in popular nightspots, such as Tokyo's Roppongi.

Traveling to and from Narita

New Tokyo International Airport at Narita, in Chiba Prefecture, is over 65 kilometers (40 miles) from Tokyo. Narita airport handles most international flights apart from those of China Airlines and Japan Asia Airways.

You can travel between Tokyo and Narita by train, bus, taxi, or private car. The JR Narita Express (N'EX) provides transportation between Narita airport and Tokyo Station, with extended service to Ikebukuro, Shinjuku, and Yokohama. The travel time between Narita and Tokyo is 53 minutes, and trains depart once or twice an hour. From downtown, the train goes directly to the terminal buildings, and space for luggage is provided. Seat reservations are required and are available up to one month before the day of travel; the special first-class Green Car service is also available. Ticket prices start at ¥2,890.

The Keisei Skyliner leaves from Keisei Ueno Station and Nippori Station every half hour and also goes to the terminal buildings. The Skyliner takes 60 minutes and costs ¥1,740. Reservations can be made through the Japan Travel Bureau or other travel agencies, or tickets can be bought at either of the train stations.

JR East operates two trains to Narita Station; the bus ride from there to the airport takes an additional 25 minutes. The Special Express on the JR Sobu Line leaves from Tokyo Station, takes 90 minutes, and costs ¥2,520; the Rapid Express on the JR Joban Line leaves from Ueno Station, takes 100 minutes, and costs ¥1,090. All seats on these trains are nonreserved.

Airport Limousine buses leave from Tokyo City Air Terminal (TCAT), at Hakozaki, and major Tokyo hotels, Yokohama City Air Terminal, and Haneda airport. The Hanzomon subway line goes directly to TCAT (Suitengumae Station); parking is also available at the terminal. A number of airlines have luggage check-in facilities at TCAT, and it is possible to go through immigration procedures there before boarding the bus. This can often save you the trouble of standing in long lines at Narita. Travel time to the airport is usually between 70 minutes and 90 minutes, and the cost is ¥2,500. Buses leave TCAT frequently, and there is no need to book ahead.

You can also catch a taxi from Tokyo to Narita. The traveling time will be about the same as the limousine bus, as both are subject to the vagaries of traffic conditions. The fare will be approximately ¥20,000.

If you have a car, it is quite easy to drive to Narita, although you should leave plenty of time for your first attempt or make a practice run first by using the Shuto Expressway to drive down to Chiba for a day's sight-seeing. Especially if you have young children, you may find it easier to drive than cope with public transportation. There are parking areas at the Narita terminal, and it is possible to drop your car off in front of the terminal buildings as you leave and, upon your return, have it delivered to the same place. Reservations are necessary for this service.

Traveling to and from Haneda

Domestic flights and China Airlines and Japan Asia Airways flights arrive at and depart from Tokyo International Airport at Haneda. The airport is accessible by monorail, Airport Limousine bus, taxi, or private car.

The monorail leaves frequently from Hamamatsucho Station, which is conveniently located on the JR Yamanote Line. The trip is comfortable and takes only 20 minutes. The problem with using the monorail to travel to Haneda is that you have to walk quite a distance carrying your luggage. The somewhat slower limousine bus service or taxi can be more convenient if you have a lot of luggage, although you run the risk of encountering a traffic jam caused by rush hour, bad weather, or an accident.

Private Transportation
Driving in Japan

Westerners, and Americans in particular, tend to take their cars for granted and hop into the driver's seat to travel any distance greater than a city block. Before running out to buy a car in Japan, however, there are a number of factors you should think about. The conditions, costs, and efficiency of traveling in your own car are not what they are at home.

The key issues for consideration are licensing requirements for the driver; procedures for obtaining and maintaining a car, including inspections and insurance; and the particular problems associated with operating a motor vehicle in Japan, such as parking and differences in driving conditions and traffic regulations.

Before starting to drive in Japan it is a good idea to obtain a copy of *Rules of the Road,* a booklet put out by the Japan Automobile Federation (JAF, see end of this chapter) and distributed by the Traffic Bureau at licensing offices. It will answer many of your questions about driving in Japan.

Japanese Driver's Licenses

A foreign driver's license is not valid for driving in Japan. However, if you possess a valid U.S. or other foreign driver's license (not an international license) and have had it for at least three months, obtaining a Japanese driver's license is relatively easy. The minimum age for obtaining a Japanese driver's license is 18 years (16 years for small motorcycles or motor scooters).

To obtain a Japanese driver's license you must apply at the license office nearest your place of residence in Japan. Your ward, town, or city office can tell you where this is located. Most Tokyo residents use the Samezu licensing office in the Shinagawa area, the Fuchu licensing office in western Tokyo, or the Toyocho licensing office in eastern Tokyo.

You must have with you your passport, current driver's license, Certificate of Alien Registration, passport, and one black-and-white or color photo (2.4 by 3 centimeters) taken within the preceding six months. (There are photo shops nearby that can provide you with one in five minutes.) Also, it is advisable to bring an official Japanese translation of your driver's license, although this may not be necessary if you are applying for your license in Tokyo. You will be asked to take an eye examination and a color blindness test.

Your Japanese driver's license is valid until your third birthday after the date of issue. The police authorities have recently proposed extending the validity of driver's licenses to five years, but only for drivers who have good records. Elderly drivers will not be eligible for this extended validity. It is strongly recommended that you renew your driver's license within one month prior to its expiration date. Only an eye examination is conducted for a renewal, and renewed licenses can be obtained the same day you apply for renewal if you have had a perfect driving record over the previous three years. You should be especially careful not to allow your driver's license to expire, as you will have to go through a considerable amount of red tape to obtain a new one. If you will be out of the country for the month during which you must renew your license, you may apply the month before, in which case your new license will be sent to you about two weeks after you apply.

Also, if you plan to return to your home country in the foreseeable future, it is recommended that you keep renewing your foreign driver's license. First, you may want to drive on home leave, and second, if you let your license expire and for some reason you cannot renew your Japanese driver's license in time, it may be difficult to get another Japanese license. Moreover, without a valid foreign driver's license, starting to drive in Japan is starting the hard way. You will be required to take two written tests (in English) and two practical driving tests. Once you have passed the first written test you will drive with an instructor on a special course; passing this qualifies you for a learner's permit. This permit allows you to drive on the street for experience, as long as you are accompanied by a licensed driver. After logging a required number of hours, both day and night, you may take the second written test, which, in addition to requiring you to answer the normal driving questions, will determine the extent of your knowledge of automobile engines and mechanics, including how to make basic repairs. Only after passing may you take the road test that qualifies you for a regular license.

This is the way Japanese people must obtain their licenses, and many of them find it necessary to repeat the examinations several times before they are able to pass. To prepare for these stringent examinations, the Japanese usually attend expensive driving schools.

Obtaining and Maintaining a Car

There are two ways to obtain a car in Japan—bring your own or purchase locally. If you are considering the purchase of a new U.S.-made car here, remember that not only will the price generally be more than double that in the States but the steering wheel will usually be on the "wrong" side for driving in Japan.

If you are set on owning a U.S.-made car, there is an active market in used cars. They may be purchased from diplomats, U.S. military personnel in Japan, or the occasional dealer specializing in used U.S.-made cars. Although there is no import duty, the person buying the car must usually pay the import costs, if any. This, of course, can and should be established between the buyer and seller.

A Japanese car, whether new or used, is probably more practical for local road conditions and certainly less costly. The prices of new Japanese cars in Japan are approximately the same as those of comparable Japanese cars in the United States. If, however, you buy a new car with a view toward taking it back to your home country after completing your assignment, you will face problems regarding safety standards and emission control regulations as well as the costs of importation.

Used cars can often be purchased from foreigners leaving Japan, and English-language publications, for example, the *Tokyo Weekender,* carry advertisements offering such vehicles. It is best to be wary, however; prices of secondhand cars will sometimes seem ridiculously low, but there are sometimes hidden costs related to registration and the mandatory periodic inspections that you must investigate carefully before making a purchase. This cannot be overemphasized. Also, the Japanese government will assess a value on the car to which taxes will be applied. If you buy a foreign car of recent vintage, you should expect both the assessed value and the accompanying taxes to be rather high.

An Automobile Tax is charged according to engine size and wheelbase. For larger cars you pay considerably higher taxes. Taxes vary depending on the type of car you are driving, and they do not decline as the car becomes older. Payment is made annually, in May. In addition to the Automobile Tax, there is a national Weight Tax for private passenger cars, collected at the time your car is first registered and also when your car undergoes the required periodic inspections. The amount of this tax varies according to the weight of your automobile. Anyone associated with the U.S. government is exempt from some of the registration requirements and taxes.

Importing Your Own Car

It is possible to import your own car, but you would be well advised not to attempt to do so; the bureaucratic barriers are formidable. If you have had your car outside Japan for a designated period, the vehicle can theoretically be brought into Japan free of duty. However, other regulations, such as exhaust emission controls, must be observed, and generally the entire process is more trouble than it is worth. This applies whether the car is Japanese-made or not.

Inspections

Private passenger cars registered in Japan must undergo an inspection (*shaken*) once every two years by a repair shop or garage designated by the Road Transportation Office (Riku-un Jimusho). A sticker will be placed on the windshield denoting the month and year the car is due for its next inspection. This inspection is expensive, at well over ¥100,000, and is one of the reasons that you will so seldom see older cars on the road. A mandatory procedure must be followed that includes verification of the serial and engine numbers and examination of the various mechanical parts of the car.

Keep this requirement in mind when considering the purchase of a used car. Many owners decide to sell their cars as the mandatory inspection nears. A deal that you thought was a bargain may strike you differently when the *shaken* becomes due, especially if repairs are needed.

Passenger cars in Japan must also undergo a periodic maintenance check every six months. These are in addition to the regular inspections every two years. A record of these inspections must be carried in your car and submitted to the Road Transportation Office when your vehicle undergoes *shaken*.

Insurance

Compulsory automobile liability insurance (CALI) is mandatory for all motor vehicles in Japan. Unless you show an insurance policy when you register your car and at the periodic inspections, the Road Transportation Office will not give you clearance to use it. You must carry the compulsory insurance policy in your car at all times. Maximum benefits are limited to ¥20 million per accident, bodily injury liability only. Policies are valid for 25 months.

No provisions are made for property damage liability coverage. It is therefore strongly recommended that additional private insurance be obtained (see Chapter 14). The liability of the owner of a car that injures a pedestrian or the occupant of another car can be enormous. In practice, the owner of the car causing the injury is generally assumed to be responsible for the injured person. Court decisions from the 1980s onward have held the owners of stolen cars responsible if the keys were left in the car. In one notable case, the owner of the car was held responsible when the thief driving the stolen car hit and killed a pedestrian, because the keys had been left in the car, thus "tempting" someone to steal it.

If you have occasion to drive on one of the American military bases in Japan, you will be required to have additional coverage of ¥10 million to ¥15 million for bodily injury liability and property damage liability. Your certificate must be shown at the gate.

Not all American insurance companies operate in Japan, but there are a number of excellent companies represented. Also, there are brokers who can handle your needs very capably. Policy provisions are similar to those in effect in the United States and can include comprehensive and collision coverage, bodily injury liability, property damage liability, and medical payments.

Parking

To register your car and obtain license plates, you must provide proof that you have an off-street parking space, certified by the local police. No all-night street parking is permitted, and this regulation has been rigorously enforced in recent years, with severe penalties for violators; fines as high as ¥100,000 are not uncommon. You can rent a parking space, which may cost as much as ¥30,000 or ¥40,000 a month or even more, depending upon where you reside—the closer to downtown, the higher the rent.

Short-term parking is relatively limited. There are a few parking meters, generally restricted to a 40-to-60-minute maximum. This period cannot be extended unless you drive the car out of the space and reenter. Illegally parked cars are frequently towed off at the owner's expense, although 10 to 15 minutes are often allowed prior to ticketing, even in on-street "no parking" areas.

You will usually have to put the car in a parking lot or garage; the rates are between ¥500 and ¥1,000 per hour. Monthly rates may be available, although in the business districts, these can run ¥80,000 a month and up. One tip is to park in a department store car park; it is usually free if you purchase a specific value of goods and have the parking ticket validated at the cashier's desk. Some hotels offer free parking to people using their facilities.

Driving Conditions

If you have driven in other large cities, such as New York, Paris, or Rome, you will probably find conditions in Japan rather similar. Many foreigners drive here and say they wouldn't be without a car. Others feel just the opposite and depend solely on public transportation. The most obvious difference between Japan and America when it comes to driving is that traffic travels on the left side of the road. But there are a few other differences that merit special attention in Japan.

International traffic signs are used. Even if you have never seen them before, they are easy to understand. For a comprehensive list of international traffic signs, see *Safe Driving in Japan,* obtainable from the Driving Licensing Office, Metropolitan Police Department, 3-1-1, Tama-machi, Fuchu-shi, Tokyo.

Road signs in English are becoming increasingly common, but don't count on one being there when you need it. Driving on the expressways can be especially confusing, as signs are not in English in most cases. When you enter an expressway, it is a good idea to memorize the number of the exit you will be using; the numbers are always clearly marked.

Be aware that motorcycles pass on the left, or inside, side of cars on expressways and city streets alike—even where there is no lane for them to do so. This is quite legal in Japan. For this reason, it is important to check your side mirrors carefully before making a left turn.

The city streets have their own particular hazards. They are usually extremely narrow, and often there are no sidewalks. The number of bicycles has increased dramatically in recent years, and careless cyclists are a constant nuisance for both drivers and pedestrians. Motorcycles, scooters, trucks, and pedestrians make many smaller streets virtually impassable.

The best advice is to drive cautiously, use your rearview and side mirrors frequently, try to get used to the tempo of the traffic, and never make assumptions about what other drivers are going to do.

Regulations

To prevent unsafe road conditions in Japan, the government imposes harsh penalties for traffic violations. A penalty point system has been in effect since 1969. Your new Japanese driver's license has 20 points, and these are subtracted as infractions are committed. Point assessments range from 1, for parking violations, to 15, for drunken driving. Major traffic accidents carry point assessments of 4 to 13, depending on the determination of prime responsibility.

Penalty points are cumulative, but if a driver completes one year of driving without an offense, his previous penalty points are canceled. However, a record of convictions or a license revocation during the past three years will have the effect of reducing the number of points allowed before suspension or revocation of a renewed license—a driver whose license has been suspended or revoked during the past three years will have the new license suspended when the total number of points reaches 6 and revoked when this total reaches 15.

A driver who has accumulated 6 points through repeated minor offenses, such as parking violations, has the option of attending traffic safety lectures instead of license suspension.

The Road Traffic Law was partially amended several years ago in a crackdown on drunken driving. The main points of the amendment are as follows:

• The penalty for driving under the influence of alcohol (alcohol concentration of 0.5 milligrams in one milliliter of blood or 0.25 milligrams in one liter of exhalation) was increased to up to three months' imprisonment or a fine of up to ¥30,000, plus a penalty assessment of 6 points and suspension of the license for one month.

• The penalty points for drunken driving were increased from 12 to 15 with up to two years' imprisonment or a fine of up to ¥50,000. The license is revoked for one year.

• Refusing a breath test or interfering, as a third person, with a policeman making the test calls for a fine of up to ¥30,000.

• The owner or administrator of a vehicle may be held equally liable if he has knowledge that a person has been drinking and allows that person to drive.

In the event of an accident, the law requires the driver and/or owner (if involved) of a vehicle involved in an accident to:

1. Stop and remain at the scene,

2. Aid the injured,

3. Remove obstacles to traffic (In practice, this extends to damaged vehicles only when they present a serious hazard. If it is necessary to move a vehicle, its position at the point of impact and at rest should be clearly marked on the road.),

4. Call or send for a policeman,

5. Follow the instructions of any policeman who comes to the scene of the accident, and

6. If no policeman appears, report to the nearest police station and give full particulars. If the accident is of a serious nature, involving injury, the foreign owner or driver would do well to contact bilingual legal counsel at the earliest opportunity.

Many insurance policies contain a clause that voids any claim if you admit responsibility for an accident. If you are in an accident, you should keep this in mind when talking to the police, who almost invariably attempt to obtain such an admission.

Legal action is less likely to be taken if an accident occurs in your personal, and not a company-owned, car—be sure that both the police and the other driver are informed if this is the case.

Additional Driving Information

The booklet *Rules of the Road,* mentioned earlier, is available from the Japan Automobile Federation (JAF), which is located at 3-5-4, Shiba Koen, Minato-ku, Tokyo 105 (directly across from Tokyo Tower), for ¥1,860. The booklet is available by mail if you enclose ¥2,070 in postage stamps. Address your letter to: Kanto Honbu Jigyo Ka (Kanto Headquarters, Business Division), Japan Automobile Federation, at the above address. JAF's telephone number is (03) 5976-9720.

If you drive in Japan, it is a good idea to join JAF. The enrollment fee is ¥2,000, and annual membership fees are ¥4,000, worthwhile considering the services offered. For additional information concerning JAF, call the JAF office at the number provided above; the staff will be more than happy to help you.

Getting to Know Tokyo

by Rick Kennedy

Ask a friend who does not know Tokyo to close his eyes and describe the city, and you are likely to hear something like this: "Oh, Tokyo is a monster! All the buildings are concrete and the lighting is all neon, and it is terribly crowded, with everyone rushing everywhere like ants."

They will make Tokyo sound like hell paved over. You should realize, however, that this vision of Tokyo is simply a product of a thousand lurid photographs of Tokyo's fabled rush hour, showing trains at 500% capacity and battalions of pedestrians stepping off the curb in front of Shibuya Station every time the light changes. The denser the crowd, the more salable the photo. Editors around the world have decided that Tokyo is a brute and that its denizens are automatons and that is just the way it is.

All I can say is that these familiar postcards from hell have nothing to do with the Tokyo I know and love.

I live in the middle of a vast cabbage patch 20 minutes from Shibuya. The farmers in our neighborhood consider Shibuya a distant fairytale kingdom. It would never occur to them to go there. In Roppongi, on the roof of an apartment building, there is a chicken farm that supplies fresh eggs to the community. Not many major cities are happy to accommodate working farms within their boundaries.

As the Tokyo city government has not got around to hammering out a city plan and shows no sign of ever doing so, the city grows like an amoeba, only stitched together by the world's best municipal transportation system. This leads to endearing juxtapositions—a *kimono* shop next door to a garage specializing in the maintenance of Ferraris, a purveyor of used earth-moving equipment next to a tiny shop known for its exquisite handmade jewelry. The varied drama of human commerce and concern is displayed on the streets of Tokyo for all to see, with many Tokyo shops and houses opening right onto the street. This variety makes Tokyo one of the world's great cities for walking.

Tokyo is awash with street festivals, with the most casual passerby welcome to join in. The city is as dedicated to gambling as Las Vegas, with as many *pachinko* parlors as gas stations.

Horse racing, bicycle racing, and hydroplane racing add a touch of raucous color. Tokyo is a proving ground for high-tech penny arcades. Akihabara, or Electric Town, as you know, is a wonder. Tsukiji, the local fish market, sells a tenth of all fish sold worldwide and every day sells many mysterious delicacies available nowhere else.

In the evening, especially in autumn, I love to drop by a *yatai* street cart for a plate of *oden* stew with a slap of sharp mustard on the side. I feel that Nombei Yokocho (Drunkards Alley) nestled up against the tracks across from Shibuya Station is a national treasure, with its little six-stool drinking places where in 10 minutes everyone knows everyone. Tokyo's coffee shops serve better coffee than Vienna's, and the alternative theater groups, some say, number over 2,000, all doing original plays, many eccentric to the point of genius. Tokyo has a multiplicity of parks, from Shinjuku Gyoen, which is landscaped to imitate heaven, to hidden gardens with little teahouses of which entry requires a discreet knock at a door. Tokyo's endearing quirkiness can be seen in its tiny revival movie theaters with no seats, where you view the screen by lying on the floor with a pillow under your head; its antique public baths, open to anyone, with soap and a towel for sale in case you forgot yours; its mad tangle of overhead wires and cables; its impossible jumble of bicycles at every train station; and its rogue cats commanding the back alleys.

Tokyo is the most comfortable city I have ever lived in. It is possible that you will find it so, too.

Rick Kennedy has written a book about his experiences in Japan and is a regular contributor to the *Tokyo Weekender* and other publications.

Chapter

10

Medical Care and Facilities

Japan has some of Asia's most advanced medical services and facilities, and in general, medical care is good. A government health insurance system is subscribed to by almost the entire population, and advanced research facilities and superior rehabilitation facilities are available. Many doctors and dentists have completed studies at leading institutions outside Japan, and Japanese physicians are frequent participants in and contributors to international medical research and symposia. On the other hand, a chronic shortage of nursing staff and trained paramedics, the overprescription of medicine, and a weakness in diagnostic techniques hamper the efficiency of the system.

Until World War II, the average life span of both sexes in Japan was only about 50 years. Significant improvements in the standard of living, diet, and medical, particularly prenatal and infant, care in recent years have given the Japanese the longest life expectancy in the world; in 1991, the average life expectancy was 82.1 years for women and 75.8 years for men.

The Japanese medical system is quite different from and in many ways more complex than that of the United States or European nations in terms of organization, insurance, hospitalization, and prescriptions. Although in recent years the government and industry have been moving to standardize and streamline the system, there remain disparities in medical training, certifications, and licensing as well as in standards, which vary from hospital to hospital and even among the departments in each hospital.

Japanese Health Insurance

Comprehensive private health insurance schemes do not exist. *Shakai Hoken*, Employees' Health Insurance, covers factory workers, employees of manufacturers, firms that lack their own health insurance organizations, day laborers, civil servants in the Japanese government, and staff of private schools. *Shakai Hoken* is operated by health insurance societies or mutual aid associations and by the national government.

People not falling into any of the aforementioned categories are eligible for *Kokumin Kenko Hoken,* or National Health Insurance (NHI), a government-sponsored, tax-supported program that makes treatment available at a very low cost to the patient, as it covers from 50% to 70% of the cost of medical care. About 97% of all Japanese medical services are administered through this program. A card is issued and must be presented each time a patient is treated. This program is also available to foreigners, but the premiums as well as medical charges are administered on a sliding income level rate and may be excessively expensive for the average expatriate. If you are not covered by U.S. or other foreign health insurance or by your company's Employees' Health Insurance, you may enroll in the NHI program. To be eligible for NHI, you must have a visa valid for one year or longer, have received a Certificate of Alien Registration, and not be enrolled with another insurance program through your employer or as a dependent of the householder.

If you elect to join the NHI program, you will not be able to withdraw unless you lose eligibility for membership. You will also have to report, within 14 days of their occurrence, any changes in the name of the head of your household, your domicile, and the number of persons in your household.

The benefits to you under the NHI program vary depending on where you live in Japan. Foreign doctors and dentists in Japan usually operate private clinics that do not accept Japanese health insurance. It is wise to call these clinics before you visit to determine what insurance coverage, if any, will be available.

Japanese medical services outside the NHI system are also available, but only about 2.5% of all doctors in Japan have a private practice. If you do not join the NHI program, you will probably find that medical and dental costs in Japan are very expensive. For this reason, many Americans coming to Japan have all major medical and dental needs attended to before leaving home or during visits to the United States.

Medical Insurance with Foreign Companies

Most U.S. medical insurance policies, such as Blue Cross/Blue Shield and AIU, can be used in Japan. Frequently, however, you are expected to pay the bill for medical services upon presentation (usually in cash, since personal checks are not widely used in Japan). The insurance company then reimburses you directly by check after receiving your claim.

Most doctors and hospitals that treat foreigners are

familiar with claim forms and will help you complete them. You should make sure that you (or your office) have these forms available.

Family Doctors

Patients seeking care under the NHI program have the choice of either visiting a hospital or a local doctor operating his or her own practice. A patient is free to change hospitals or doctors at any time. In Tokyo, Yokohama, and Kobe and in a few other areas, English-speaking, Western-trained physicians operating from clinics or their own practice are prepared to serve as family physicians in the usual American sense of the term. These doctors seldom participate in the NHI system, and you will have to pay full fees.

Although attitudes toward disclosure are beginning to change, most Japanese doctors are very reluctant to discuss a patient's condition in detail, describe the side effects of a given medicine or treatment, or venture an opinion on the chances of a treatment/cure being successful. If you feel you need to discuss your health problem in this way, you might prefer a foreign doctor or one who has been trained abroad and is familiar with a different style of consultation.

Be Prepared

• It is advisable to contact a doctor soon after your arrival and discuss your medical needs, especially if you or members of your family have chronic ailments or are susceptible to certain disorders or diseases.
• Ascertain how to reach a doctor in cases of emergency.
• It is also advisable to familiarize yourself with your neighborhood and determine the location of hospitals where you can obtain treatment.
• Likewise, find pharmacies that can fill prescriptions written in English; in Tokyo, perhaps the best known is the American Pharmacy in Yurakucho.
• Carry with you the yellow, bilingual medical data card that is available from the Consular Section of the British Embassy in Tokyo (Tel: (03) 3265-4001). In an emergency or in cases of severe incapacitation and/or if you are unable to communicate, this information will be of assistance to the medical professionals treating you. Also, if you are covered under the NHI program, it is advisable to always have your membership card with you, especially if traveling in Japan, as this must be presented or the full charge will have to be paid for treatment.

Ambulance Service

The municipal or prefectural fire departments operate Japan's ambulance service, which is free of charge. If you dial **119** and ask for an ambulance (in Japanese), you can expect one to arrive in 5 to 10 minutes, depending on traffic conditions and how far away you are from the fire station. If you do not speak Japanese, the 119 answering staff have been taught how to ask your address and name in English, but be sure to speak slowly. If possible, speak in Japanese, as follows:

1. Request an ambulance   *Kyukyu desu*
2. Give your address   *—ku, —machi,*
                                            —chome, —ban, —go,
                                            —(apartment name)
3. Give your name   *—desu*
4. Give your telephone number   *—*

5. If possible, mention a nearby shop or other landmark to help staff find their way quicker.

As soon as the 119 answering service has determined your address, an ambulance will be dispatched. If you cannot communicate effectively with the 119 staff, do not hang up, as the fire department will try to trace your call and dispatch an ambulance.

You may also call from a public telephone. All modern public telephones have an emergency button for 119 and 110 (the police). Push the button, insert two ¥10 coins (one ¥10 coin is good for only three minutes). From pink and red public telephones, however, you will not be able to dial 119 or 110 even if you insert a coin. You will have to ask the storekeeper to call the emergency numbers, as the old public phones can only connect with emergency numbers when a key is inserted.

All ambulance attendants are trained in limited first aid, and the ambulance is equipped for standard first aid but nothing more. The authorities have recently launched a system to train ambulance attendants as paramedics. Some ambulances are already equipped with paramedics, but the majority of vehicles still have ordinary attendants who are not permitted to administer any emergency treatment except the most basic first aid. After reaching the patient, the attendants try to determine what help is needed and then contact their headquarters to get the name of an appropriate hospital that has space for an emergency patient.

Ambulance attendants consult with doctors through a mobile phone system to determine which hospital the patient should be taken to. Some hospitals may refuse admission to a patient if they do not have the equipment to administer specialized treatment.

Hospitalization and Outpatient Services

Almost all Japanese hospitals have outpatient departments where consultation and treatment can be obtained. For general medical care under the NHI system, it is usually not necessary to make an appointment with the doctor, but you should expect to wait anywhere from one to three hours for treatment. The staff doctors, either specialists or younger, less-experienced physicians, examine patients on a rotation basis. Patients can designate a specific doctor, but doing so will often mean a longer waiting period.

Hospitals in Japan usually have more general wards than private rooms. Nurses may not understand much English, and the hospital diet is, of course, a Japanese one.

In the event that hospitalization is required, the following points should be kept in mind:

•Due to the language barrier, some Japanese hospitals are reluctant to accept patients who do not speak Japanese. Most doctors, however, can understand some English. There are several major hospitals that have sections that are staffed with personnel who can speak English and specialize in treating foreigners who cannot speak Japanese.

•Considering the inevitable language problems if you don't speak Japanese and the differences in hospital methods and procedures, you are strongly advised to seek admission at one of the hospitals that specialize in treating foreigners.

•All Japanese hospitals, including those that specialize in caring for foreigners, operate on a "closed" system. Hospitals rely completely on their own staff and do not permit outside medical personnel, such as a family doctor, to administer any form of treatment.

Prescriptions and Medications

Prescriptions written by doctors in the United States or other foreign countries will generally not be honored by pharmacists in Japan unless the prescriptions have been approved by a local physician. There are some major differences in the availability of pharmaceuticals here. Some medicines that are prescription drugs in the United States are available over the counter in Japan. Also, many OTC medications in the United States, for example, Sudafed and Vick's Nasal Inhaler, are illegal in Japan. Standard dosages in Japan are slightly smaller, since Japanese are generally lighter in build than Americans.

If you require any kind of medication on a regular basis, consult your local doctor and, if possible, bring an adequate supply with you—enough for two or three months—until you can be assured of finding a local source or an acceptable substitute. If the drug is not available in Japan, there may be some method by which it can be imported; you should ask your doctor. There are pharmacies in Tokyo, including the American Pharmacy, and in the other large cities that specialize in drugs and remedies manufactured outside Japan.

Contraceptives

Condoms are by far the most common form of birth control in Japan and are available at most pharmacies as well as at convenience stores and from vending machines. The Ministry of Health and Welfare has declined to approve birth control pills for general use because of fears about side effects. Although concerns about the side effects have abated somewhat now, the authorities are not permitting the over-the-counter sale of the pill as they are concerned that it would result in lower use of condoms and thereby encourage the spread of AIDS. However, oral contraceptives are available if you have a prescription from a doctor. Abortion is generally available on demand in Japan and is considered a matter to be determined solely by the woman and her physician.

Dental Care

The quality of dental services in Japan is, on the whole, good. Many dentists have studied abroad and can speak at least some English, and specialists in all fields of dentistry are available. Dental care, however, can be expensive if you are not covered by NHI.

Having a Baby in Japan

Medical care for pregnancy in Japan follows international standards, and the quality is generally high. Some maternity hospitals will expect the patient to understand Japanese. Other hospitals, however, have considerable experience with foreign patients who do not understand Japanese.

Women who think they are pregnant should select a

sankai, or obstetrician, as soon as possible. Once pregnancy is confirmed, the patient can file a pregnancy report with the local ward, town, or city office and, by so doing, receive the *Boshi Kenko Techo,* or Mother's Pocket Book, which records the condition of the mother and the infant both before and after delivery as well as postnatal growth of the child. You can obtain a translation of this book for a nominal cost from the Japanese Organization for International Cooperation in Family Planning, at Hoken Kaikan Bekkan, 1-1, Sadoharacho, Ichigaya, Shinjuku-ku, Tokyo (Tel: (03) 3268-5875). Possession of this book gives the mother access to various forms of free assistance, such as classes for mothers and health-related guidance.

Pregnancy and delivery are not considered to be illnesses and thus are not fully covered by NHI, unless there are complications, in which case the coverage is generally good. Maternity-related medical expenses are now exempt from the general 3% consumption tax.

Blood-typing, hepatitis B, anemia, and rubella (German measles) tests are generally conducted early in pregnancy. Regular examinations during pregnancy include blood pressure measurement, urine testing, and weight monitoring. The fetus's health is tested by measurement of uterine size and heart monitoring.

Consultations with obstetricians are generally very short, and the physician will not expect to answer questions from the patient. Midwives in clinics and hospitals, however, are always willing to answer questions (in Japanese) and play a leading role in the education and care of pregnant women.

The number of regular visits pregnant women should make to their obstetrician in Japan conforms to the standards of the World Health Organization (WHO). In Japan this translates into visits once every four weeks through the sixth month of pregnancy, once every two weeks during the seventh and eighth months, and once a week in the ninth month. If the pregnancy continues beyond the expected date of birth, the doctor will devise a new visit schedule.

Licensed midwives are eligible to operate small clinics of their own. They can only handle normal pregnancies, and few have staff who can speak English. As most births now take place in hospitals, the number of midwives' clinics in Tokyo and other large cities is limited. These clinics provide an alternative to the traditional hospital delivery in Japan but involve a small risk as they are not hospitals per se. They do, however, have affiliations with hospitals and obstetricians for emergency cases.

Hospitalization and Labor

Japanese women usually have a natural delivery derived from the British "natural childbirth method," as do foreign women who give birth in ordinary Japanese hospitals, as opposed to those that specialize in treating foreigners. Pain relievers are generally not given during labor or before or after delivery. Medication is usually administered to alleviate bleeding, and antibiotics are used to prevent infection.

Postnatal Care

Women are usually discharged one week after a normal delivery and two weeks after a cesarean section. Postnatal treatment includes breast massage and weighing of the baby before and after feeding. The baby will be routinely tested for congenital diseases and will receive regular pediatric examinations after becoming one month old. Circumcision is not a routine procedure in most Japanese hospitals but may be available on request at certain hospitals and clinics.

Immunizations

Under the Japanese health regulations, polio, DPT (diphtheria/pertussis/tetanus), measles, rubella, and TB (after a negative skin test) immunizations are mandatory and free of charge for children at *hokenjo,* or public health centers. Inoculations against mumps, chicken pox, cholera, hepatitis A, hepatitis B, rabies, and yellow fever (available only at the quarantine office) are optional, and the payment of a fee is required. Immunization against influenza, Japanese encephalitis B, and Weil's disease is only offered at designated times. For other immunizations that may be necessary for travel to tropical regions, such as typhoid fever and bubonic plague, you are advised to consult one of the clinics or hospitals that specialize in treatment for foreigners.

Mental Health and Support Organizations

Mental health, psychiatric, and counseling services are available in Japan and include the following organizations:

• Alcoholics Anonymous (AA). AA offers meetings for anyone with a drinking problem, for mutual support and the exchange of information. AA has no professional counselor, and meetings are conducted by the members. In Tokyo, the AA center is 10 minutes from the west exit of Ikebukuro Station and is open from 9:00 A.M.

to 7:00 P.M. Monday to Friday and from 9:00 A.M. to 5:00 P.M. on Saturdays, Sundays, and holidays (Tel: (03) 3971-1471).

•Counseling International. This organization offers psychotherapy centered on individual and family matters. An appointment is required for face-to-face counseling. Opening hours are on Mondays from 1:00 P.M. to 3:00 P.M. and 9:00 P.M. to 11:00 P.M. (Tel: (03) 3408-0496).

•Overeaters Anonymous. Support meetings are offered for people with weight problems and eating disorders, such as compulsive eating. Regular meetings are held several times each week (Tel: (03) 3630-3118).

•The Counseling Center of Tokyo. This organization is community based and dedicated to offering clients a range of services that foster personal growth and understanding. The fully confidential services include counseling for addiction and disorders, including alcohol abuse and sexual disorders; counseling for individuals, couples, and groups; cross-cultural counseling; bodywork, including rolfing, rebalancing, and deep tissue massage; and crisis intervention (Tel: (03) 3953-2495).

•Tokyo Medical and Surgical Clinic. This clinic has an American consultant who deals with the full range of personal and psychological problems experienced by foreign executives, their spouses, and their families. The clinic can also provide a referral to a psychiatrist if necessary. Call only on weekday mornings (Tel: (03) 3436-3028).

Medical Vocabulary

Here are some useful medical words in Japanese:

abortion	*ninshin chuzetsu*
accident	*jiko*
allergy	*arerugii*
ambulance	*kyukyusha*
anemia	*hinketsu*
antibiotics	*kosei busshitsu*
appendicitis	*mochoen*
asthma	*zensoku*
backache	*yotsuu (koshi ga itai)*
blood	*chi*
broken bone	*kossetsu*
burn	*yakedo*

cancer	*gan*
cold	*kaze*
constipation	*benpi*
cough	*seki*
cure/get better	*naoru*
dentist	*haisha*
diabetes	*tonyobyo*
diarrhea	*geri*
discharge (from hospital)	*taiin*
disease	*byoki*
doctor	*isha*
earache	*mimi ga itai*
electric shock	*kanden*
emergency	*kinkyu*
eye(s)	*me*
fall	*korobu*
fever	*netsu*
fracture	*kossetsu*
gynaecologist	*fujinkai*
headache	*zutsuu (atama ga itai)*
heart	*shinzo*
heart attack	*shinzo mahi* or
	shinkin kosoku
hemorrhage	*shukketsu*
hernia	*herunia*
high blood pressure	*koketsuatsu*
hospital	*byoin*
hospitalize	*nyuin*
insomnia	*fuminsho*
kidney	*jinzo*
laceration/cut	*ressho* or *kirikizu*
liver	*kanzo*
low blood pressure	*teiketsuatsu*
lung	*hai*
medical test	*kensa*
medical treatment	*chiryo*
medicine	*kusuri*
menstruation	*gekkei* or *seiri*
mental hospital/clinic	*seishin byoin*
miscarriage	*ryusan*
nausea	*hakike*

nurse	*kangofu* (female) or *kangoshi* (male)
obstetrician	*sankai*
pain	*itami*
pancreas	*suizo*
paralyzed	*mahi* or *ugokenai*
physical (full checkup)	*ningen dokku*
pneumonia	*haien*
poison	*doku*
poisonous	*yudoku*
pregnant	*ninshin*
psychiatrist	*seishinbyogakusha*
sore throat	*nodo ga itai*
specialist	*senmonka*
sprain	*nenza*
stomachache	*itsuu (onaka ga itai)*
strangle (choke)	*chossoku*
stroke	*noikketsu* (hemorrhage) or *nokosoku* (thrombosis)
toothache	*hatsu (ha ga itai)*
ulcer	*kaiyo*
unconscious	*kizetsu* or *ishiki fumei*
vomit	*haku* or *modosu*
X-ray	*rentogen*

Put the U.S. in your pocket.

If you're living in Japan, we'd like to give you an *AT&T Calling Card.* You'll find it's a big help.

Getting one is free. All you need is a VISA®, MasterCard® or American Express® Card account.

With your *AT&T Calling Card*, you can use *AT&T USADirect*® Service. Just dial 0039-111 from Japan and follow the simple voice promts or stay on the line for the AT&T operator. And when you're traveling in the States, it makes calling everywhere easier. Using the card, you'll get an itemized record of all your calls too, with your monthly credit card statement.

To apply for your free *AT&T Calling Card*, simply call us toll-free at **0120-4-10288**, or call **03-5561-3219**. Or write for an application to: AT&T Japan, Mori Building 25, 18th Floor, 1-4-30 Roppongi, Minato-ku, Tokyo 106.

You'll like having the U.S. in your pocket. And all the help you'll be able to get from AT&T.

Chapter

11

Family Life

Adjusting to Japan

Moving to Japan can be an exciting experience for a family. At first, however, many adults and children alike may feel out of place and lonely because they miss their friends and the familiar environment they left behind. The length of time it takes to adjust is of course different for different people.

The initial stage can be particularly difficult for a spouse who accompanies a husband or wife who has been transferred to Japan. The person who is employed full-time is able to step straight into a life structured by the demands of the workplace and a network of social relationships, while the partner must relearn basic, everyday survival techniques, such as how to buy shoelaces, catch a bus, or find people to talk to during the day.

It is important for a family, as a unit and as individuals, to start to develop relationships with a variety of people as soon as possible after arriving in Japan. Work will provide a starting point for some, as will schools, community groups, family clubs, and religious organizations. This chapter concentrates on these groups and organizations, while other activities for families to enjoy together or with friends are covered in other chapters of this book.

Community Organizations

There are a number of organizations established in Japan to cater to a wide range of interests: culture, the environment, politics, and community service. The TELL *International Community Calendar* lists approximately 100 of these, ranging from Ikebana International, the Japan International Friendship Club, and the Foreign Residents' Advisory Center to Sweet Adelines International and UNICEF.

Some groups are specifically for women, such as the College Women's Association of Japan and the Tokyo Union Church Women's Society; some focus on one country but have international membership, such as the Australian Society; and many have facilities where members can meet.

Contact telephone numbers for most groups can be found in the TELL calendar, which is widely available in Japan. Many place notices in the classified sections of newspapers and such publications as *Tokyo Journal*.

In general, there are more organizations that cater to the needs of women who accompany their husbands to Japan than there are for men who come with their wives. Both groups, if they do not intend to join the work force immediately, will find that their first few months in Japan will be spent exploring a range of new social situations and handing out the inevitable *meishi*.

This can be trying at times; however, after a relatively short time spent meeting a large number of new people, you will find that you are making friendships, many of which you will maintain over the years, regardless of where you are living.

In addition to the organizations already mentioned, parent groups associated with international schools play an important role for many newcomers to Japan. These groups not only provide social opportunities but also serve as fund-raising organizations for their respective schools. Members often hold school bazaars—unique because of their international flavor—bingo games, dinner dances, and many other activities. If you have school-age children, taking an active part in parent groups is a good way of developing closer ties with the school and, at the same time, meeting interesting people and enjoying new experiences.

Family Clubs

In addition to the organizations and groups just mentioned, there are two major clubs, one in Tokyo and the other in Yokohama, that provide a range of facilities and activities suitable for foreign families.

The Tokyo American Club

Centrally located, the Tokyo American Club offers a variety of recreational facilities and activities. Sporting facilities, including an outdoor swimming pool, squash courts, and a gymnasium as well as other recreational facilities, such as a print library, a video library, and restaurants, are available. A wide range of classes are also provided, sponsored by the Tokyo American Club Women's Group.

Yokohama Country and Athletic Club

This club, founded in 1868 as the Yokohama Cricket Club and

renamed in 1912, offers the widest variety of sporting and social facilities of any club in Japan. Covering an area of 33,000 square meters (about 355,000 square feet), the club has facilities for rugby, soccer, hockey, cricket, and baseball as well as four clay tennis courts, three all-weather tennis courts equipped with floodlights, a bowling green, a swimming pool, a gymnasium, squash courts, a bowling alley, a billiards room, and a children's playground. Sporting activities are organized for all ages, as are various social functions for families and for adult members. Many Tokyo residents find that the quality of facilities for families at this club more than compensates for its distance from central Tokyo.

Activities for Children

The first and perhaps most comforting point to emphasize is that the vast majority of children who are brought to Japan adjust quickly and enjoy their lives here. This fact is obvious to parents and observers and has been confirmed through professional research.

The supportive attitude of Japanese people, the high degree of personal safety, and the convenient and efficient public transportation system are identified by young people as major reasons for the positive feelings they have toward Japan. Indeed, children usually learn Japanese and master the transit system long before their parents do.

The importance of the family unit is significantly greater here than in the United States. A major reason for this is the absence of "neighborhoods" as we know them in suburban America. For many children, friends and playgrounds are no longer next door or just around the corner. An afternoon with a friend, especially for younger children, may entail complex logistical organization by parents; often the struggle with map reading alone is enough to discourage frequent visits. Inevitably, the family as a social unit must compensate for the absence of much of the formal and informal social activity that is taken for granted in U.S. suburbia.

Additionally, there is a change in the nature, and perhaps in the amount, of information children receive in Japan: films of great interest may arrive late or not at all, school and club libraries substitute for public libraries. While most parents may welcome a reduction in their children's TV viewing time, Japanese television does offer some children's programs in English, and within a short time, young children are often able to understand and enjoy programs in Japanese.

Paradoxically, the study and discussion of pressing issues in the United States are probably more important for young Americans going to school in Japan than for their peers at home, simply because of the lack of information on those topics in the Japanese media. As a result, it falls to parents to provide richer sources of information. Books, tapes, records, periodicals, and the like should be readily available. With older children, especially, there is a great need for discussion of current issues. Parents who are sensitive to this problem of awareness will find many ways to deal with it in a fashion suited to the family's interests and needs.

Children need help in developing both the attitude and the knowledge necessary to "tune in" to the action around them in Japan. For those who succeed, the rewards are many and varied, and life in Japan becomes much more interesting. There is the satisfaction that comes from learning about another culture, and perhaps more importantly, there is a deepened understanding of one's own culture and oneself.

Here again the parents' role is crucial, for it is primarily the parents who determine the children's reaction to life in Japan. If the parents are enthusiastic about the opportunities presented by living here, the chances are that the children will be, too. If, on the other hand, the parents are somewhat unenthusiastic, the children may make no attempt to develop a positive attitude at school or elsewhere.

Children's Camps

There are a number of camps for children and teenagers in the Kanto region and elsewhere, some sponsored by the international schools. Several of the schools also operate summer camps and have annual spring outings.

These camps enable children to meet and develop a camaraderie with each other, and friendships are often formed within a short time. The camps also encourage self-sufficiency, a degree of independence, and a sense of community. Finally, they offer parents a chance to free themselves of family responsibilities for a short time with the knowledge that their children are in safe hands and having fun.

Summer Student Employment

What do such tasks as fumigating *tansu* chests, cleaning swimming pools, pruning azaleas, assisting airline passengers, and researching international trade have in common?

These are just some of the different types of jobs enthusiastic and energetic Tokyo area students take during school vacation. Cosponsored by the ACCJ, the Tokyo American Club, and the U.S. Embassy, the Summer Student Internship Program successfully arranges these and many other interesting summer jobs, including work permits and insurance. The program, formerly known as Teens in Community, started in 1975 and is open to students 16 to 24 years of age who are dependents of Japan residents.

With student preferences running the gamut from physical labor to intellectual pursuits, volunteer program coordinators attempt to find a commensurately broad spectrum of summer jobs, and each year, between 100 and 200 students are placed in jobs during June, July, and August. Bookkeeping for an international computer company may intrigue one student, while another may choose to scan figures of a different sort—those swimming past the lifeguard's post at a local swimming pool. Unusual jobs undertaken in the past included refurbishing a 17-meter yacht, working at a farm lodge in Yamanashi Prefecture, tutoring young invalids in a Tokyo area hospital, and updating geological maps for a major international petroleum company.

Three months of uninterrupted vacation may seem idyllic to the book-weary student, but the long-awaited summer days soon acquire a sameness and relaxation turns to monotony. There may be plenty of leisure, but as one applicant put it, "free time in Tokyo isn't free...it costs money."

Students not only want to escape boredom and earn pocket money but also desire practical work experience that will be beneficial to their educational pursuits or career objectives. Starting in April, students or parents can pick up application forms from the coordinator's office at the Tokyo American Club.

Religious Activities

There are many places for Christian worship in the Greater Tokyo/Yokohama area, including Catholic, Anglican, Baptist, Quaker, Mormon, Greek/Russian Orthodox, and Lutheran churches. Services are usually conducted in English, although some churches also have regular services in Tagalog or German. There is worship for the Jewish community in English and Hebrew and for the Islamic community in English and Arabic. Some Buddhist temples also have services in English; further information is available from the International Buddhist Association.

Different churches offer different types of fellowship. Many of the churches here offer culturally oriented classes, usually from September to May, corresponding to the school year at most of the international schools. There are also small-group activities for members of every age group, from children to adults. Churches and other religious centers often combine their resources to provide social services for the foreign community. The Tokyo Union Church Women's Society, the Franciscan Chapel Center, and the Jewish Community Center, for example, all offer a variety of activities and are centrally located in Tokyo.

Information about times of worship and the groups associated with religious organizations can be obtained from the newspapers and periodicals published for the foreign community; telephone numbers are printed in the TELL calendar. (A listing of religious organizations is also given in the telephone directory at the end of this book.)

SAINT MAUR INTERNATIONAL SCHOOL
Established in 1872
Coeducational Christian School

A school with a long history, well established quality program, caring family atmosphere, and outstanding record of achievement.

Programs Offered:	Montessori from age 2 1/2 - 5 Elementary, Grades 1 - 5 Middle School, Grades 6 - 8 High School, Grades 9 - 12
Accredited by:	Western Association of Schools & Colleges European Council of International Schools
External Examinations:	International Baccalaureate Advanced Placement
Situated in historical Yokohama:	83, Yamate-cho, Naka-ku, Yokohama 231 Telephone: 045-641-5751 Fax: 045-641-6688
Headmistress:	Jeanette K. Thomas
Principal:	Richard B. Rucci

ST. MICHAEL'S INTERNATIONAL SCHOOL
17-2, NAKAYAMATE-DORI 3-CHOME CHUO-KU
KOBE 650 JAPAN
TEL: (078) 231-8885 FAX: (078) 231-8899

Headmaster
George E. Gibbons, M.A., B.Ed., F.R.G.S.

- **Pre-School to Grade Six**

- **Central Location**

- **Friendly atmosphere**

- **Much emphasis placed on personal development and character building**

- **Stimulating learning environment**

AOBA INTERNATIONAL SCHOOL

2-10-34 Aobadai
Meguro-ku, Tokyo 153

Tel: (03) 3461-1442
Fax: (03) 3463-9873

Aoba International School is a unique bi-lingual and multicultural nursery, kindergarten-pre-first grade for boys and girls ages 1-1/2 to 6. It provides a complete academic program in English geared to each age level, with strong English enrichment in the Language Arts. Also included are English as a Second Language (for Japanese and non-English-speaking children in Japan) and Japanese as a Second Language (for foreign children resident in Japan) programs. Japanese writing and reading are also introduced to all children from age 4. All-day programs with lunch and busing are available for the older children, ages 4 to 6.

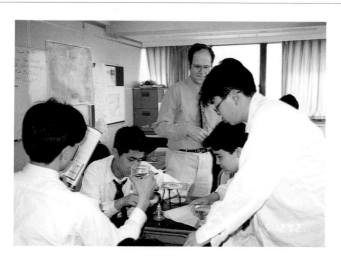

JAPAN INTERNATIONAL SCHOOL

2-10-7 Miyamae
Suginami-ku, Tokyo 168

Tel: (03) 3335-6620
Fax: (03) 3332-6930

Japan International School is a bi-lingual and cross-cultural elementary and junior high school, with a full academic program for grades 1 through 9 taught in English. It also has English as a Second Language and Japanese as a First or Second Language programs designed to meet the specific needs of both Japanese and foreign children resident in Tokyo who come from a wide variety of educational and cultural backgrounds. Music, Art, and Computer are offered at all grade levels. There is a full lunch program which recognizes cultural and religious diversity. Japan International School moved to a beautiful new facility which can house up to 600 students in air-conditioned comfort in August 1992. School bus service is available.

St. Mary's International School

THE SCHOOL

St. Mary's International School was founded in 1954 and is sponsored by the Brothers of Christian Instruction, a worldwide Catholic teaching order whose home base is Pointe du Lac, Quebec. The school provides educational services to male students of all nationalities and religious denominations. Currently, over 60 nations are represented. Each year, 98% to 100% of St. Mary's graduates are accepted into colleges throughout the world.

FACILITIES

St. Mary's International School is located on a seven-acre campus in a residential area of Setagaya-ku within a half hour from downtown residential areas. In addition to being served by ten school buses, the school is close to two railway stations.

SPECIALIZATION

St. Mary's secondary school is patterned after private preparatory schools in the United States. All students are expected to pursue a course of studies that challenges their academic potential. The elementary school program includes art, music, and physical education. Phonetics and computation skills are emphasized in the primary grades, while reading comprehension, problem solving, and social awareness are stressed in the intermediate grades. At the high school level, International Baccalaureate courses are offered.

Japanese, French, and Latin are language options at both the junior and senior high levels. Well-equipped science laboratories, computer centers, audio-visual rooms and typing rooms allow students a variety of hands-on learning experiences.

EXTRA-CURRICULAR ACTIVITIES

Participation in extra-curricular activities such as instrumental and choral music, arts, debate, speech, drama, and journalism is strongly encouraged. St. Mary's offers an excellent fine arts program with year-long exhibitions and public performances. In sports, basketball, wrestling, baseball, swimming, soccer, ice hockey, tennis, and track and field are the primary focus. The school boasts an astro-turf field and four tennis courts.

ADMISSION

Proficiency in English, previous educational records, a successful placement examination, and a positive attitude toward school regulations constitute St. Mary's entrance requirements. Standardized tests such as the IOWA BASIC, KUDER, DAT, PSAT/NMSQT, SAT, and TOEFL are administered.

FOR INFORMATION

Brother Michel Jutras, Headmaster
St. Mary's International School
1-6-19, Seta, Setagaya-ku, Tokyo 158, Japan
Tel: (03) 3709-3411/6
Fax: (03) 3707-1950

YOKOHAMA INTERNATIONAL SCHOOL

Yokohama International School is non-sectarian and accepts children of all nationalities regardless of their competency in English, unless it is felt that local schools in other languages would provide a better education. The school is to some extent a microcosm of the world's society and there is an attempt to promote an understanding and respect among students of the differences between cultures and a sensitivity towards those who are less privileged either economically or physically.

The school was established in 1924 and accepts children from nursery to grade 12. Yokohama International School is accredited by the New England Association of Schools and Colleges and the European Council of International Schools. It offers the International Baccalaureate at the 11th and 12th grade levels and is the G.C.E. (London University) centre for Japan.

258 Yamate-cho, Naka-ku
Yokohama, 231 Japan
Tel.: 045-622-0084
Fax: 045-621-0379

Chapter

12

Education

Education is a major concern for families moving overseas with children. The number of international schools in Japan that offer educational programs in English from nursery school through to the secondary level has risen to 25. Of these, 13 are in the Tokyo/Yokohama area, while the other 12 are in Sapporo, Sendai, Nagoya, Kyoto, Nara, Osaka, Kobe, Hiroshima, Fukuoka, and Okinawa. In addition, there are French, German, Indonesian, Chinese, and Korean schools in Tokyo and German and Norwegian schools in Kobe.

Vacancies at the international schools have been declining with the growing number of English-speaking families residing in Japan, particularly in the Tokyo area. As a consequence, admission to these schools is becoming increasingly competitive and waiting lists are common, especially for the lower grades. Application for admission should be made at least six months before the start of the academic year or even earlier if possible.

If there are no vacancies in the international schools and if you are a U.S. citizen, your children can attend the base schools in the Kanto region, at the Yokota, Zama, Atsugi, and Yokosuka bases, on a space-available basis. Some of the international schools outside the Kanto region—which tend to have a greater number of vacancies than schools in Tokyo—offer facilities for boarders.

Also, foreigners in Japan who are Japanese taxpayers are welcome to send their children to Japanese schools. Public education is free from elementary school to high school, and incidental charges, such as for uniforms, are reasonable. All instruction is of course in Japanese, and at the intermediate and upper levels this may prove a problem. Also, the curriculum differs significantly from that of schools in the United States.

Sending your children to a Japanese school is a viable option if either you or your spouse can speak Japanese reasonably well (for communication with teachers), if you intend to stay in Japan for many years, and if you feel your children can handle the academic pressure and long hours of study that Japanese students must face. On the positive side, the academic levels of Japanese schools are very high. Information on public schools is available at your local ward, town, or city office.

International Schools

The academic standards of the international schools in Japan are high, and an average of over 90% of graduates of these schools attend university. Standardized test scores at all grade levels are significantly higher than in the United States. In some cases, parents and children may worry whether they will be able to find an institution of equal quality once they return home.

The tuition at many of the international schools is high, up to as much as ¥1.2 million a year or more. Your company may be prepared to cover the schooling fees of your children. These schools are independent and receive no tax support (although the Japanese government does grant taxation benefits to schools that meet certain minimum standards). The international schools also face high and usually rising procurement costs in Japan, such as the attractive wages needed to retain qualified teachers, and substantial expenses for maintaining and improving buildings and equipment. In fact, tuition and other fees fall short, in some cases, of covering costs and providing for expansion to meet growing demand. Most international schools raise additional funds by soliciting the support of parents and corporations and by holding fund-raising events, such as bingo nights, carnivals, and food fairs.

The following points should be considered when selecting a school:

•Entrance requirements vary. It is a good idea to ask the administration at your child's present school for an unofficial transcript. Usually the official document is sent directly from one school to the other. Up-to-date health examination reports are also required by most of the schools.

•Programs and facilities for children with physical, emotional, or learning disabilities are extremely limited; however, there is a specialized international school for children with handicaps in Tokyo, the Tokyo International Learning Community. Parents should consider the options carefully before accepting an assignment to Japan.

•Some schools have religious or national affiliations, but enrollment is by no means always restricted along these lines.

•The academic year is from early September to early June or mid-June, and the school day is generally from 9:00 A.M. to 3:00 P.M., five days a week.

•Uniforms, when required, are available locally.

•Not all schools provide accident insurance. Medical facilities are not always available, but emergency cases are treated at nearby hospitals or clinics.

•While international schools make every effort to accommodate all students wishing to enroll, many schools are operating at capacity levels and waiting lists are common, particularly at the elementary level. Recent sudies project continued growth in the number of new students. While the schools are implementing long-range development plans to handle the increase, there is still a shortage of vacancies, its severity varying from school to school and from grade to grade. Generally, the international schools in areas outside Tokyo and its environs have a greater capacity for new students than those in the Tokyo metropolitan area.

•In the unlikely event of an American family finding itself in an area with no suitable educational facilities, if there is a U.S. military base in the vicinity an application can be made for a child to attend the base school on a space-available basis.

Brief descriptions of English-language international schools in Japan, listed in alphabetical order, are given in the following pages. All schools are members of the Japan Council of Overseas Schools. The ACCJ makes no evaluation of the schools and encourages parents to contact the administrative offices of the schools for further information and to visit the schools to examine the facilities firsthand.

The American School in Japan

Developing Compassionate, Inquisitive
Learners Prepared for Global Responsibility

- Co-educational, pre-school (ages 3-5)
  through 12th grade; post-graduate
  year option
- The largest and most complete inter-
  national school facilities in Japan
- An extensive Japanese language and culture
  program
- College preparatory, fully accredited
- Advanced computer education curriculum
- Progressive athletic and fine arts departments

Chofu Campus

Tel: (0422) 34-5300 Ext. 721

Fax: (0422) 34-5304

Nursery-Kindergarten

Tel: (03) 3461-4523

Fax: (03) 3461-2505

Chofu Address: 1-1-1 Nomizu, Chofu-shi, Tokyo 182

International Schools in the Kanto Area

The American School in Japan (ASIJ),
Chofu, Tokyo
Tel: (0422) 34-5300
A coeducational elementary and second-
ary school in northwest Tokyo, about one
hour from the city center by school bus.

The British School in Tokyo, Shibuya
1-chome, Shibuya, Tokyo
Tel: (03) 3400-7353
A coeducational day school for children
from the ages of 3 to 11, close to Shibuya
Station on the JR Yamanote Line and the
Ginza and Hanzomon/Shin-Tamagawa
subway lines. The school offers a curriculum based on the British educational system.

Christian Academy in Japan, Shinkawa-
cho, Higashi-Kurume, Tokyo
Tel: (0424) 71-0022
A coeducational elementary and secondary day/boarding school, kindergarten through grade 12, close to
Higashi-Kurume Station on the Seibu
Ikebukuro Line, in the northwestern
outskirts of Tokyo. Two thirds of the
students are children of Protestant missionaries, but the school also accepts a
limited number of non-Christian students.

**International School of the Sacred
Heart,** Hiroo, Shibuya-ku, Tokyo
Tel: (03) 3400-3951
An elementary and secondary day school
for girls (boys in kindergarten only) on
the campus of the University of the
Sacred Heart, near Hiroo Station on the
Hibiya subway line.

*The campus of the American
School in Japan (ASIJ),
in Tokyo*

Japan International School (JIS), Miyamae, Suginami-ku, Tokyo
Tel: (03) 3468-8476
A coeducational elementary and junior-high day school, grades 1 through 9, in northwestern Tokyo.

Nishimachi International School, Moto-Azabu, Minato-ku, Tokyo
Tel: (03) 3451-5520
A coeducational school, kindergarten through grade 9, on various bus routes and 10 minutes' walk from either Roppongi or Hiroo stations on the Hibiya subway line.

St. Joseph International School, Yamate-cho, Naka-ku, Yokohama
Tel: (045) 641-0065
A coeducational day/boarding school, preschool through grade 12, 10 minutes' walk from Ishikawa-cho Station on the JR Negishi Line in Yokohama.

St. Mary's International School, Yoga, Setagaya-ku, Tokyo
Tel: (03) 3709-3411
An elementary and secondary day school for boys, near Yoga Station on the Shin-Tamagawa Line.

St. Maur International School, Yamate-cho, Naka-ku, Yokohama
Tel: (045) 641-5751
A coeducational school, nursery through grade 12, 10 minutes' walk from Ishikawa-cho Station on the JR Negishi Line in Yokohama.

Santa Maria International School, Minami-Tanaka, Nerima-ku, Tokyo
Tel: (03) 3904-0517
A coeducational school, kindergarten through grade 6, close to Fujimidai Station on the Seibu Ikebukuro Line and Iogi Station on the Seibu Shinjuku Line.

Seisen International School, Yoga, Setagaya-ku, Tokyo
Tel: (03) 3704-2661
An elementary and secondary day school for girls (boys in kinder-garten only), 10 minutes' walk from Yoga Station on the Shin-Tamagawa Line or 15 minutes by bus from Denenchofu Station on the Toyoko Line.

Tokyo International Learning Community, Osawa, Mitaka, Tokyo
Tel: (0422) 31-9611
A coeducational school providing education and psychological counseling for children between the ages of 3 and 16 with handicaps or special needs, close to Tamabochimae Station on the JR Chuo Line.

Yokohama International School, Yamate-cho, Naka-ku, Yokohama
Tel: (045) 622-0084
A coeducational nursery and day school through grade 13. The school adjoins the Yokohama Country and Athletic Club and is within walking distance of Yamate Station on the Keihin Tohoku Line.

International Schools in the Kansai Region and Outlying Areas

Canadian Academy, Naka, Higashi Nada-ku, Kobe
Tel: (078) 857-0100
A coeducational kindergarten through grade 12 day school. The closest station is JR Sumiyoshi Station.

Fukuoka International School, Momochi, Sawa-ku, Fukuoka
Tel: (092) 641-0326
A coeducational kindergarten through grade 12 day school, close to Fujisaki Station on the Fukuoka subway.

Hiroshima International School, Kurakake, Asakita-ku, Hiroshima
Tel: (082) 843-4411
A coeducational day school, kindergarten through grade 8, close to Hiroshima Station.

Hokkaido International School, Fukuzumi, Toyohira-ku, Sapporo
Tel: (011) 851-1205
A coeducational day school, kindergarten through grade 12, close to Fukuzumi Sanjo Itchome bus stop.

Kansai Christian School, Tawaraguchi-shi, Ikoma, Nara
Tel: (07437) 4-1781
A coeducational day school, grades 1 through 12, near Ikoma Station on the Kintetsu Line. Most students are the children of Protestant missionaries, but the school also accepts a limited number of non-Christian students.

Kyoto International School, Kamimiyanomae, Shishigatari, Sakyo-ku, Kyoto

Tel: (075) 771-4022

A coeducational day school, kindergarten through grade 8, in northeastern Kyoto, near Ginkakuji Temple.

Marist Brothers International School, Chimori-cho, Suma-ku, Kobe

Tel: (078) 732-6266

A coeducational day school, kindergarten through grade 12, near Suma Dentetsu Station on the Hankyu and Hanshin lines and Suma Station on the JR Tokaido Line.

Nagoya International School, Nakashidami, Moriyama-ku, Nagoya

Tel: (052) 736-2025

A coeducational day school, nursery through grade 12, close to Kozoji Station on the JR Chuo Line, a roughly 30-minute ride from Nagoya Station.

Okinawa Christian School, Urasoe, Okinawa

Tel: (0988) 77-3661

A coeducational day school, kindergarten through grade 12, on Hacksaw Ridge in central Okinawa, near Camp Kinser.

Osaka International School, Mino-shi, Osaka

Tel: (0727) 27-5050

A coeducational day school, kindergarten through grade 12, near Kita-Senri Station on the Hankyu Line.

St. Michael's International School, Nakayamate-dori, Chuo-ku, Kobe

Tel: (078) 231-8885

A coeducational day school, preschool through grade 6, close to Sannomiya Station. The school offers a curriculum based on the British educational system.

Sendai American School, Komatsushima 4-chome, Aoba-ku, Sendai

Tel: (022) 234-8567

A coeducational day school, grades 1 through 9, close to Dainohara Station.

International Schools in Japan

Name	Est.	Location	Principal	Grades	Affiliation	Coed	Enroll.	Tel	Fax
The American School in Japan (ASIJ)	1902	Tokyo	Mr. Peter Cooper	K-G12	Nonsectarian	Yes	1,261	(0422) 34-5300	(0422) 33-0608
The British School in Tokyo	1989	Tokyo	Ms. Gillian Greenwood	N-G6	Nonsectarian[3]	Yes	240	(03) 3400-7353	(03) 5485-5340
Canadian Academy	1913	Kobe	Dr. Stuart J. Young	K-G12	Nonsectarian	Yes	675	(078) 857-0100	(078) 857-3250
Christian Academy in Japan	1950	Tokyo	Dr. Bruce Hekman	K-G12	Missionary[1]	Yes	335	(0424) 71-0022	(0424) 76-2200
Fukuoka International School	1972	Fukuoka	Ms. Clara Furukawa	K-G12	Nonsectarian	Yes	94	(092) 641-0326	(092) 841-7602
Hiroshima International School	1962	Hiroshima	Mr. Terry Donaldson	K-G8	Nonsectarian	Yes	42	(082) 843-4411	(082) 843-4111
Hokkaido International School	1958	Sapporo	Dr. Richard McClain	K-G12	Nonsectarian	Yes	106	(011) 851-1205	(011) 855-1435
International School of the Sacred Heart	1908	Tokyo	Sr. Ruth Sheehy	K-G12	Catholic[2]	Girls[5]	683	(03) 3400-3951	(03) 3400-3496
Japan International School (JIS)	1980	Tokyo	Ms. Regina Doi	K-G12	Nonsectarian	Yes	315	(03) 3468-8476	(03) 3468-8448
Kansai Christian School	1970	Nara	Ms. Kenelee Proctor	G1-G12	Missionary[1]	Yes	32	(07437) 4-1781	(07437) 4-1781
Kyoto International School	1957	Kyoto	Ms. Cheryl Burghardt	K-G8	Nonsectarian	Yes	76	(075) 771-4022	(075) 752-1184
Marist Brothers International School	1951	Kobe	Br. George Fontana	K-G12	Catholic[2]	Yes	252	(078) 732-6266	(078) 732-6268
Nagoya International School	1963	Nagoya	Mr. Gerald F. Craig	N-G12	Nonsectarian	Yes	380	(052) 736-2025	(052) 736-3883
Nishimachi International School	1949	Tokyo	Mr. Hikojiro Katsuhisa	K-G9	Nonsectarian	Yes	380	(03) 3451-5520	(03) 3456-0197
Okinawa Christian School	1957	Urasoe	Mr. Paul Gieschen	K-G12	Nonsectarian	Yes	296	(0988) 77-3661	(0988) 76-2655
Osaka International School	1991	Osaka	Mr. James Wiese	K-G12	Nonsectarian	Yes	94	(0727) 27-5050	(0727) 27-5055
St. Joseph International School	1901	Yokohama	Fr. James J. Mueller	P-G12	Catholic[2]	Boys	282	(045) 641-0065	(045) 641-6572
St. Mary's International School	1954	Tokyo	Br. Michel Jutras	K-G12	Catholic[2]	Boys	950	(03) 3709-3411	(03) 3707-1950
St. Maur International School	1872	Yokohama	Ms. J.K. Thomas	N-G12	Christian[2]	Yes	470	(045) 641-5751	(045) 641-6688
St. Michael's International School	1945	Kobe	Mr. George Gibbons	P-G6	Protestant[2]	Yes	159	(078) 231-8885	(078) 231-8899
Santa Maria International School	1959	Tokyo	Sr. Raphael	K-G6	Catholic[2]	Yes	158	(03) 3904-0517	(03) 3904-9552
Seisen International School	1962	Tokyo	Sr. Asuncion Lecubarri	K-G12	Catholic[2]	Girls[5]	600	(03) 3704-2661	(03) 3701-1033
Sendai American School	1984	Sendai	Dr. Maynard F. Yutzy	G1-G9	Nonsectarian	Yes	23	(022) 234-8567	(022) 272-7161
Tokyo International Learning Community[4]	1987	Tokyo	Mr. Ross Anderson	Ages 3-16	Nonsectarian	Yes	17	(0422) 31-9611	(0422) 31-9611
Yokohama International School	1924	Yokohama	Mr. John Tanner	N-G13	Nonsectarian	Yes	495	(045) 622-0084	(045) 621-0379

N=Nursery, P=Preschool, K=Kindergarten, G=Grade   [1]20% of each class may be non-Christian.   [2]Open to all.   [3]50% of students may be non-British.   [4]For children with handicaps or special needs.   [5]Kindergarten is coed.

Note: Enrollment figures are approximate.

Nursery Schools for Foreign Children

Name	Est.	Location	Principal	Grades	Affiliation	Coed	Enroll.	Tel	Fax
The American School in Japan Nursery/Kindergarten	1902	Tokyo	Mr. Doug Roe	N-K	Nonsectarian	Yes	118	(03) 3461-4523	(03) 3461-2505
Aoba International School	1976	Tokyo	Ms. Regina Doi	N-K	Nonsectarian	Yes	220	(03) 3461-1442	(03) 3463-9873
Child's Play		Tokyo	Ms. Naomi Fujita	N-P	Nonsectarian	Yes	40	(03) 3460-8841	(03) 5709-0552
Global Garden	1992	Tokyo	Ms. Maureen Ilg	N-K	Nonsectarian	Yes		(03) 3449-8060	(03) 3449-8020
Gregg International School	1987	Tokyo	Ms. LeMay, Mrs. Okada	P-K	Nonsectarian	Yes	100	(03) 3725-6495	(03) 3724-0577
J.A.C. International Kindergarten	1982	Tokyo	Ms. Asai	N-P	Nonsectarian	Yes		(03) 3445-6326	(03) 3473-3219
Maria's Babies	1987	Tokyo	Mrs. Matsuoka	N-K	Nonsectarian	Yes	50	(03) 3404-2945	(03) 3404-3625
PTC Pacific International School	1982	Tokyo	Mrs. Takatsuka	P-K	Nonsectarian	Yes	30	(03) 3793-0438	(03) 3793-0438
Shirogane International Pre-School	1984	Tokyo	Ms. Keiko Shoji	P	Nonsectarian	Yes	45	(03) 3442-1941	(03) 3442-1942
Tokyo Union Church Preschool/Kindergarten	1985	Tokyo	Ms. Vivian Consul	P-K	Protestant[1]	Yes	72	(03) 3400-1579	(03) 3400-1942
Unida International School		Tokyo	Ms. Harumi Shimura	N-K	Nonsectarian	Yes	60	(03) 3443-6850	(03) 3443-7867

N=Nursery; P=Preschool; K=Kindergarten.   [1]Open to all.

Note: Enrollment figures are approximate.

Adult Education

Graduate and undergraduate credits and degrees can be earned in the Tokyo area by foreigners at institutions of higher education where classes are conducted in English. Three institutions offer regular programs throughout the year: International Christian University, the International Division of Sophia University, and Temple University, Japan.

Each institution has its own admission requirements. Courses can be taken as part of a degree program or for further education only and may, at the discretion of the institution, be audited or taken for credit. Classes start in September, and it is advisable to contact the school well in advance to ensure compliance with deadlines for application.

Information concerning courses and entrance requirements can be obtained directly from these institutions by contacting:

International Christian University
3-10-12, Osawa, Mitaka-shi, Tokyo 181
Tel: (0422) 33-3131

International Division, Sophia University
Ichigaya Campus,
4, Yonbancho, Chiyoda-ku, Tokyo 102
Tel: (03) 3264-7337

Temple University, Japan
2-2, Minami-Osawa, Hachioji-shi, Tokyo 192-03
Tel: (0426) 77-5111

Several other adult education options also exist in Japan. For example, the International University of Japan in Niigata offers graduate degree programs. Courses are all in English and an MBA program is offered. Also, some American universities, such as Chaminade University of Honolulu and the University of Maryland, among others, offer extension courses, usually through one of the international schools. The availability and content of such courses vary, and it is best to ascertain what is being offered and where from newspapers and other sources. Extension programs are usually scheduled in the late afternoon, in the evening, or on weekends for the convenience of those who have business or other obligations.

Chapter

13

Working Spouses

Challenges and Opportunities

In recent years, the number of foreigners coming to Japan for personal or professional reasons—with their companies, for overseas work experience after completing graduate studies, or to learn more about Japanese business and culture—has increased dramatically. Among these are many women and an increasing number of men who are accompanying their spouses. The following sections are intended for those coming to Japan not on assignment and hoping to find employment of some kind during their stay.

For spouses wanting to work in Japan, there are many rewards besides the purely financial. You will find yourself a part of the Japanese business community and come to know an aspect of Japan that nonworking people never experience. Work can also speed cultural adjustment and give added insight and understanding in such areas as cross-cultural communication, which future employers are likely to appreciate.

However, foreigners who plan to work in Japan may also face a number of issues related to managing expectations, the type of employment to consider, handling job interviews and negotiating benefits, and various practical arrangements.

Managing Your Expectations

Many professional people who have interrupted a well-established career to come to Japan can expect to work at a lower level and at a lower salary than they are accustomed to; this often happens when entering a new market with skills obtained elsewhere. The number of jobs available is limited in many areas, particularly in the professional areas, and people wanting to work in Japan may have to accept jobs that would not necessarily be their first choice. Some people are lucky, of course, and find exactly the type of job they were hoping for, but others might have to adjust their expectations a little.

For example, a lawyer without at least five years of active practice in the United States will not be able to practice in Japan, even as a foreign law consultative attorney; however, he or she can be an aide or a consultant in a Japanese law firm. A pharmacist cannot legally practice but can write advertising brochures for a Japanese pharmaceutical firm for overseas markets. Teachers with credentials are an exception and generally have few problems in finding work in their particular area.

Besides trying to continue along your present career path, there are two ways of approaching working in Japan. The first is to look for a position that will add something unique to your résumé. Working in Japan can add a breadth to your experience that is not easily obtained by others in your profession who do not leave home and can thus make your position more competitive when you return.

The second is to use your time in Japan to pursue work-related activities in a different field. Many people have successfully made use of their stay in Japan to engage in such entrepreneurial activities as starting their own business or to give their time and professional expertise to nonprofit work. Others have decided to make a radical career change and undertake new training to develop a business from a personal hobby or interest.

Types of Employment

Recently, the job market has tightened somewhat as foreign firms, especially, have rationalized their operations. As in any job market, the right skills and experience are the key to finding employment. Options you might consider in addition to full-time employment are part-time employment and working as a free lance for more than one employer.

Visas

If you wish to work in a full-time capacity, or for more than 20 hours a week, you will have to apply for a working visa, for which you will need a sponsor, usually your employer. With your employer's sponsorship and the appropriate documentation, you are likely to be granted a visa. If you already have another type of visa—such as a dependent's visa—you may work up to 20 hours a week, with the permission of the immigration authorities. Obtaining this is a relatively simple procedure, provided you have the necessary documentation. If you are the spouse or child of a Japanese national or permanent resident, there is no restriction on your activities. Further information on obtaining a visa is given in Chapter 4.

Looking For a Job

Positions available in Japan are advertised in several English-language dailies, in particular the Monday edition of the *Japan Times*. Many foreigners, however, find that they hear about openings through contacts rather than through newspaper advertisements. Among associations that meet regularly and may be useful in developing your own network of contacts are: Foreign Executive Women (FEW), the Kaisha Society, the Japan branch of your alumni association, the ACCJ, Forum for Corporate Communication, and Toastmasters clubs. Most of these groups advertise their meetings in the English-language press, and their telephone numbers are given in TELL's *International Community Calendar*. One of the advantages of looking for a job in Japan is that people are usually more accessible; it is quite acceptable to use your network to contact the managing director of a foreign company in person.

In other respects, looking for employment in Japan is similar to the job search elsewhere. You should have a well-presented résumé that lists your experience and achievements, select the companies you are interested in working for, contact the appropriate person in each company, send your résumé, and make a follow-up call. If you are targeting a Japanese company, going through someone you know who can introduce you to a contact within the company will usually be an enormous help.

Job Interviews

In Japan, job interviews are often granted as a courtesy even when no employment is available. Although you should be encouraged by an interview, you should not make the mistake of thinking a good interview will automatically result in a job offer. The interview itself may be somewhat different in Japan from what you are used to, especially if the interviewer is a Japanese businessperson conducting the interview in English. Do not be surprised if your Japanese interviewer appears to be more interested in you than in your credentials; he or she has probably examined your credentials already and now wants to meet you in person.

In Japan, a positive assessment of character is considered essential to employment and may even be more important than credentials. In such an interview, show your ability to communicate by listening respectfully and speaking slowly and clearly. Resist the temptation to speak rapidly and idiomatically if you are speaking to a Japanese person, even one who speaks English well.

You can expect a number of personal questions during the interview; Japan has no legal limitations on information that can be requested, so you might be asked questions about your age, marital status, and even your plans for a family. The best way to handle such questions is to be polite but vague about those you do not wish to answer. Not answering such questions at all or, worse, displaying a hostile attitude when asked may reduce your chances of success significantly. Try not to show your displeasure during the interview, even if you are unhappy with the way it is going—keeping good relations is useful in Japan, and more often than not problems are simply due to misunderstanding. This is a particularly important point if you are new to Japan, as you will learn that even those Japanese who appear to speak good English often use words differently and have difficulty understanding everything you say.

Although you should know what is expected of you in a prospective position, be aware that jobs in Japan often "evolve." If you prove yourself over time, responsibility will be pushed your way to test your talents. Such a gradual change in capacity is more important to consider in the long run than your initial job title.

Negotiating Benefits

Besides your salary, benefits also can be negotiated with a new employer, particularly in a smaller firm. Before your interview, you should have a clear idea about which benefits will be important to your life in Japan. For example, you may wish to think about:

• Your Job Title. Although in Japan traditional titles come only with time and experience, you may be able to negotiate a Western title that appears impressive on your résumé.

• Working Hours. You may wish to negotiate working hours that are suitable to your lifestyle.

• Language Lessons. As mentioned previously, some employers will be agreeable to paying the cost of Japanese language lessons at a school or with a private teacher.

• Home Leave/Vacations. If you are accompanying a partner who is employed under expatriate conditions, you may wish to negotiate longer vacations than would usually be available or unpaid time off for home leave.

• Expatriate Fringe Benefits. With the right skills, you can often negotiate a number of the fringe benefits generally associated with overseas hires.

•Salary. You should obtain some idea of the usual salary paid to Japanese people for the type of job you would like and expect to be compensated fairly.

Child Care

For foreign working spouses who have children too young to attend school, the type of full-time child care available may be different than expected. There is no formal training for nannies or child-care assistants in Japan, but despite this, the quality of child care available from babysitters or day-care centers is generally good, and there will be few worries about safety or reliability. For further information on child care, see the chapter on everyday life.

Language and Working Environment

Although many jobs require bilingual capabilities, some jobs in which only English is required are available. Even when no knowledge of Japanese is required, however, you will probably be more comfortable and able to achieve a great deal more if you have some grasp of basic conversational Japanese. Many companies are willing to subsidize or pay for Japanese language lessons.

More often than not, you will work with a largely Japanese work force, and there may be some problems related to adjustment, communication, expectations, and different cultural perspectives. Successful foreign employees are usually flexible, have a strong desire to be a success in their new environment, and maintain a sense of humor in most circumstances. With a similar approach, working in Japan may turn out to be one of the most interesting, valuable, and fulfilling experiences on your résumé.

A JR Sobu Line train passes cherry trees in bloom along the canal near Tokyo's Yotsuya Station. (Courtesy of Shinjuku Ward, Tokyo)

Students at St. Joseph International School, in Yokohama.

Children in the playground of Santa Maria International School, in Tokyo's Nerima Ward.

Most deposits and withdrawals
are now made through
automated teller machines, and
an increasing number of banks
are providing instructions in
English for the convenience
of the foreign community.

Many of Tokyo's commuter trains are so crowded during the morning rush hour that it is impossible to move, let alone read a book or newspaper. The government has pledged to reduce the overcapacity of trains to 180% by 1999.

The Mikuni Junction links three major expressways in Saitama Prefecture. (Courtesy of Saitama Prefectural Government)

A peaceful bamboo grove

A performance of traditional Japanese music at Kumano Shrine, Tokyo (Courtesy of Meguro Ward, Tokyo)

The ACCJ office in Tokyo

The Yokohama Bay Bridge is one of Japan's newest. (Courtesy of Kanagawa Prefectural Government)

About 40 kilometers from downtown Tokyo, Makuhari, in Chiba Prefecture, has been developed extensively and features Japan's largest exhibition halls, several office buildings, hotels, and a baseball stadium for one of Japan's professional baseball teams, the Chiba Lotte Marines. (Courtesy of Chiba Prefectural Government)

Cherry blossom season at Himonya Hachiman Shrine, Tokyo (Courtesy of Meguro Ward, Tokyo)

In summer, many amusement parks, like this one in Osaka, are open until 10:00 P.M.

Tokyo's Harajuku on Sundays is a stage for young dancers and musicians.

A festival at sea, Kanagawa Prefecture (Courtesy of Kanagawa Prefectural Government)

The annual Snow Festival held every February in Sapporo, Hokkaido, attracts thousands of visitors from all around Japan and from overseas. (Courtesy of Hokkaido Prefectural Government)

The Chichibu-no-Yomatsuri *is held every December in Chichibu, only about 60 kilometers from Tokyo. (Courtesy of Saitama Prefectural Government)*

*Demonstrations of traditional
Japanese archery are held
annually in Tokyo's Meiji
Jingu. (Courtesy of Shinjuku
Ward, Tokyo)*

*A festival at Narita temple,
Chiba Prefecture (Courtesy
of Chiba Prefectural
Government)*

*The Tanabata festival in
Hiratsuka, Kanagawa
Prefecture (Courtesy of
Kanagawa Prefectural
Government)*

A mikoshi, or portable shrine,
is carried through the
grounds of Narita temple.
Mikoshi can weigh up
to as much as a ton.

The photo shows the **AIU** Japan Building at Marunouchi, Tokyo.

AIU is proud to provide you with various types of insurance that meets the needs of each of you, not only in Japan, but around the world.

AIU Japan started its business in Japan in 1946. It now employs more than 2,400 staff in over 100 offices spread throughout Japan.

AIU INSURANCE COMPANY

1-3, Marunouchi 1-chome, Chiyoda-ku, Tokyo Japan Tel.03-3216-6611

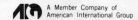
A Member Company of
American International Group

Chapter

14

Business and Finance

The American Chamber of Commerce in Japan

People coming to Japan in a business capacity will find the American Chamber of Commerce in Japan (ACCJ) of prime interest.

The ACCJ was founded in 1948 by representatives of 38 U.S. companies in early postwar Japan. Today, the ACCJ has a membership of more than 700 companies and 2,100 individuals. The ACCJ's work is conducted through over 40 standing committees and subcommittees, which focus on trade expansion, bilateral investment, employment practices, marketing, intellectual property, technology, tax and legal matters, and a variety of other business areas.

The ACCJ has its headquarters in Toranomon, in downtown Tokyo, and maintains an office in Kobe. The Tokyo office has a permanent full-time staff of 14, including 4 Americans. The office in Kobe, which serves the ACCJ's Kansai Chapter in the Kansai region (centered on Osaka and Kobe), is staffed by a full-time administrator.

The addresses and telephone and fax numbers of the ACCJ offices are as follows:

The American Chamber of Commerce in Japan
7th Floor, Fukide Bldg. No.2, 4-1-21, Toranomon, Minato-ku, Tokyo 105
Tel: (03) 3433-5381 Fax: (03) 3436-1446

The American Chamber of Commerce in Japan
  Kansai Chapter
Business Center 301, East Court Two,
1-14, Koyocho Naka, Higashi Nada-ku, Kobe 658
Tel: (078) 857-9745 Fax: (078) 857-6714

The ACCJ conducts monthly committee meetings and open programs to help U.S. businesspeople further their understanding and knowledge of Japan and the Japanese market. Also, the ACCJ produces a number of publications in addition to the one you are now reading, including the following:

- *ACCJ Journal.* A monthly magazine containing timely articles about doing business in Japan. The *Journal* is free to ACCJ members and is sold to the general public.
- *ACCJ Pictorial Directory.* Published annually, this directory lists all members, both resident and nonresident, and supporting associates of the Chamber. A classified section lists firms by sector.
- *ACCJ Newsletter.* A monthly newsletter that contains committee reports and information about business opportunities, trade fairs, and other items of interest to members.
- *Setting Up an Office in Japan.* This guide, scheduled for publication in spring 1993, explains how to set up an office in Japan and includes detailed sections on real estate in Tokyo, contract negotiations and fees, legal services, banking, patents, staffing, and other issues.
- *U.S.-Japan Trade White Paper.* This annual publication provides a current update of business issues by sector.

(An order form for ACCJ publications can be found at the end of Chapter 19.)

Occasionally, the ACCJ also issues special publications concerning investment, patents and trademarks, trade, joint ventures, marketing, and employment practices.

Briefing breakfast meetings for visiting home office VIPs are especially popular. Regular members can contact the ACCJ Tokyo office if they care to have a breakfast meeting arranged; the office will do the rest, including making arrangements for the room and breakfast and inviting guests in similar fields for a networking session.

Personal Banking

Japan's consumer banking market is served by a wide range of financial organizations: city banks, regional banks, mutual savings and loan banks, credit associations, the postal savings system, and foreign banks, including most of the major U.S. banks.

In addition to establishing an account with a Japanese bank, which will probably be necessary for paying bills and receiving salaries and other payments, you may want to open an account with an authorized foreign exchange bank to facilitate overseas transactions. Any institution designated as an authorized foreign exchange bank can handle remittances overseas and currency exchange transactions, although the quality and speed of

IBI, Inc.

Market Research & Strategic Planning for Japan

Founded in Tokyo in 1972, IBI is a leading market research and strategy consulting services firm dedicated to helping companies succeed in Japan's rewarding, but challenging, marketplace. With a staff of over 100 in Japan, we have a proven track record working with high-technology companies, financial services firms, and other clients in the following areas:

Market research
Market entry studies
Competitor analysis
Distributor search
High-technology studies
Customer opinion surveys
Strategic alliance consultancy
Mergers and acquisitions counsel
Strategy consulting programs

International Business Information

For further information contact:
Thomas R. Zengage, Director, IBI, Inc., Izumiya Bldg., 3-1-1 Kojimachi, Chiyoda-ku, Tokyo 102, Japan Tel: (03)3230-1835 Fax: (03)3234-8264

service will vary depending on the English-language proficiency (if you do not understand Japanese) and experience of the staff. Branches of the larger Japanese banks in urban areas, especially those in or close to the city center, are likely to have the most experience and skill in handling foreign currency transactions. U.S. banks, including Citibank, have Japan branches that can offer a range of retail banking in local yen and foreign currency services. Most Japanese banks have foreign customer service representatives to assist you in your banking needs.

Ordinary Deposit Accounts Offered by Japanese Banks

•General Deposit Accounts (*futsu yokin*). The most common type of Japanese bank accounts, general deposit accounts can be used for remittances and payments, including payrolls. They are not normally used for long-term savings, as the interest offered is a mere 2%, minus the 20% government tax on interest. To open a deposit account you must present some form of ID, such as your driver's license, passport, or Certificate of Alien Registration—and ¥100 for the minimum initial deposit. You will probably be issued a passbook the same day, with your bank card mailed to you about a week later.

As a non-Japanese, you will have the option of using either your signature or an *inkan* (an official personal or company seal, also known as a *hanko*) when opening an account. Thereafter, you may occasionally need to sign or stamp your *inkan* on certain bank-related documents. (If you happen to have an *inkan,* keep in mind that it is considered extremely important; once you have had it officially registered at your ward, town, or city office, you will have to use it for all official paperwork, and your signature will then not be enough without your *inkan.*)

If you are a company director or are thinking of establishing your own company in Japan, you will need to have an official seal (*jitsuin*) made and have it registered with your ward, town, or city office. Seals used for banking may be either *jitsuin* or *bon'in* (an unofficial personal seal, such as those for Japanese names sold at stationery shops).

For security, the bank clerk handling your account application will ask you to designate a secret four-digit number for access to your account through automated teller machines (ATMs). You must have your ATM card to make withdrawals from your account, and if you have your passbook, you are able to update it at the same time. If you have used your *inkan,* rather than your signature, to open your account, you will need to have it with you whenever you make a withdrawal at the counter using just your passbook.

•Time Deposits (*teiki yokin*). Deposits are made for fixed periods, such as three months, six months, one year, or two years. Interest rates are higher than those of general deposit accounts, and the size of the deposit depends on the investment instrument you choose.

Long-Term Deposit Accounts

•Super Teiki. The minimum deposit for this type of account, offered by various banks, is ¥3 million. No withdrawals can be made for a specified period. The interest was about 4% per annum in late 1992.

•Super MMCs (money market certificates). For these deposit accounts, also offered by banks, the minimum deposit, once ¥10 million, is now only ¥100,000. No withdrawals can be made for a specified period. The interest was about two percentage points above interest (after government tax) on passbook savings accounts in late 1992.

•Super Gold. This type of deposit account is offered by securities companies, such as Nomura, Kokusai, and Yamaichi. The minimum deposit is only ¥100,000. With an annual interest rate about 2% higher than that of Super MMCs, Super Gold is one of the better options for interest-bearing accounts in Japan. Maturity can be set for periods varying from one week to over one year. Additional deposits are in units of ¥10,000.

•Chuki Kokusai Fund (Chukoku Fund). This investment instrument is also offered by the major securities companies and has a minimum deposit of ¥100,000. Withdrawals can be made at any time after the first month, in any amount; however, deposits must be in units of ¥10,000. The yield on these funds is sometimes higher than that of Super Gold.

•MMFs (money management funds). These deposit accounts are U.S.-type money market funds offered by securities companies. The minimum investment is ¥1 million. The interest rate is higher than that of Super Gold, and withdrawals can be made in the same way as with Chuki Kokusai Fund deposits.

•Postal Savings. This savings deposit instrument is available at any post office in Japan. Anyone can start a postal savings account with a deposit as small as ¥100 or as large as ¥3 million. Interest rates are higher than ordinary bank savings accounts, but the maximum deposit limit makes postal savings suitable only for small-volume savings.

For more information on long-term savings accounts, contact any bank or securities company in Japan. Most have materials in English and an international department with staff who can speak English.

Accounts with Foreign Bank Branches in Japan

Until relatively recently, due to the language barrier, many expatriates held accounts only with branches of foreign banks. However, some foreign banks have downsized their consumer banking operations in Japan and require a substantial minimum deposit, sometimes as much as ¥1 million, while Japanese banks have made significant efforts to offer information and services in English.

You may wish to have accounts with both a Japanese bank and a foreign bank. Foreign banks may be able to offer you checking accounts that are generally unavailable at Japanese banks.

Availability of Checking Accounts

Checking accounts held by individuals are still rare in Japan. Few establishments accept personal checks. If you intend to use personal checks, when doing so you may find a business card may help. Cashing such checks is tediously slow, if not impossible, and can be a nuisance for smaller shops. Other reasons behind the unpopularity of checking accounts in Japan include the following:

•Japanese banks have a clear-cut responsibility to screen those who have checking accounts, as the negotiability of checks issued by the bank will be adversely affected if a large number need to be returned for approval by the local bank authority. For this reason, penalties for the misuse of checking accounts are quite severe. If within any six-month period two checks bounce, the depositor is barred from opening another checking account for two years. Checking accounts, also called "current accounts," must not be overdrawn unless a separate overdraft agreement has been made between the bank and the customer. Certain foreign banks also offer such overdraft facilities.

•Payment by check does not offer the same kind of protection as in the United States. Banks are not required to ascertain the authenticity of endorsement, as checks in Japan usually include the words "or bearer" on the face of the check. Also, Japanese banks do not normally return canceled checks.

•It is sometimes difficult to stop payments on checks issued, and banks are not legally bound to honor such a request until 10 days after the date of the check.

Due to the relative unpopularity of checking accounts, most Japanese maintain savings accounts only and withdraw funds as needed, settling transactions via cash payment, bank or postal transfer, or credit card. Foreigners who are accustomed to maintaining a checking account may desire to continue doing so in Japan. Being a foreigner in Japan may, to some extent, expedite the use of a checking account, as shops, restaurants, and other establishments frequented by foreigners are more likely to accept checks than are other outlets.

Opening a checking account with a Japanese bank will usually entail an introduction from your company. (Thus, it is generally necessary to use the same bank that your company uses.) Foreign banks do not usually have such a requirement.

Credit Cards

The use of credit cards in Japan has increased dramatically in the past few years. Many kinds of credit cards are available, and cardholders are offered a comprehensive range of services.

The cards most commonly accepted in Japan are American Express, Diner's Club, JCB, Master Charge (UC, DC, and MC), and Visa. It may be difficult for you to acquire a credit card in Japan; foreigners—especially those who have not been in the country long and those who do not have a Japanese sponsor—are often denied all forms of credit by Japanese financial institutions.

Your chances of obtaining a credit card in Japan will be significantly enhanced if your company has a long-standing relationship with a Japanese bank or credit card company and is prepared to sponsor your application. Failing this, substantial deposits with the institution in question, a Japanese spouse, or permanent residence may increase your chances of success.

Credit card bills are usually paid through automatic debit or bank transfer, but some companies will accept a yen-denominated check.

Making Remittances Overseas

If you have a dollar checking account, you will be able to readily make remittances overseas. If you do not, you will need to purchase a cashier's check from either a foreign bank branch or one of the Japanese city banks. The handling fee for issuing the check ranges from ¥4,500 at a main branch to ¥7,500 at a small rural branch. Some foreign banks can issue a cashier's check in less than 10 minutes, but be prepared to wait at least an hour at a smaller branch of a Japanese bank. For paying bills in the United States, many people find it most convenient to maintain a U.S. account.

Post offices in Japan issue money orders for sums of up to ¥200,000 for a fee of only ¥1,000. The handling charge rises to ¥1,500 for sums between ¥201,000 and ¥500,000, with an additional incremental charge of ¥500 per ¥500,000 thereafter.

All banks in Japan that are authorized to handle money exchange will buy and sell convertible foreign currencies (but no coins will be bought).

U.S. Tax Liabilities

Taxes are a complex subject in any country. For expatriates, especially Americans, taxation is further complicated by the possibility of double-taxation obligations: to Japan as the country in which you are resident and from which you derive employment income and, depending on citizenship, the tax authorities back home.

The following is a brief and basic outline of the taxation liabilities of U.S. citizens living in Japan.

The United States is one of the very few countries that taxes its citizens and permanent residents (Green Card holders) on income earned both domestically and overseas and regardless of where they live. Accordingly, even living overseas, you are obliged to file a U.S. Internal Revenue Service (IRS) return, no matter if you work for a U.S. or non-U.S. company and if you are paid in dollars, yen, or any other currency. You must report as income any payments made by your company on your behalf for rent, utilities, tax reimbursements, education, home leave, and any other fringe benefits.

To alleviate the U.S. tax burden, qualified U.S. citizens abroad may exclude up to $70,000 of foreign earned income and are also entitled to a housing exclusion or deduction for certain housing expenses that exceed an amount specified by IRS regulations.

To avoid double taxation by both the U.S. and Japanese tax authorities, each country provides a credit for certain income taxes paid to the other.

Since the IRS is concerned not only with your income after arrival in Japan but also with moving costs paid by your company and the costs of temporary accommodation on arrival, it is important to keep thorough records of the payments made by you or on your behalf relating to your move to Japan. The IRS publishes a pamphlet (Publication 54) that provides a summary of your obligations during your residence abroad and a special set of forms and instructions designed to help you comply with these complicated rules. However, we recommend that you consult an international tax accountant for assistance. There are many international accounting and law firms in Japan. Also, your company may have an in-house accountant who provides personalized accounting services.

You may file your U.S. tax return, obtain extensions of the time period to file your return, make tax payments, and obtain IRS publications and forms at the IRS office at the U.S. Embassy in Tokyo during the tax-filing season. The local IRS office at the U.S. Embassy has been obliged to scale down its operations due to budget restraints, and IRS representatives are present only during the tax-filing season from late January to June 15.

It is worth noting that Americans residing overseas automatically benefit from a two-month extension of the filing deadline (from April 15 to June 15), but interest is charged on any taxes not paid by the former date. The IRS does not handle any state tax matters.

As U.S. income tax laws and regulations become more complex, it is increasingly important to establish and maintain a good record-keeping system. The amount, date of payment, and complete description of all items of income and expenses, whether paid by you or on your behalf by your employer, should be gathered throughout the year so that you or your tax return preparer will be able to complete your return promptly and efficiently before the deadline.

The responsibility for filing a U.S. income tax return is yours. Thus, it is advisable to plan and manage your tax affairs accordingly.

Japanese Tax Liabilities

Japanese income tax liabilities consist of national income tax (similar to federal income tax) and local inhabitants' taxes (similar to state taxes). For income tax purposes, individual taxpayers are classified into three categories based on residency and are taxed as follows:

• A nonpermanent resident taxpayer is an individual who has no intention of permanently residing in Japan and has maintained his or her residence or domicile in Japan for a period of not more than five consecutive years. (Almost all U.S. expatriates on temporary assignments are considered nonpermanent resident taxpayers.) The taxpayer is taxed at graduated rates on income from sources within Japan and income from sources outside Japan that is paid in Japan or remitted into Japan. Noncompensation income (for example, interest and dividends) from sources outside Japan are subject to tax at graduated rates.

• A permanent resident taxpayer is an individual who has maintained his residence or domicile in Japan for a period of more than five years. Income from worldwide sources, including interest and dividends from sources outside Japan, are subject to tax at the graduated rates. (You should note that you may be defined as a permanent resident in this respect without having permanent resident status from the immigration point of view.)

• A nonresident taxpayer is any individual other than a resident (permanent or nonpermanent). Income from sources within Japan is generally taxed at a flat rate of 20%.

Salaries, wages, and other income for services performed in Japan are deemed to be earned income from sources within Japan, irrespective of who pays them or where they are paid, and are thus subject to tax. As in the United States, there are a number of deductions, exemptions, and dependency allowances that are taken into consideration when determining taxable income for a resident taxpayer.

Reimbursements for rent on company-owned or company-leased accommodation are subject to different tax rules. Normally only a portion of the rent is considered as income. For most people, this will vary from between 5% and 10% of the total rent. This rule does not apply to company directors.

Except as stated below, resident taxpayers must file a Japanese national tax return by March 15, reporting on the previous year's income, and pay the balance of any tax due or claim a refund for tax overpaid. A resident departing from Japan for good should file his or her return and pay the balance due before departure or appoint a representative who will file the return and pay the tax by March 15 of the following year.

A U.S. resident whose taxable income in Japan consists of employment income received from one employer that is subject to Japanese withholding income tax and does not exceed ¥20 million need not file a national tax return. (Your employer will make an adjustment at the year-end so that your total taxes withheld will equal your tax liability.)

A resident taxpayer who files a national tax return and pays tax may be required to make predetermined tax payments in July and November of the following year. A taxpayer who declares gross taxable income over ¥20 million in his or her final return is required to submit a statement of personal assets and liabilities in Japan as of the end of the period covered by the return.

A nonresident individual whose total taxable income in Japan is subject to withholding is not required to file a national tax return. A nonresident individual not subject to withholding tax should file a tax return before departing from Japan or by March 15 of the following year. A nonresident individual who has taxable income in Japan and who is not physically present in Japan at the time when tax returns must be filed should appoint a tax consultant in Japan to administer his or her affairs.

You do not normally need to file an inhabitants' tax return. Your local taxes are assessed based on information contained in your national tax return. The tax is levied on all residents in Japan as of January 1 of each calendar year and is based on income earned during the previous year. The taxes are payable through withholding and/or installment payments.

Consumption Tax

From April 1, 1989, a blanket 3% consumption tax was imposed on nearly all goods and services in Japan. The imposition of this new tax coincided with small reductions in the withholding tax of salaried workers and the elimination or reduction of various taxes on luxury goods.

The consumption tax system is not as straightforward as it may appear, however. Businesses that have revenues that do not exceed ¥500 million are not required to submit detailed accounting reports on the consumption tax they have passed on to consumers. Furthermore, companies or free-lance operations with income not exceeding ¥50 million are not required to forward information to the Japanese tax authorities. Since it is impossible for the consumer, or anyone else for that matter, to determine precisely whether a business has revenues exceeding ¥50 million per annum, a retailer can legally pocket the consumption tax.

Initially, all purchases of goods or services of any kind, including government services, were subject to the 3% consumption tax. However, in 1991, the government decided to exempt rents, school fees, medical expenses related to childbirth, and funeral expenses related to cremation.

Insurance

The Japanese buy more insurance per person than any other people in the world, and most products and services available abroad have their equivalent here. Unlike in most countries, however,

the Ministry of Finance controls types of insurance and rates very strictly, resulting in standardized policies and fixed premiums, so there is no need to "shop" around for insurance. Like most things in Japan, prices for insurance will be a bit more expensive than you may be used to at home.

As a word of caution, local law requires that any insurance purchased for persons or property in Japan must be sold by a company licensed to do business here. A number of the larger U.S. insurance companies and insurance brokers do have Japanese licenses and have been doing business in Japan for many years. These companies can provide English-language services and applications printed in English and have branches and claims networks nationwide. If you are in Japan with the U.S. military, special policies and conditions may apply—check with an agent near your base or your base legal office for further information.

Personal Insurance

Automobile

Compulsory automobile liability insurance (CALI) is required to drive all automobiles, motorcycles, and motor scooters registered in Japan. This insurance covers medical expenses for people injured in vehicular accidents caused by the insured. CALI is available at all vehicle dealerships and most insurance agencies. Another policy covering bodily injury and property damage liability as well as physical damage to your own car is strongly recommended. Three types of policies that cover the latter damages are available: the Basic Auto Policy (BAP), the Personal Auto Policy (PAP), and the Special Auto Policy (SAP). The PAP or SAP are recommended for foreign residents as these provide for the insurance company to negotiate on your behalf in the event of an accident.

Personal Property/Household Goods

Natural disasters are never easy to prepare for, and in Japan, you should expect to experience an occasional earthquake and heavy rainfall during the typhoon season. You should consider insuring your household goods and personal property just as you would in your home country. As you will probably not be a homeowner in Japan, you will be more interested in policies similar to renter's insurance, which covers household contents and valuables, such as jewelry, cameras, furs, works of art, family heirlooms, and other valuables as well as personal liability. This insurance is offered on an all-risk basis, including protection against fire, earthquakes, windstorms, burglary, and other disastrous or damaging occurrences.

Comprehensive Personal Liability

You can purchase basic liability insurance, plus "fire legal liability," separately or with a renter's or homeowner's insurance package as previously described. Since most personal liability insurance policies carried in the United States are not effective in Japan, you should consider local coverage.

Personal Accident/Overseas Travel Accident/Medical Expenses

The Japanese insurance market has a wide variety of products designed to cover your medical expenses if you or a member of your family is accidentally injured here or elsewhere abroad. These insurance instruments can be especially valuable to foreign residents unfamiliar with the national health care system. For basic protection, you should consider "personal accident," "family accident," or "children's accident" coverage.

Personal accident insurance basically covers loss of life, physical impediment, and hospital confinement and provides daily indemnity against bodily injury sustained by the insured and caused by any sudden and accidental happening of external origin. As an option, nonconfinement daily indemnity and medical expense indemnity are also available for bodily injury.

As for insurance to cover medical expenses, see the sections at the beginning of Chapter 10.

Business Insurance

All major forms of business insurance coverage are available in Japan, including fire and business interruption, general liability, marine, and worker's compensation. In addition, employee group life and pension plans are widely available from life insurance companies and are benefits typically offered to Japanese employees. Just like personal policies, all nonlife rates are set by tariffs and forms are standardized.

While many of the basic risks insured against in a corporate insurance program are the same in Japan as elsewhere, local conditions in Japan may warrant some changes in any standardized companywide program offered by your employer. For example, earthquakes are a much greater threat here. Legislative and legal environments are considerably different from those in the United States or Europe.

When making the transition to starting up operations or continuing them here, to make insurance matters easier, you will be happy to hear that the largest foreign capitalized insurance companies and brokers in Japan are American and that they are prepared to help you map out insurance and employee benefit programs for your Japan operations either on a stand-alone basis or as a part of a worldwide or regional property or casualty program.

Investments

If you are an experienced investor and follow the investment markets closely, continuing to play the market once you move to Japan poses few problems. Establishing an account at a securities company is relatively easy, and usually at least one staff member will be able to understand English to handle your account. You will also find that virtually every kind of product or service that is available in the United States is also available in Japan, and with the ongoing liberalization of the financial industry, you are able to choose from a wide variety of investment instruments.

In the early 1990s, a series of scandals shook the Japanese securities industry, and since then, stock prices have tended downward. Japanese securities companies welcome investments from individuals of any income level. However, the best advice invariably goes to institutional investors and private investors willing to assemble a portfolio in excess of ¥50 million. For this reason, small investors would well be advised to study the Japanese markets carefully and make their own purchasing and selling decisions.

As a general rule, those purchasing securities in Japan are investing solely for stock price appreciation purposes; cash dividends here are negligible.

Establishing Your Own Company in Japan

If you are an entrepreneur or self-employed, you may consider establishing a company in Japan. Sole proprietorship, or *kojin jigyosha,* is the simplest form of doing business and may be chosen instead of a corporate form. Sole proprietors are not entitled to limited liability, and obligations for debts and taxes remain with the proprietor.

Alternatively, there are two types of companies under Japanese law: *kabushiki kaisha,* or K.K., a fully fledged corporation; and *yugen gaisha,* or Y.K., a company with limited liability. The minimum capitalization required for the former is ¥10 million and for the latter ¥3 million. Of the two, *kabushiki kaisha* are generally considered more creditworthy; *yugen kaisha* sometimes have difficulty securing loans from banks or leasing equipment. On the other hand, a *yugen kaisha* will probably pay less in taxes than a *kabushiki kaisha*. Foreigners can establish Japanese companies, but unless you have increased capitalization to at least ¥40 million and generated substantial revenues, you will find it difficult to use your new company as a sponsor for visa purposes.

To establish a company, you will probably need the services of a Japanese *konin kaikeishi* (CPA) or *zeirishi* (tax accountant). The paperwork for registration is likely to take a few weeks to process. When you start a Japanese company you will be asked to specify the fields of business you will be engaging in. These business categories can be quite vague, but if you engage in a field not covered by the original specifications, you will need to have your company's registration papers amended, which will require the assistance of an accountant.

Chapter

15

Consular and Legal Matters

The United States maintains an embassy in Tokyo, consulates general in Naha, Osaka, and Sapporo, and a consulate in Fukuoka. These offices provide a variety of services for Americans visiting or residing in Japan and are open to the public Monday through Friday; opening hours vary, so it is wise to call in advance to confirm times. The embassy and other consular offices in Japan are closed on Japanese and U.S. national holidays.

U.S. citizens who plan to be in Japan for six months or longer should register themselves and any U.S. citizen family members in Japan at the embassy or the U.S. consular office in their particular area. To do this, you must appear in person with your passport and the passports of any U.S. citizen family members to be registered. No fee is charged for registration.

Your passport should be renewed before the expiration date and should be kept in a safe place. Do not allow it to pass into the possession of an unauthorized person, and it must not be used as collateral. A mutilated or altered passport is invalid and should be reported promptly to the nearest consular office. You will be requested to submit a detailed affidavit explaining the circumstances surrounding the mutilation, alteration, or loss. Loss or theft should also be promptly reported to the police.

Application for a new passport should be made well in advance of the expiration date of your current one to ensure that you do not find yourself without a valid passport in the event of an emergency. Also, it is impossible to renew the Certificate of Alien Registration issued by the Japanese government if your passport or visa has expired.

The birth of a child in Japan to a U.S. parent or parents should be reported promptly to the embassy's consular section or to the consular office in the appropriate district to establish the child's claim to U.S. citizenship. An application for the child's passport can be filed at the same time. The embassy requests that parents contact the consular section prior to the birth of their child.

A U.S. citizen planning to marry in Japan may consult the consular section for information regarding the documentation required by the Japanese government office having jurisdiction.

The consular section at the embassy and consular offices will assist in making the necessary arrangements in the event of the death of a U.S. citizen in Japan. There is a duty officer who can be reached at the embassy 24 hours a day (Tel: (03) 3224-5000). Notary services are also available at the embassy and consulates.

In imprisonment or welfare cases, consular personnel will be as helpful as possible. Assistance in cases involving a violation of Japanese law is largely limited to ensuring that the individual receives proper treatment from the authorities. In welfare cases, the consular offices will help as much as possible, but there is no official funding available to assist U.S. citizens, and officers are prohibited by law from extending loans drawn from personal funds. Completely destitute Americans may be repatriated at the U.S. government's expense, but only after all possible sources of funds from family or associates have been exhausted. The expenses are treated as a loan from the U.S. government and must be repaid.

Documentation of Children Born in Japan

The following information concerns the birth of Americans in Japan. Fees, documentary requirements, etc., may change without notice. It is best to check with the embassy to determine the exact requirements at the time of birth.

Documentation of a Child Born Abroad of Parents Who Are Both U.S. Citizens

Consular Report of Birth (Form FS-240)

A Consular Report of Birth is not a birth certificate but a certification of the birth of a U.S. citizen abroad. A report of birth should be made at the consular office of the district in which the child is born as soon as possible after the birth—ordinarily, within a few days. It may be made by either parent.

A child born abroad of parents who are both citizens of the United States, and one of whom has resided in the United States or one of its outlying possessions prior to the birth of the child, is a U.S. citizen at birth.

Documents Required for a Consular Report of Birth
- Proof of Child's Birth. Signed copy of the hospital record of

birth or signed statement of the doctor or midwife in attendance; the full name of the child and other pertinent data must be shown on this document.

• Proof of Parents' Citizenship.

— Passport and, if applicable and available, a naturalization certificate.

— Military ID card with certified copy of birth certificate if born in the United States; if born abroad, the ID card and a naturalization certificate (or certificate of citizenship if available) and a sealed copy of Consular Report of Birth (Form FS-240).

— Military ID card with certified copy of birth certificate for regular commissioned officer on active duty if born in the United States; if born abroad, the ID card and a naturalization certificate (or certificate of citizenship if available) and a sealed copy of Consular Report of Birth (Form FS-240).

• Proof of Parents' Marriage. The existence of a valid marriage, if applicable, must be established. If the parents were married in the United States, a marriage certificate issued by the Vital Statistics Office of the state, county, city, or other local government office should be presented. If they were married abroad, satisfactory evidence of a valid foreign marriage must be presented.

• Proof of Termination of Prior Marriage(s) of Parent(s). A divorce decree, annulment decree, death certificate, or any positive proof, sealed and certified by appropriate government authorities where the record is kept, is required to establish the termination of a prior marriage, if applicable.

It should also be noted that

• The birth certificate(s) of the parent(s) as well as the marriage record and proof of termination of prior marriage(s) should be the originals or certified copies with the seal of the issuing office. If not in conflict with the laws of the state issuing the document, a copy can be made and the original returned after examination by the consular officer.

• Documents in foreign languages must be accompanied by accurate English translations.

The consular office will furnish the parent with a copy of the report. The original copy of the report with its attachments is forwarded to Washington, D.C., to be retained in the archives of the State Department.

Documentation of a Child Born Abroad of One U.S. Citizen and One Noncitizen Parent

A child born abroad on or after November 14, 1986, of one U.S. citizen and one noncitizen parent is a U.S. citizen if the U.S. citizen parent was physically present in the United States or its outlying possessions before the birth of the child for a period of or periods totaling not less than five years, at least two of which were after the age of 14.

Any period(s) of honorable service by the U.S. citizen parent in the United States Armed Forces or period(s) of employment with the U.S. government or with an international organization as that term is defined in Section 1 of the International Organizations Immunities Act may be included to satisfy the physical presence requirement. Any period(s) of presence abroad by the citizen parent as the unmarried son or daughter or member of the household of a person honorably serving with the United States Armed Forces or employed by the U.S. government or an international organization as described above may also be included in the physical presence requirement.

A child whose parents are not married and who is born abroad of a U.S. citizen mother takes the mother's citizenship if she was physically present in the United States for a continuous period of one year previous to the birth of the child.

In general, the requirements and documentation required are the same as those for a child born of parents who are both U.S. citizens. The report should be made by the U.S. citizen parent. In the absence of the citizen parent, the report may be made by the noncitizen parent or by any other person who can provide the appropriate documentation, as follows:

•Proof of Child's Birth. Signed copy of the hospital record of birth or signed statement of doctor or midwife in attendance; the full name of the child and other pertinent data must be shown on this document. If the child's father is Japanese, a certified copy of his family register, showing the name of the child.

Special cases:

•A U.S. citizen parent not making the report of birth should submit an affidavit attesting to his or her residence in the United States and abroad.

•If the child was born before the marriage or less than eight months afterward, the citizen father may be asked to execute an affidavit of residence and paternity.

—If the child was born out of wedlock to a U.S. citizen father, additional evidence to prove the existence of blood relationship will be required. Also, if the mother is Japanese, a certified copy of her family register, indicating the father's acknowledgement of the child's paternity, is required.

It should be noted that

•The birth certificate(s) of the parent(s) as well as the marriage record and proof of termination of prior marriage(s) should be the original or certified copies with the seal of the issuing office. If not in conflict with the laws of the state issuing the document, a copy can be made and the originals returned after examination by the consular officer.

•Documents in foreign languages must be accompanied by accurate English translations.

Passport Documentation of the Child

Application for a passport for the child should be made at the time that the child's birth is reported. The following are needed:

•Photographs. Three identical photographs of the child. The photographs must be 5 by 5 centimeters (2 by 2 inches). Snapshots, full-length photographs, or Polaroid photographs are not acceptable. The image size, measured from the bottom of the chin to the top of the head (including hair), must not be less than 2.5 centimeters (1 inch) nor more than 3.5 centimeters (1⅜ inches). The photographs must be printed on thin, unglazed paper, show a full front view of the applicant (child) with a plain, light background, and can be either black-and-white or color.

•Passport Fees. $40 or the yen equivalent ($10 for the application and $30 for the issuance). There is no fee for authorized dependents of military personnel who are above the fourth pay grade (E-4) and those of the fourth pay grade who have two years of service or for authorized dependents of certain government employees.

•Letter of Dependency. If the passport applicant (child) is the authorized dependent of a member of the United States Armed Forces or of a government employee, a letter of dependency from the parent's personnel office should be submitted.

Marriage of U.S. Citizens

The following information concerns the marriage of Americans in Japan. Fees, documentary requirements, etc., may change without notice. It is best to check with the embassy to determine the exact requirements at the time of marriage.

All persons, including U.S. citizens, who wish to marry in Japan must do so according to Japanese law. The marriage process in Japan consists of a civil registration of the marriage by the couple at a Japanese ward, town, or city office. This registration itself constitutes legal marriage and is recognized as such throughout the United States. Religious ceremonies and rites performed by fraternal or other organizations are not valid as legal marriages, although, of course, they may take place in addition to the civil registration.

Marriages may not be performed by an embassy diplomatic or consular officer under U.S. law. However, to register a marriage under Japanese law, foreign nationals must present to the Japanese government office where the marriage is to be registered certain registration documents, including an Affidavit of Competency to Marry, signed and sworn before his or her country's consular officer in Japan. U.S. consular officers will advise Americans of these marriage procedures and assist them with the preparation of the Affidavit of Competency to Marry. This service is provided at the U.S. Embassy in Tokyo and at U.S. consular offices in Sapporo, Osaka, Fukuoka, and Naha. U.S. military members and others associated with the Department of Defense in Japan may obtain the necessary documentation from their base legal office.

Marriages in Japan involving Americans may be completed as follows:

1. The couple goes to a consular office to prepare and sign the Affidavit of Competency to Marry.

2. The couple then proceeds to the appropriate Japanese government office for registration of the marriage. Two witnesses, of any nationality and over 21 years of age, must be present at the signing of the Japanese forms. The witnesses should be provided by the couple. Japanese, Korean, or Chinese witnesses must be in possession of their *inkan* (seals). A personal identification document is required of all witnesses. Upon presentation of the forms, the local government office will issue a Certificate of Acceptance of Notification of Marriage.

Appointments at U.S. consular offices for the preparation of marriage forms are not required. There is no Japanese requirement for a premarital physical examination or blood test.

For more information concerning marriage procedures, contact the U.S. Embassy or, if you are not a U.S. citizen, your country's embassy (see the Telephone Directory at the end of this book for a listing of embassies in Tokyo).

Death of a U.S. Citizen

Procedures established by the authorities concerning the death of a U.S. citizen in Japan must be followed at the time of death. We urge you to familiarize yourself with these and, in case such a tragic event occurs, follow them carefully. Any deviation may cause you legal problems.

1. DO NOT MOVE THE BODY. You are not authorized to move a corpse, for any reason, until after examination by the Japanese medical examiner and issuance of release. (This applies only if a doctor is not present at the time of death.)

2. Call a doctor. If you can reach the private physician of the deceased, do so, as he or she will know the medical history of the deceased. If the private physician is not available, have another physician examine the body.

3. Call the police. If you speak Japanese, dial **110**; otherwise, in Tokyo, dial (03) 3581-4321 and ask for extension 5290 (in Japanese, *go-ni-kyu-maru*). Give the following details: location of the body, telephone number, address, and your name as well as that of the deceased. The police will call a medical examiner and instruct him or her to go the scene. Remain with the body until the examiner arrives, arranges for the inspection, and issues the death certificate.

4. Call the U.S. Embassy. In Tokyo, dial (03) 3224-5000 and, during regular office hours, ask for the American Citizens' Services Branch of the Consular Section. After hours and on Sundays or holidays, ask for the embassy duty officer. Tell the officer what has happened, giving all the details you can. Identify yourself and the deceased and give the location of the corpse. If possible, give the passport number, address at time of death, social security number, permanent address, and name of the deceased's next of kin. The embassy is in a position to help you in a number of ways. If the next of kin is not in Japan, the embassy will assist in arranging for the embalming, if needed, and shipment of the corpse or ashes to the United States after receiving instructions and funds for this purpose from the next of kin.

5. Disposition of the corpse. The options available are embalming of the corpse with burial either in Japan, the United States, or elsewhere; burial in Japan without embalming; or cremation with interment of the ashes in Japan, the United States, or elsewhere. The embassy can provide you with further details.

Police and Legal Matters

Police in Japan are generally polite and helpful. Police boxes, or *koban,* can be found in almost every neighborhood in Japan, and as a result, Japanese police tend to be more visible and accessible than their American counterparts. They are required to know those who live in their precinct, and it is considered proper to introduce yourself to the local police when you move into a new neighborhood.

The police emergency number is **110**. You will be connected to an English translator if you do not speak Japanese. In Tokyo, a police car arrives on the scene in an average of about four minutes.

The Japanese constitution guarantees equal treatment under the law; thus, if a foreigner is suspected of breaking a law in Japan or is arrested, the constitution requires that he or she be treated the same as a Japanese citizen. Any person, upon arrest or questioning, has the right to refuse to answer questions that may be incriminating to him or her. The person may also first ask to see a lawyer and may ask to talk to a consular officer. The consular officer can provide a list of lawyers upon request if legal assistance is needed. Some Japanese law offices have lawyers who speak English.

It is important to remember that the Japanese like to solve problems out of court and try to prevent disputes from becoming formal legal proceedings. Sincere apologies and respect for the law prevent many arguments from reaching the courts. Foreigners should remember that a small problem can often be resolved by offering an honest display of contrition and perhaps gifts to the offended party. It should also be remembered that uncontrolled anger and arguing usually serve only to exacerbate the problem at hand.

Illegal acts that foreigners are most likely to be involved in include visa violations, tax violations, drug offenses, and traffic violations and accidents.

Visa Violations

It is absolutely essential to keep your visa status current at all times. Any changes in your status must be reported immediately to the immigration office. A delay in reporting changes or any tardiness in obtaining renewals requires a letter of apology. Obviously, the immigration authorities will take into account such factors as, for example, a sudden departure due to a death in the family.

Keep your Certificate of Alien Registration or passport with you. This applies to anyone over 16 years of age. You will very seldom, if ever, be asked by the police to produce it, but the law requires that you carry it at all times. Although rarely imposed, the punishment for violations of the Alien Registration Law is a period of up to one year in jail and/or a fine of up to ¥30,000.

Tax Violations

Forgetfulness is not considered an excuse for failure to file tax returns in Japan. In addition, the tax authorities have the authority to conduct thorough audits, which are often random and unexpected. For information on taxation and filing a return, see Chapter 14.

Drug Offenses

Antidrug legislation and its enforcement are strict in Japan. Fortunately, Japan has far fewer drug addicts and drug-related offenses than the United States.

Search and seizure laws are administered to maintain law and order, and judges tend to have almost unquestioning faith in a policeman's testimony. Drug laws are strict. The amount of drugs required to secure a conviction is quite small, and penalties are relatively severe.

Cannabis-related convictions can result in a maximum seven-year sentence for importation and up to five years for possession. Be warned that the Japanese police may arrest groups en masse for drug offenses. A member of a group can be penalized for drug possession even if that person was not using or was not directly in possession of the substance.

Traffic Violations and Accidents

Given Japan's crowded cities and the number of vehicles in use, it is not surprising that driving conditions in Japan are quite different from what most Americans are accustomed to.

Most driving is done on narrow streets or on highways, and it is quickly apparent that widespread drunken driving would prove disastrous. Therefore, just a hint of alcohol at a random police traffic checkpoint can result in arrest and the suspension of your license. In short, do not drive if you have consumed alcohol, no matter how small the amount.

Drivers are expected to maintain a high standard of safety.

The allocation of damages is usually decided by the parties at the nearest *koban* under pressure from the police, who actually have no legal authority to force a settlement. Courts and lawyers are used only as a last resort and are a sign that all else has failed, proving that at least one party has been unreasonable.

When driving in Japan, it is most important to remember that negligent driving is a criminal offense—penalties can be severe.

Legal Procedures

It is often said that Japanese people prefer to resolve their disputes through such informal and private means as personal negotiations, conciliation proceedings, or mediation. Nevertheless, Japan's system of formal institutions for settling disputes is often overburdened.

The court system is administered on a national level by the Supreme Court. The court of first instance for cases involving domestic matters or persons under 20 years of age is generally one of the 49 district courts or family courts. Usually a single judge will hear cases involving Japanese citizens. However, cases involving foreigners are frequently heard by a three-judge panel, presided over by a chief judge. Although Japan briefly adopted a jury system for criminal trials in the early postwar years, it proved unpopular and was suspended indefinitely.

The party against whom judgment is awarded may appeal to one of the eight High Courts, where a three-judge panel will rehear the case, sometimes recalling witnesses, bringing in new evidence, and generally retrying the case from the beginning. This is one reason for the slow pace of lawsuits in Japan. With both the prosecution and defense having the right to appeal, some major cases have dragged on for decades, and a few cases from the 1950s are still being appealed.

An appeal from a High Court to the 15-member Supreme Court (called "revision") is at the discretion of the latter. The Supreme Court usually sits in three petty benches, one each for civil, criminal, and administrative appeals. In special cases, the Supreme Court will decide a case as a grand bench with all 15 judges.

Japan also has a network of summary courts for cases involving amounts of ¥100,000 or less, similar to small claims courts in the United States.

Judges in Japan are career civil servants supervised by the Supreme Court. They are not elected by local communities and do not necessarily stay in any one community for an extended period of time.

Generally speaking, Japanese judges have a strong tradition of independent thinking and personal integrity. As in the United States, the Diet can impeach judges, although it has rarely done so. In Japan, the public also has the right to disapprove new justices of the Supreme Court, including the Chief Justice. In the first national election held after a new judge is installed, the ballot includes a section for disapproval votes against new justices. If there are disapproval votes from more than 50% of the voters, the justice is removed from office. To this day, however, a justice has never been rejected by the public.

The Supreme Court has always acted conservatively and seldom overturns criminal convictions. When the Supreme Court does make a new interpretation of legislation or reverses a criminal conviction, the ruling is a very significant one for the judicial system as a whole.

Litigation in Japan proceeds along the European model of the discontinuous trial. Unlike in the United States, where there is extensive pretrial investigation and preparation by the respective attorneys followed by a short court trial, a litigant in Japan can get into court almost immediately after filing the complaint.

The hearing is brief, and the proceedings are largely conducted by the judge. In its initial phase, the court concentrates on familiarizing itself with the documentary evidence. Then, a schedule for witness testimony is arranged. The judge is the sole arbiter of the admissibility of evidence and resolves objections by counsel.

At the end of each hearing, the parties schedule another hearing for a month or sometimes several months later. In this manner, the trial may proceed for two or more years before a judgment is handed down. The losing party often appeals to a High Court, and the appeals process is also lengthy. Thus, civil suits often extend over a long period, and as time passes, the pressure to settle out of court increases. Despite this pressure and Japanese tradition, some litigants are intractable and uncompromising, especially if they feel they are in a superior position.

The judge in the Japanese legal system plays a far more active role than his or her U.S. counterpart. Not simply a referee between competing attorneys, the judge will interrogate witnesses, instruct the attorneys on the kinds of evidence that should be presented, direct the attorneys to revise their submissions, and so forth.

Japan experimented with a full adversarial system based on the U.S. model just after World War II. However, the Japanese bar was ill-prepared for the active role suddenly thrust upon it, and consequently the conduct of litigation partially returned to that of the prewar system.

Japanese attorneys generally work on a dual-fee basis— an initial retainer (*chakushukin*) of about 10% of the amount in contention and a success fee (*seiko hoshu*) of 8% to 15% of the portion gained or saved if the case is concluded successfully for the client. The retainer, however, is not refundable, even if the attorney loses. Thus it can be to the lawyer's financial advantage to settle the case quickly and move on to the next case after receiving the retainer. This fee arrangement is not universally employed, and many attorneys follow a policy of charging a set fee, as do U.S. attorneys, for each hour spent on a client's behalf.

The Legal Profession

There are less than 15,000 licensed attorneys (*bengoshi*) in Japan. In contrast, the United States has about 900,000 attorneys for a population only twice that of Japan. The Japanese statistics, however, are misleading. Hundreds of thousands of college students who majored in law fill positions in government, commerce, and banking and are well versed in the law. This has led to the observation that Japan has more "lawyers" per capita than any other country; however, 99% of them are unlicensed.

The ratio of licensed attorneys per capita in Japan is comparable to that in most European countries. Many legal services in Japan, however, are performed by a wide variety of paralegals, or individuals trained in law who are not *bengoshi*. For example, tax problems are handled by *zeirishi*, or tax accountants, and patent and trademark matters by *benrishi*, or patent lawyers. Much routine legal documentation is prepared by *shiho shoshi*, or judicial scriveners.

The role of the *bengoshi* is restricted primarily to representing his or her clients' interests in court matters (although *bengoshi* in large international law offices do offer a wider range of legal services). Judges and government attorneys, or "public procurators," are not in fact *bengoshi* and are generally accorded a higher status than *bengoshi*.

Foreign Attorneys in Japan

With the growth of Japan's economy, U.S. business interests have increasingly sought to participate in the Japanese market and become involved in the country's economic activities. This movement has generated a need for lawyers knowledgeable about the laws, legal institutions, cultures, and languages of both the United States and Japan.

To satisfy this demand, Japan has a small number of relatively large law firms that are staffed by foreign lawyers and Japanese attorneys who have studied overseas. In particular, as the maze of government regulations becomes a principal point of contact between foreign enterprises and Japanese law, a major service performed by these international law firms is to maneuver their clients' projects through these complicated regulatory channels and to find practical solutions to legal problems through negotiations with government officials.

Since the mid-1980s, American and other foreign lawyers have been able to practice in Japan as *gaikoku jimu bengoshi,* a status that restricts the foreign lawyer to providing advice on legal matters pertaining to the lawyer's own country. Foreign lawyers are not permitted to hire Japanese lawyers to work with them or to form joint law offices with Japanese. To qualify as foreign law advisers, U.S. lawyers must have practiced in the United States for at least five years.

Not all foreign lawyers, however, stand on the same footing. Before the Attorneys' Law was amended in 1955, completely excluding new non-Japanese lawyers until the *gaikoku jimu bengoshi* system was instituted in the 1980s, it did permit associate membership, or *junkaiin,* in the Japanese bar for certain foreign lawyers—the "Article Seven attorneys." Several of these older attorneys are still in practice, having acquired over 40 years of legal experience in Japan representing major U.S. corporate, banking, and business interests.

There are also Japanese attorneys who have studied abroad, principally in the United States. Their language skills and services can be adequate for the foreign community, but lack of experience in dealing with foreign business practices and customs may handicap some of them in terms of their ability to fully understand and support the objectives of their foreign clients.

Chapter

16

Things to Do

On weekends, don't be afraid to strike out on your own to visit the many temples, shrines, and parks located within an hour from downtown Tokyo. Or, if you have a Saturday free that is not a national holiday, it is a good opportunity to visit amusement parks and other attractions, because children will be in school and the crowds will be smaller. Consult your newspaper for suggestions about local festivals, special events, and various day hikes in the area.

Better still, pick an area on the map that includes a temple or a park of interest, hop on the subway or train, and wander around at your leisure. You will be amazed at the interesting things you will find that are not written up in any of the available guidebooks. The following are just a few suggestions as to areas and places worth visiting in and near Tokyo.

Shopping Areas

Department stores in Japan are not just for shopping; they usually offer coffee shops and restaurants and often have museums and special exhibition halls. Even the merchandise is "on view," with items attractively displayed and frequently changed. Wandering through a department store can be a fascinating excursion. In Tokyo, there is generally at least one department store in any suburban area with a major train station. The largest and best department stores, however, are concentrated in Nihonbashi (Mitsukoshi, Takashimaya, and Tokyu), Ginza/Yurakucho (Hankyu, Matsuya, Matsuzakaya, Mitsukoshi, Printemps, Seibu, and Sogo), Shibuya (Marui, Seibu, and Tokyu), Shinjuku (Keio, Isetan, Marui, Mitsukoshi, and Odakyu), and Ikebukuro (Mitsukoshi, Seibu, and Tobu).

Tokyo also has numerous specialized shopping districts where certain types of products can be found at much lower prices than elsewhere. For example, books, including a vast number of secondhand and antique books, are concentrated in the Jimbocho area; electronics in Akihabara;

decorations in Asakusabashi; office furniture in the street between Higashi-Nihonbashi and Asakusabashi; and cameras in the discount shops of Shinjuku and Ikebukuro. In Okachimachi, near Ueno, a wide range of cut-price general merchandise, from fresh fish to perfume, can be found in the street market known as Ameyoko-cho, combining the words for "America" and "alley." In such neighborhoods, even if you are not buying, "shopping" can be fun. For more information on the goods and services available in Japan's wide range of shops and other outlets, refer to Chapter 7.

Amusement Parks

Tokyo has no shortage of amusement parks. Tokyo Disneyland, at Urayasu, about a 25-minute train ride from Tokyo Station, is similar to other Disney amusement parks in California, Florida, and France. People come from all over Japan to see Tokyo Disneyland, and a significant number of tourists from Korea, Taiwan, and other nations visit the park.

Toshimaen, in Tokyo's northern suburbs, about a 20-minute train trip from Ikebukuro, is the largest and most popular amusement park other than Disneyland. It has a vast complex of outdoor swimming pools (only open in the summer months), water slides, and a wide range of rides. At the peak of the summer season, in August, it is not unusual for more than 60,000 people to crowd into Toshimaen on a hot, sunny day, and on Saturday nights during July and August there are fireworks displays.

Korakuen, next door to Tokyo Dome, an indoor baseball stadium that accommodates more than 50,000 spectators, is an aging amusement park that was Tokyo's pride in the 1950s and 1960s. It is much smaller than Tokyo Disneyland or Toshimaen, but the admission fee is modest, and the location is quite convenient. With increasing competition from other amusement complexes, the management is steadily modernizing the park.

There are other amusement parks in the Tokyo area, including Summerland, with its indoor pools, and Seibuen, a park similar to Toshimaen but further away from the center of Tokyo.

Parks and Gardens

Although Tokyo may appear to be a huge mass of concrete, the city has a number of fairly large parks open to the public. One of the lesser-known of these parks is the East Garden of the Imperial Palace, which is open free of charge year-round, from 9:00 A.M.

to 3:00 P.M., except Mondays and Fridays. It is seldom crowded, and amid its vast amount of greenery are some of the ruins of the old Edo Castle of the Tokugawa shogunate.

Rikugien, a short walk from Komagome Station on the Yamanote Line, is one of the oldest parks in Tokyo; a visit is almost like stepping back into the Edo period.

If you are in the mood for a picnic on a Sunday afternoon but don't feel like riding the trains for an hour or more, you might want to try Shinjuku Gyoen, a large park with lots of open space and gardens in a variety of styles. There is a nominal fee to enter, but there are few more pleasant or convenient places to spend the day with family or friends.

Hama Rikyu, a detached palace garden situated on Tokyo's waterfront, is one stop on the water-bus route that starts from Asakusa. The pleasant grounds are a sanctuary for many kinds of birds, and there is a reconstructed tea pavilion.

Another option is Nezu Garden, which is hilly and treed and provides a feeling of space even though it is sandwiched into a residential area just a few minutes from Omotesando Station. The small museum within is famous for its art treasures.

Temples and Shrines

Tokyo is only about 500 years old, and few of the capital's temples and shrines can match those of Kyoto and Nara. However, there are some that are certainly worth visiting.

The large Buddhist temple close to Asakusa Station, Sensoji (also known as Asakusa Kannon) survived both the Great Kanto Earthquake of 1923 and the firebombing of Tokyo during World War II. It is one of the largest and oldest temples in Tokyo, and the street leading from the main gate to the temple, Nakamise-dori, is lined with small shops selling souvenirs and traditional crafts.

Sengakuji, near Shinagawa, is not a very large temple but is famous as the site of the ritual suicide of the 47 *ronin,* or masterless *samurai,* in the early 18th century. The 47 *ronin* are buried in the temple grounds, which also house a museum dedicated to the warriors.

Meiji Jingu, or Meiji Shrine, is the largest Shinto shrine in Tokyo and is dedicated to the memory of the Meiji emperor (the great-grandfather of the present emperor), who reigned between 1868 and 1912, and his consort, Empress Shoken. The shrine was completed in 1920 and is thus relatively new, but the surrounding gardens are spectacular. It is the most popular place in Tokyo for New Year's shrine visits and usually attracts well over five million people in the first week of the year.

Yasukuni Jinja, the shrine for the war dead, was dedicated in 1869 and maintains in its sanctum lists of all those who died while on active military duty from the Meiji Restoration of 1868 to World War II. The compound is large, but corresponds to only a fraction of the area of Meiji Jingu. The shrine's museum contains a collection of articles associated with the war dead and the Japanese military. The shrine has two festivals every year; the Spring Festival in late April, of which one of the highlights is a one-day *sumo* exhibition featuring all the top *rikishi,* is very enjoyable and open to the public free of charge.

Festivals

Japan has thousands of colorful *matsuri,* or festivals, both of a religious and of a historical nature. Ranging from martial displays to purification rituals, festivals provide ample evidence of the people's love of pomp and tradition. Many are small neighborhood affairs, with a parade along the street to the local shrine and street stalls selling everything from clothes to goldfish to fried noodles. The larger celebrations are sometimes startling in the frenzy they produce in the huge crowds in attendance, while others are more dignified and restrained. If you take your camera to any one of them, you are sure to capture some memorable scenes. The following list is not comprehensive but may give you some idea of the wonder and variety of Japanese festivals. The English-language newspapers and magazines will keep you well informed of upcoming events.

A List of Major Festivals

January
1: New Year's Day (national holiday). New Year's Day is the most important festival on the Japanese calendar, and it is observed throughout the country. There is a mass exodus out of Tokyo, as millions of people head toward their hometowns to be with their families for this occasion. Once there, they celebrate with seasonal dishes called *osechi-ryori,* the equivalent of turkey with all the trimmings in the United States. There are special New Year's games, and streets and homes are adorned with colorful decorations. Most people visit a shrine or, more rarely, a temple within the first three days of the new year to pray for health and success; this visit is called *hatsu-mode.*

February

1-5: *Yuki Matsuri* (Snow Festival), Sapporo. The city's main thoroughfare is lined with elaborate sculptures of famous buildings and monuments, historical figures, and mythical beasts fashioned from snow and ice.

3 or 4: *Setsubun*, nationwide. According to the lunar calendar, *Setsubun* marks the last day of winter. In private homes and on temple grounds, the day is highlighted by a ceremony called *mame-nage*, or bean-throwing. To ensure good luck for the year and to ward off evil, roasted beans are hurled at masked *oni* (devils). As the children throw the beans, everyone participates by calling out, "*Oni wa soto, fuku wa uchi!*," which means "Devils out, fortune in!"

March

3: *Hinamatsuri* (Doll Festival), nationwide. *Hina* dolls are figures representing Heian period royalty and retainers, and it is traditional for all girl children to have a set, which is displayed on a special, tiered shelf once a year. Parents insist that the dolls are put away immediately after the festival; according to superstition, if a girl delays in this, her wedding will also be delayed.

12: *O-Mizutori*, Todaiji, Nara. This festival climaxes with a solemn Buddhist rite that has been performed continuously for over a millennium. In the early morning hours, by the light of huge torches, water is drawn from the temple well and symbolically purified with fire. If you have a chance to go, this festival is highly recommended.

April

14-15: *Sanno Matsuri*, Takayama (Chubu). This is one of the most energetic and exciting events of the year; a real not-to-be-missed display. It is most famous for the huge, ornate *yatai* (festival wagons something like floats), some of them almost 300 years old, that are paraded through the streets. The engineering of some of these *yatai* is amazing, especially the ingenious mechanical dolls, controlled by wires and rods, that dance and perform astounding tricks. There are a total of 23 *yatai*; 12 are paraded at the *Sanno Matsuri*, near Hie Jingu, and the other 11 can be seen during the autumn *Yahata Matsuri*, an equally intriguing celebration that takes place at Hachiman Jingu (October 9-10).

May

15: *Aoi Matsuri,* Kyoto. A magnificent pageant is presented, colorfully reenacting the Imperial procession to the Shimogamo and Kamigamo shrines in the days when Kyoto was Japan's capital.

16-17: *Sanja Matsuri,* Sensoji, Tokyo. This is a huge festival held in the Asakusa area of Tokyo to honor the Goddess of Mercy. Elaborate *mikoshi* (portable shrines) are carried through the streets as cheering crowds look on. Another highlight is the *Binzasara-mai,* a series of traditional dances.

17-18: Grand Festival, Toshogu Shrine, Nikko. In this most beautiful setting, a procession of armor-clad attendants escorts three huge *mikoshi* that carry the spirits of Japan's first *shogun,* Tokugawa Ieyasu, and two other lords. On the first day, the *Ennen-no-mai,* or Dance of Longevity, is performed.

July

16-17: *Gion Matsuri,* Yasaka Shrine, Kyoto. Perhaps the most famous and elaborate festival in Japan, the *Gion Matsuri* dates back to the ninth century. Thirty-one beautiful *yatai* are on display in the evenings leading up to the festival. On the morning of July 17, they are pulled through the streets to the delight of the huge crowds of spectators who make their way to Kyoto from all over Japan.

23-24: *Soma Nomaoi,* near Sendai. Hundreds of horsemen in *samurai* attire compete to retrieve flags shot by a small rocket onto a wide plain.

Mid-July to Mid-August: *O-Bon,* nationwide. *O-Bon* is celebrated to honor the spirits of ancestors who, it is believed, return to visit the homes of their families during this season. Fairs are held at most local temples across the country, and special dances are performed. In Tokyo, these usually take place sometime in mid-July, and in other parts of Japan, usually in early August or mid-August.

August

2-7: *Nebuta,* Aomori. *Nebuta* is said to have begun as an attempt to drive away the lethargy caused by Japan's hot, muggy summers. Enormous floats in the shapes of warriors and monsters are pulled through the streets, and, in a special ritual, the spirits of sleep are set adrift on the river. This is perhaps Japan's wildest festival.

6-8: *Tanabata,* Sendai and elsewhere. This festival has its origins in the ancient Chinese legend of the Weaver and the Herdsman (the stars Vega and Altair), who meet only once a year. Several places hold celebrations at this time; Sendai's is the most famous.

12-15: *Awa Odori,* Tokushima. This is one of the most interesting of Japan's many folk dances. The entire city is alive with singing and dancing.

16: *Daimonji* Festival, Kyoto. At the culmination of the *O-Bon* season, huge bonfires in the form of *kanji* characters are lighted on separate mountains surrounding Kyoto, and city lights are doused to heighten the effect.

September

16: *Yabusame,* Tsurugaoka Hachiman Shrine, Kamakura. *Yabusame* is a fascinating contest of horseback archery, a recreation of the *samurai* tests of skill in feudal Japan.

October

9-10: *Yahata Matsuri,* Takayama (Chubu). See April.

22: *Jidai Matsuri,* Heian Shrine, Kyoto. This "Festival of the Ages" is a commemoration of Kyoto's founding as the Japanese capital in 794. The highlight is a large procession of people in costumes representing the 13 main periods of the city's history.

November

3-4: *Okunchi,* Nagasaki. This festival is centered on Suwa Jinja, but the whole city participates in the festivities. It is well worth seeing, especially for the floats and the dragon dance.

December

2-3: *Chichibu-no-Yomatsuri,* Chichibu. This energetic and exciting festival celebrates the convergence of the male and female deities of two shrines. There are various performances during the day, and fireworks light up the sky on the evening of December 3.

17: *On-Matsuri,* Kasuga Shrine, Nara. Besides a gala procession of people costumed as courtiers, retainers, and athletes of old, a sacred Shinto invocation of the local deity is performed.

A fireworks display in Kobe
(Courtesy of Kobe
Municipal Government)

Chapter

17

Culture and Entertainment

Participating in Japan's Culture

Japan has a rich cultural heritage that dates back thousands of years. While in Japan, you will have countless opportunities to become involved in the local culture, either as a direct participant or simply as a spectator.

A newcomer's first few months in Japan may be frustrating, with many adjustments to be made. However, most people soon take to the people, culture, and scenery; Japan's dynamic cities each have their own distinctive character, and the beauty and diversity of the rural areas are a source of endless fascination. Short- and long-term residents alike will often find themselves wanting to learn more about their host country.

The opportunities to become more familiar with the culture and people of your adopted home are virtually limitless. Stay in shape while you get the feel for Japan by taking up a martial art, such as *aikido, karate,* or *judo*. Or, perhaps, choose from classes in a wide variety of traditional arts, including *ikebana,* flower arranging; *sumi-e,* silk-screen painting; *shodo,* calligraphy; and doll making. You will find these and many other fascinating aspects of Japanese culture waiting to be discovered.

Classes are an excellent way to learn about Japanese culture, including the arts and crafts of both ancient and modern Japan. Many of the instructors speak English, so you need not be fluent in Japanese to participate. Various organizations offer formal classes directed toward members of the foreign community, among them the Tokyo Union Church, the Tokyo Baptist Church, and the Tokyo American Club. Sophia University, Aoyama University, and a few other institutes of higher learning also have courses for foreigners.

One of the best ways of getting involved in your community is to participate in culturally oriented groups. You will find that many Japanese are interested in your country, and by joining a group or a club, such as Ikebana International, International Social Services, or the Japan-America Society, to name just a few, you will make friends cross-culturally with people from all social and age groups.

Japan is famous for its arts and crafts. *Imari, Kutani,* and *Noritake* are ceramics known throughout the world. Traditional wood-block prints or ultramodern lithographs, delicate china or pottery that exhibits strength and vitality, Mashiko ceramics, bamboo crafts, pearls, ivory, and baskets; the diversity of choices can keep you constantly entertained.

You can visit many of the places where these works of art are made on your own or with a group. Domestic travel agencies, such as Japan Travel Bureau (JTB), and JNTO Tourist Information Centers (TICs) can provide detailed information on tours available.

You may also have the opportunity to meet some of the crafters, and if you make a purchase, your newly acquired treasure will have that extra value that personal experience provides. Many of these artisans give lectures, usually with the aid of a simultaneous interpreter, at various functions, and some are so highly regarded that the government has declared them Living National Treasures.

If you have an interest in any of the arts, you will enjoy Japan for that aspect alone. Participating in Japan's beautiful and intriguing culture can be an enriching experience. Take your time and absorb as much as possible.

Theaters, Movies, and Music

Japanese theater has a long and varied tradition. *Kabuki* plays are often wildly colorful and full of action and can be appreciated without a knowledge of Japanese. Both the National Theater, near the Imperial Palace, and Kabukiza, one of the few remaining prewar buildings in Ginza, stage excellent, imaginative productions. Earphones are available at the theaters to provide you with English translation and lively explanations of settings, costumes, and theatrical history. Before attending, it is a good idea to decide on the portion of the day's program that holds the most interest for you. *Kabuki* goes on for 8 to 10 hours, and most people prefer to see either the afternoon or evening performance.

Although stylized, *kabuki* plays are far more accessible than the classical *noh* plays of old Japan, which are also staged year-round in Tokyo, notably at Nohgakudo and Kanze Kaikan. They have their own charm, with costumes of great beauty and stylistic recitations with a musical appeal. But they are are not easy— the language is often incomprehensible even to Japanese people.

Modern Japanese theater is extremely active, with presentations that include translated adaptations from modern U.S., British, and French plays as well as Japanese versions of Broadway musical comedies and even something like the nearly extinct vaudeville of the United States. You can also see modern dramas by native writers, stand-up comedy, and experimental theater.

Takarazuka Revue Company features a light, airy, musical program, renowned among Japanese and foreigners alike. This is an all-female group (male roles are played by women) that performs twice a year—spring and fall. The shows are vivid and colorful, and the young cast is full of spontaneity and life. The main theater of the troupe is at Takarazuka, near Osaka and Kobe, but shows are also presented at the Takarazuka Grand Theater in Tokyo, close to the Imperial Hotel.

Theater tickets can be purchased either at the theaters themselves or through ticket outlets, called "playguides," in various locations, including most of the larger department stores.

Japan has a thriving film industry, and some of its directors are justly praised around the world. The names of Akira Kurosawa (*The Seven Samurai; Kagemusha*), Nagisa Oshima (*In the Realm of the Senses; Merry Christmas, Mr. Lawrence*), and Juzo Itami (*Tampopo; A Taxing Woman*) are familiar to film fans everywhere. Tokyo cinemas show movies produced in Japan and overseas in considerable variety—art films as well as box-office record breakers. U.S. films are generally released in Japan shortly after their Stateside premiere. Foreign movies are not usually dubbed but are accompanied by Japanese subtitles.

Unreserved seats cost approximately ¥1,700 and reserved seats about ¥1,000 more. Also, discount tickets, priced at ¥1,300 or ¥1,400, are available at playguides. Organizations like Onkyo offer movie tickets at even lower prices, sometimes less than ¥1,000, supposedly only to members. However, these tickets are often made available to the general public through discount shops. On June 1 and December 1, movie theaters throughout Japan hold *kansha dei*, or day of appreciation of moviegoers, when all seats are available for ¥850, a 50% discount.

Video rentals are legal in Japan and very inexpensive. Most U.S. movies are locally distributed versions with the original English sound track and Japanese subtitles. Rental prices are as low as ¥280 per video per day in suburban Tokyo. To become a member of a video rental club you will need some form of identification in

Japanese, such as a driver's license or Certificate of Alien Registration. Sometimes there is no membership fee; when there is, it will be a few thousand yen at most.

The Japanese are great lovers of symphonic music, and performances may be heard regularly both at concert halls and over television and radio networks. There are instrumental music concerts every day. The Tokyo metropolitan area has well over 100 concert halls, notable among which are Tokyo Festival Hall, Suntory Hall, NHK Hall, Hitomi Memorial Hall, Shinjuku Festival Center, Shibuya Public Hall, Yuport Hall, Kenmin Hall, and Bunkamura. There are many promotional brochures announcing coming events at every concert hall, and the week's highlights are listed in varying detail in the English-language newspapers.

Great jazz and pop music are also to be found in Tokyo, and concerts by visiting foreign artists are frequent. In addition, there are many "live houses"—bars and pubs where live jazz, country and western music, or rock music can be heard. Many of the establishments feature U.S. and other foreign entertainers.

Nightlife

Through the 1960s, one of the most popular forms of entertainment for the Japanese businessman was the traditional *geisha* party. The role of the *geisha* has long been misunderstood by many foreigners. She is not a barfly or a call girl. She is trained from an early age in the traditional arts and social graces. In fact, the word *geisha* can be most closely translated as "artist." The training is difficult and takes many years to complete; a *geisha* does not reach her prime as an entertainer until she is in her 40s or 50s. Although *maiko* (apprentice *geisha*) are still being trained in Kyoto, their number is dwindling, and true *geisha* have become something of a rarity.

Traditionally, the *geisha* party is restricted to male guests. Food, beer, *sake,* and whiskey are served, and entertainment in the form of songs and dances accompanied by the *shamisen* (a three-stringed instrument resembling a banjo) is provided by the *geisha,* who also wait upon the guests. Nowadays, women can attend package tours to *geisha* restaurants, but these are generally pale imitations of the real thing.

There are thousands of cabarets, bars, and live houses in Tokyo, varying widely in service and price. The high-class cabarets of Akasaka, Ginza, and Roppongi can be astronomically expensive, directed as they are toward the expense-account trade.

The clientele in cabarets is usually made up exclusively of executives indulging in the uniquely Japanese custom of "business drinking."

Their needs are attended to by hostesses (who are not to be confused with *geisha*), for whose presence a steep charge is added to the bill. If a customer requests a specific hostess, an extra fee, called *shimeiryo,* will also go on the tab. If you do enter an unfamiliar establishment, it would be prudent to ask about "table charges," "service charges," and "charm charges" before sitting down, to avoid a nasty shock when the bill arrives.

Of course, cabarets are not your only choice when it comes to nightlife in Tokyo. At the opposite end of the scale are the thousands of *izakaya,* eating and drinking places that are lively, loud, and cheap. *Izakaya* usually feature a large menu and are just the thing for a large group of hungry and thirsty friends.

Much of Tokyo's nightlife is concentrated in a few "entertainment districts," the most famous being Ginza, Roppongi, and Shinjuku, with its famous Kabukicho, which has nothing whatsoever to do with *kabuki* theater. Other areas around the larger train stations, such as Shibuya, Ueno, and Ikebukuro, have their own warrens of restaurants, bars, and cabarets. In some of these places, notably Kabukicho and Ikebukuro, many of the establishments are controlled by the *yakuza,* Japan's version of the Mafia, and are best avoided.

Conventional bars in Tokyo most often close at about 11:30 P.M., to give patrons time to catch their last trains home. But the entertainment districts are full of places that remain open until 4:00 A.M. or 5:00 A.M.

Roppongi is especially popular with the foreign community. The area is perhaps best known for its cabarets and the discos that are the center of Tokyo's "singles' scene," but there are also any number of fine restaurants, friendly pubs, and live houses featuring jazz or rock music.

Nightlife in Tokyo

by Davis Barrager

During the late 1950s and early 1960s, I was privileged to spend lavish evenings in posh Shimbashi and Ginza bars, pubs, clubs, and restaurants as the guest of a pleasant, dark, and handsome Japanese gourmet. His famous design company paid me a modest retainer to drop by now and then and provide editorial assistance and my opinion about designs. Later, he would invite me out for some expense-account indulgence at places where we enjoyed a warm rapport with lovely, elegant women, most of whom wore *kimono*.

If his nocturnal style was intended to impress me, it succeeded. I marveled at his unpretentious joie de vivre while reveling in the first-class *sushi,* whole crab, turtle soup, and scallops sauteed in *miso* and butter, all usually chased with high-grade Japanese *sake*.

All this was 30 years ago. My nightlife in Tokyo has never been as lavish as it was then because I would never think of going to the expensive bars and clubs my old friend took me to and dropping the equivalent of a few thousand dollars in one night.

In the meantime, nightlife in Tokyo has changed rather little compared with Japan's dramatically changing food culture. Nightlife is not all bars, clubs, and cabarets, of course. Thank heavens. But these places are still the mainstays of Japan's expense-account set. Still, the *karaoke* bar is surely the single most significant development in Japan's nightlife. Despite its international appeal, it strikes me as being essentially Japanese because people go there to relax and enjoy the spotlight, a place usually denied by Japanese society.

In Japan, as in the West, the 1980s ushered in tidal waves of change in eating habits. This will no doubt continue, but certain things remain tenaciously constant. The Japanese are still obsessively fond of *sushi, sashimi, yakizakana* (Japanese-style grilled fish), *yakitori,* and such noodle dishes as *soba, somen, udon,* and *yakisoba.* All of these dishes, even if often attended by fanfare disproportionate to their culinary sophistication, are delightful.

So are you ready for some nightlife in Tokyo? It needn't cost a lot of money, but you will find that it almost invariably involves food, because the Japanese, wisely, never drink without eating. That is a good principle to follow, and as you stroll through Tokyo's neon-lit streets, you'll discover that Tokyo is a vast and varied place to live in.

Davis Barrager's close involvement in the food and health-care business began in the New York advertising business. A long-time resident of Japan, Barrager writes articles on food, wine, and spirits that are published in North America, Latin America, Europe, and Japan, both in English and in translation.

Chapter

18

Sports and Recreation

Despite the rather limited amount of space available for sports and recreational facilities, Japan is one of the most sports-conscious nations in the world. Almost all the major sports that are played in the United States and Europe have taken root in Japan. There are also a number of sports unique to Japan that are earning increasing recognition worldwide. Participating in sports in Japan provides foreign residents with an opportunity to make Japanese friends and gain additional insights into the local culture.

The following is an overview of some of the more popular participation and spectator sports.

Golf

Golf is extremely popular in Japan, but as land in metropolitan areas is prohibitively expensive, most golf courses are in distant suburbs or in the countryside, sometimes even on mountain slopes.

Most golfers in Japan are men, many of whom play golf more for business-related purposes, such as entertaining clients, than for relaxation. However, since about 1987, golf has also become a favorite pastime among young Japanese women. This trend stems at least in part from golf's perceived high status, and the game's popularity among women appears set to stay.

Unfortunately, there are only a few public golf courses in Japan, while private clubs are abundant but very expensive. Even with the large number of private courses, memberships may be so oversubscribed that play on weekends is impossible without making reservations months in advance. Membership fees range from ¥2.5 million to ¥75 million, depending on the location, and some memberships are sold on the Tokyo Stock Exchange. Not surprisingly, most memberships are held by corporations, but even then members must pay an additional ¥15,000 to ¥35,000 in green fees each time they play a round.

These high prices prevent most Japanese from playing a full round of golf. Their golf "outings" are usually limited to the numerous driving ranges, covered in green netting and including four-story and rooftop ranges, that can be seen in major cities. Some of these can accommodate several hundred golfers simultaneously.

Another reason that people limit their golf outings is the inaccessibility of courses. For example, while a number of courses can be reached from Tokyo in 45 minutes to an hour, traveling time to others may stretch to two hours or more, especially in weekend traffic. Moreover, with private clubs, the number of guests a member is permitted to bring is limited, and on Saturdays and Sundays guest fees are higher than on weekdays. For any tentatively planned golf date, it is advisable to make arrangements well in advance and reserve a specified starting time.

For competitive but friendly golf, as opposed to a business golfing outing, you can participate in the Tokyo American Club's golfing group, if you are a club member. The Tokyo American Club golf competitions are held at a variety of attractive and relatively convenient courses. Also, ACCJ membership offers playing privileges at local U.S. military courses.

Golf tournaments are held by the following organizations, among others:

The American Chamber of Commerce in Japan (spring and fall),
Japan-America Society (spring, summer, and fall), and
Foreign Correspondents' Club of Japan (spring and fall).

When golfing in Japan, here are a few points to remember:

• On a typical golf outing, you will leave Tokyo at the crack of dawn and arrive at the course early enough to complete nine holes in the morning. You will then have lunch in the clubhouse. (Don't forget to take off your hat when you sit down to eat!) The game is completed in the afternoon—if Japanese friends or associates invite you to play, be prepared to play 27 holes. They themselves enjoy playing as much golf as possible and, having paid the green fees, intend to use the opportunity to the fullest.

• Play tends to be slow. Unless you are in the first foursome of your group, be prepared to spend easily two hours or more to play each nine holes.

• Most golfers dream of achieving a hole-in-one, if just once in a lifetime. However, in Japan, your "reward" for hitting the hole-in-one will be to pay for dinner and drinks for the entire group you are playing with. Furthermore, the golf course will plant a tree to commemorate your accomplishment that you will be expected to pay for. Since these expenses are likely to total several hundred thousand yen, "hole-in-one insurance" is available at a very modest premium at most courses and covers the cost of dinner and drinks and the tree.

•No one carries their own clubs in Japan, at least on private courses. Caddies will carry your clubs, but be prepared to walk, as everybody does; there are no golf carts.

•Golf balls of almost all leading brands can be purchased in Japan.

•One of the most enjoyable experiences at golf course club-houses is the *ofuro*, or bath, which everyone takes when the round is concluded. Most private courses also offer massage services.

•Memberships at privately owned golf courses in Japan are extremely expensive. In the unlikely event that you are offered a membership at what appears to be a bargain price, it is wise to be cautious. Recently, memberships to new courses have tended to be oversubscribed—often massively—and fly-by-night companies on the verge of bankruptcy have sold memberships in courses that never opened.

In Japan, golf can be very enjoyable. It is considered a prestigious activity, and a round of golf with lunch and drinks afterward goes far toward overcoming some of the difficulties caused by the language barrier.

Skiing

Skiing has a loyal following in Japan, especially among young people, and snow-boarding is also catching on fast. Japan's topography is especially suited to skiing, with rugged mountains in the central regions of Honshu and Hokkaido.

The most popular ski resort areas for people in the Kanto region are Japan's Northern and Southern Alps, the ranges of snowcapped peaks in central and northern Honshu. The Hakuba ski resort area in Nagano Prefecture is particularly popular with Tokyoites and will be the site of some of the events at the 1998 Winter Olympics.

Hokkaido, about an hour north of Tokyo by plane, has probably the best skiing in Japan. There is more powder snow than in Honshu, and both the slopes and the accommodations are well worth the trip. Recommended ski resort areas near Sapporo, the island's capital, are Mount Moiwa, Mount Arai, and Teine, the site of the 1972 Winter Olympics; about two hours away is Niseko, said to have the best snow in Japan. Ski areas on Honshu tend to be overcrowded, while the more distant courses in Hokkaido are far less so.

Most Japanese prefer to go to ski resorts by bus or train. Until a few years ago, traveling to the ski slopes in Nagano and Niigata prefectures (about 240 kilometers, or 150 miles, from Tokyo) entailed a tedious all-night journey by car on a bumper-to-bumper highway or standing several hours on a train or bus in rush-hour conditions. Now, skiers can use a much more comfortable alternative, the Joetsu Shinkansen Line, which links Tokyo with Niigata Prefecture and passes close to some of the most popular ski resort areas in this part of Japan. One such resort, Gala Yuzawa, has ski lifts only a few minutes' walk from Gala Yuzawa Station, making it convenient for day trips. JR East offers discount packages combining the train fare and lift ticket and occasionally accommodation.

In Japan, rather than carrying a heavy and cumbersome load of skis and winter clothing to and from your destination, you should consider sending your equipment by delivery service (*takyubin*). Please note, however, that skis and poles must be stored in proper ski bags or in plastic bags purchased from the delivery companies. Rental ski gear is also available at each resort and is probably cheaper to use than sending your own gear via a delivery company. You should call ahead to check the sizes available and make reservations. If you choose not to use these services, you should plan your traveling arrangements carefully. Most Japanese skiers use a ski gear bag that is large enough to hold both clothes and boots and has wheels as well as shoulder straps, so that they have the choice of pulling the bag along the ground or carrying it in a backpack style. Skis and poles are carried in a separate ski bag that can be hung from the overhead baggage rack on the trains.

Adult skiers coming to Japan should bring boots and skiwear. Even though younger Japanese are getting taller, boots larger than men's U.S. size eight or skiwear for a six-footer (183 cm) are hard to find. On the other hand, there is a wide selection of boots and skiwear for children. Skis and bindings are available in almost all sizes. You can buy them at large department stores and ski shops in Tokyo, Osaka, and Kobe. In Tokyo, check the Isetan department store, Mizuno, the various Victoria outlets, or some of the many stores near Kanda; in Kobe or Osaka, try Kojitsu-Sanso.

For those going skiing in Japan for the first time, it is strongly recommended to go as part of a group or with experienced friends. This not only eases any language problems but also saves time and eliminates other problems, as your friends will have learned all the shortcuts after skiing here for a few years. It can also save you money.

Skiing can be expensive if you make your own reservations. Traveling in groups and thereby taking advantage of package-tour discounts can bring the price of a skiing weekend down from between ¥60,000 and ¥100,000 to between ¥25,000 and ¥40,000.

The Tokyo American Club arranges ski trips for members, and most of the large international schools organize weekend excursions for their students.

Physical Fitness

Physical fitness has been a booming business in the past 10 to 15 years. A wide variety of facilities are available, and the quality of equipment is generally good, nearly on a par with facilities in the United States.

Aerobics classes are quite popular among young Japanese, particularly women, and many of the instructors go to the United States to learn the latest moves at aerobics clubs there. Step and low-impact aerobics are especially popular at health clubs and dance studios.

Health club membership fees vary, with some as reasonable as ¥10,000 and others as exorbitant as ¥1 million to ¥2 million; in the latter cases, a sizable portion of the entry charges may be deposits that will be returned to you once you resign your membership. Monthly dues of about ¥10,000, which may be paid every month or annually, are common. Also, there may be fees for each visit and each facility used (for example, squash, racquetball, and tennis courts and the swimming pool) as well as charges for towels, uniforms, and toiletries used. Some clubs offer rental training clothes and shoes. Certain health clubs are part of a chain, allowing you to visit—at a small extra charge—any of the clubs in the chain. The Tokyo American Club has a health club, as do some health centers run by local wards, which are open to the public on a pay-as-you-go basis.

Before deciding on a health club, do a little research. The general rules to follow are:

- Do not be fooled by the decor; look carefully at the facilities offered and the equipment you will actually be using as well as its condition. Some clubs offer only aerobics classes and/or weights, while others have swimming pools and racquetball and tennis courts. Jacuzzis and saunas can be found at most clubs.

- Look for a strong central management and knowledgeable staff; some clubs go out of business within three years of opening due to poor management.
- Consider the proximity of the club to your office, home, and train stations.
- Take into consideration the size of the membership. Health clubs in Japan are smaller than those in the States, yet their memberships are, on average, large. Usage, particularly in the evenings after work, is extremely high.
- Carefully check the operating hours of any club you are considering joining, especially its peak hours, to see if they conflict with your schedule. Also, check on which day(s), if any, the club is closed.

Martial Arts

Many martial arts, or *budo,* have either originated or been adopted and refined in Japan. World-class experts instruct or oversee some of these classes, and instruction in English is occasionally possible. Usually tuition at *dojo* (schools) of *judo, karate, kendo,* or *aikido* is extremely reasonable, normally less than ¥10,000 per month (for one or two evenings a week) in Tokyo. A sincere desire to learn is the most important requirement in applying to enter a *dojo,* and age and sex are largely irrelevant. Children of five or six can begin practicing *karate* or *judo* either as part of the school curriculum or at after-school lessons, and elderly men and women in their 70s and 80s can still actively take part. Foreign men and women are also generally welcome to join the thousands of *judo, karate, kendo, aikido,* and other kinds of *dojo* throughout Japan.

The basic technique of *judo,* probably the best known of the martial arts, is to utilize the strength of the opponent to one's own advantage. *Karate* is an art of self-defense that uses hands, elbows, feet, and other parts of the body as weapons. Both involve rigorous training to condition the body.

Less well-known traditional Japanese martial arts are *aikido* and *kendo. Aikido* has a more meditative, ascetic aspect than *judo* or *karate*—it depends on muscular flexibility and is good for keeping physically fit since it promotes smooth and supple movement of the body.

If you are thinking about joining a martial arts class, remember:

- To visit a class or two to get a feeling for the *dojo*'s atmosphere. The atmosphere may vary between *dojo,* from very relaxed to strictly traditional, with a strong emphasis on the *sempai-kohai* system, or relationships based on seniority, which may carry over into social situations. Class sizes, and thus the degree of personalized instruction, also vary widely.
- The training can be quite rigorous and may include full-contact sparring.
- Politeness goes a long way; first impressions of your sincerity are important.

Other Participation Sports

A wide variety of other stimulating recreational activities await you in Japan, including anything from hiking and mountain climbing to scuba diving in Okinawa's subtropical waters. Newcomers are always warmly welcomed to groups of enthusiasts, and socializing is often the most important element of being a member.

Tennis has long been popular in Japan. However, public tennis courts are difficult to reserve, and private clubs, such as the Tokyo Lawn Tennis Club, are expensive and have long waiting lists. Most courts have clay surfaces and play tends to be rather slow. The sport is taken very seriously in Japan, so be prepared to wear immaculate whites.

The cost of playing tennis depends on where you play. Indoor tennis courts at public sports centers cost about ¥2,000 to ¥2,500 per hour during the day on weekdays or about ¥4,000 per hour on weekday evenings or on weekends. You can also play, for only ¥200 per hour, at sports centers operated by local governments, but you will have to reserve at least a month in advance. One of the famous tennis clubs in Japan is the Tokyo Lawn Tennis Club, in Azabu. The membership is not very expensive, but the waiting list is long, probably at least several years. The Imperial Family has sometimes used the club, and the present Emperor and Empress are said to have first met at this club.

Among other racket sports, squash is fairly new to Japan, but the number of courts is gradually increasing. Courts are available at some health clubs, and the Tokyo American Club has squash courts for its members and their guests.

During the summer months, water sports are popular, particularly surfing, windsurfing, and scuba diving. Seawater in Tokyo Bay, although improving in quality, is still polluted, and the beaches near Tokyo, especially on hot summer weekends, tend to be extremely crowded. On the east coast of Chiba Prefecture, however, the sandy beaches of Kujukurihama are quite clean. If you are willing to travel further out of Tokyo—as far as the Izu Peninsula—the beaches are considerably cleaner and less crowded.

There are numerous public and private swimming pools in Tokyo, but these are often crowded. Sports centers run by local governments have pools that can be used for few hundred yen. The Tokyo American Club and some of the apartment buildings rented to expatriates also have swimming pools, as do many health clubs. In addition, it is possible to use the facilities at major hotels on a daily basis—the average charge is about ¥6,000 (reduced rates are available for the late afternoon)—or just for the summer months (June to September)—passes cost about ¥30,000 to ¥40,000. Alternatively, the Toshimaen amusement park in northwestern Tokyo, 20 minutes from Ikebukuro on the Seibu Ikebukuro Line, has the largest outdoor pool complex in Tokyo, and although the pools are often very crowded, family passes valid for a year are available for less than ¥35,000.

Sailing enthusiasts arriving in Tokyo can quickly become involved in the yachting scene by contacting members (membership is available to anyone interested, regardless of nationality) of the Tokyo Power Squadron, part of the U.S. Power Squadron, which regularly meets at the New Sanno Hotel (the hotel for the U.S. military in Tokyo). Although pleasure boating is popular, good harbors and marinas are, unfortunately, limited. Tokyo Bay is crowded with commercial shipping, and most of the popular marinas in the Tokyo area are some 65 kilometers (or about two hours' drive) southwest on Sagami Bay, on the west side of the Miura Peninsula, at places like Abaratsubo, Hayama, Enoshima, Sajima, and Kuwajiro.

Cruising on Sagami Bay can be a delightful experience, but a visiting sailor is well advised to check with an experienced "salt" before setting out. Winds can shift suddenly and the weather on the bay changes quickly. There are also other potential hazards, such as strong currents and unmarked fishing nets.

A Japanese operator's license is required for all motor-powered boats, regardless of size. Examinations are normally given only in Japanese, but through the efforts of the squadron, these can be arranged in English. Squadron members regularly conduct classes in Tokyo to prepare would-be sailors for these exams.

Scuba diving licenses are also easily obtained, although not cheaply, with English-speaking instructors available to teach you the ropes. Diving certificates obtained overseas through such organizations as PADI and NAVI are normally honored in Japan. The Izu Peninsula, about three hours' drive south of Tokyo, the Izu chain of islands, the Ogasawara Islands, and Okinawa are the best spots for scuba diving in Japan. Also, many people enjoy diving holidays in such nearby tropical destinations as Thailand, the Philippines, Guam, and Saipan.

Fishing is also a popular recreational activity. Both freshwater and saltwater fishing is within a half-day's travel any-where in Japan. Trout fishing is particularly good, and the trout streams around Lake Chuzenji, near Nikko (two and a half hours from Tokyo by car), not only have fine fishing but beautiful mountain scenery as an added bonus. Some diehards even fish in Tokyo's rivers and canals. The water is moderately polluted with sludge, although less so than in the 1960s, so whatever fish you catch should not be eaten raw.

Four-fifths of Japan's landmass is mountainous, a fact that makes hiking and climbing popular forms of recreation. Climbs range from sheer faces of over 3,000 meters (9,840 feet) for the experienced climber to the relatively easy hike up Mount Takao, one and a half hours from central Tokyo by train. During your stay in Japan you will probably develop the urge to trek up Mount Fuji, the world's most heavily climbed peak, to see the sunrise from its summit. The Japanese have a saying, "If you climb Mount Fuji once, you are blessed for life. Twice or more and you are a fool." No matter what, dress appropriately, bring rain gear, and carry with you a survival kit, including a flashlight and extra food rations in case of emergency, as the weather is unpredictable, even in summer.

Ice skating, both indoors and outdoors, is enjoyed during the winter months. Tokyo and other major cities have many good public rinks, where you can rent skates at moderate prices; the average charge for two hours on the ice is about ¥800. Roller skating may take place at the same facilities during off months. Roller blading, however, is just beginning to catch on here.

In the mid-to-late 1960s, Japan experienced a bowling boom. After the inevitable bust, many bowling alleys closed down, but some of the larger bowling centers in Tokyo survived and are still thriving. The Tokyo American Club has its own bowling alley and an organized league.

Archery ranges and cycling courses—with high-performance mountain bikes experiencing a recent surge in popularity—have been set up in the suburbs of Tokyo and other cities. Equestrian facilities can also be found not too far from city centers. Riding lessons are available in English but are quite expensive.

Spectator Sports

Japan is blessed with a wide variety of spectator sports, including baseball, track and field, basketball, American football, soccer, ice hockey, horse racing, bicycle racing, boat racing, ping-pong, volleyball, rugby, marathon races, and traditional Japanese sports like *sumo, judo,* and *karate.* In addition, the country boasts professional and amateur sports facilities that are among the best in the world.

Major international sporting events are frequently held in Japan. For example, Japan hosted the 1964 Summer Olympics and the 1972 Winter Olympics in Sapporo, and the city of Nagano, less than a two-hour train ride from Tokyo, has been chosen for the 1998 Winter Olympics. Track and field meets are also often held, usually at the Kokuritsu Kyogijo, or National Stadium (the main venue of the 1964 Tokyo Olympics). Regular season NBA basketball games were played here originally in 1990 and are now held occasionally. NCAA basketball and football games are held annually. Another popular event is the preseason exhibition NFL game, which is played each year at the Tokyo Dome.

Although *sumo* is Japan's unofficial *kokugi,* or national sport, baseball draws the greatest crowds. Professional baseball began in Japan in 1936 and has reached a level where some of the best players could compete evenly with those in the majors. Japanese pro baseball has two leagues, the Pacific and Central leagues, with six teams in each. The Central League Yomiuri Giants (who borrowed their name, and even uniform, from the old N.Y. Giants) once dominated Japanese pro baseball—with a remarkable nine consecutive Japan Series victories between 1965 and 1973—but are now less impressive, although still by far the most popular team. Giants games are invariably sold out, and even standing-room-only tickets are difficult to obtain. It is fairly easy to buy even the best tickets for games between teams other than the Giants, and there are usually seats available on the day of the game itself.

From June through September, most pro baseball games are held at night to avoid the oppressive summer heat and humidity. Mondays and sometimes Fridays are days off; with these exceptions, games are played daily, although doubleheaders are rare. Compared with a 162-game schedule in the United States, only 130 games are played each season here. Nearly every other year, a U.S. major league team or a group of U.S. all-stars plays the best Japanese players and/or the Giants in a series of goodwill games.

Rivaling professional baseball in spectator support are the annual high-school baseball tournaments held each spring and summer at Koshien Stadium in Nishinomiya, near Osaka and Kobe, home of the Central League Hanshin Tigers. The nation nearly comes to a standstill as salarymen become absorbed in the team spirit of dedicated players and dream of their own playing days of yesteryear.

Sumo is the most popular of Japan's traditional sports. Not only a spectator sport, *sumo* is part of the physical education curriculum for both boys and girls in Japanese schools. Professional *sumo,* in which only men compete and including a number of non-Japanese, has experienced a boom in recent years, and its popularity is now at an all-time high. Takanohana, Wakahanada, Kotonishiki, Mainoumi, and others are heroes throughout the nation and even overseas. Three of the top-ranked *rikishi,* Akebono, Konishiki, and Musashimaru, are Americans from Hawaii.

Rikishi, or competitors (literally, "strong men"), in the top *makunouchi* division weigh an average of 145 kilograms (320 pounds), but as there is no classification by weight—only by rank—it is not at all uncommon for a 90-kilogram (200-pound) lightweight to be matched against a behemoth more than twice his weight and a good two heads taller. These bouts are always crowd pleasers.

The rules of *sumo* are relatively simple. The *rikishi* fight, using a variety of techniques, to push each other out of the ring or make any part of the opponent's body other than the soles of his feet touch the ground. The *shikiri,* or prematch ritual, takes four minutes at the top level, while the bout itself, for which both spectators and *rikishi* have been psyching themselves up, is usually over in less than 20 seconds.

Six *honbasho,* or official tournaments, each lasting 15 days, are held every year. These tournaments are held in Tokyo in January, May, and September, in Osaka in March, in Nagoya in July, and in Fukuoka in November. *Sumo* tournaments are televised daily from 3:10 P.M. to 6:00 P.M. on NHK (Channel 1) and are reviewed in digest form for 30 minutes from 11:15 P.M. (from 11:00 P.M. on Saturdays and Sundays) on TV Asahi (Channel 10).

Tickets for *sumo* have become hard to obtain in recent years, but prices are not expensive by Japanese standards. The most expensive boxes are priced at ¥10,000 per person (box tickets are sold in fours), while the cheapest standing-room tickets are ¥2,300 for adults and ¥500 for children. However, a limited number of tickets are reserved for sale on each day of the tournament, and if you line up in front of the Kokugikan (the *sumo* arena in Tokyo's Ryogoku) or at the venues in Osaka, Nagoya, and Fukuoka before 7:00 A.M., you will probably be able to obtain a standing-room ticket. Retirement ceremonies and other unofficial *sumo* events, known as *hanazumo,* offer a good chance to obtain a better view, and you will be able to purchase tickets to most of these events on the day itself, except for the retirement ceremonies for very popular *rikishi.* Tickets for these events range from ¥1,000 to ¥9,000.

Soccer, rugby, and American football are also very popular in Japan. Famous soccer teams, such as Bayern München, have played in Japan; J League, a professional league, began its first season in 1992; and Japan will host the 2002 World Cup.

Winter sports also attract much attention. World Cup skiing events are held annually; ice hockey and figure and speed skating, while they do not have nearly the following of skiing, are growing in popularity, and major international events in these sports are held in Japan each year.

Boxing generates keen spectator interest in Japan. The country has produced some excellent world champions, such as Yoshio Shirai, Masahiko "Fighting" Harada, Shozo "Guts" Ishimatsu, and Yoko Gushiken. In 1992, there were five Japanese world champions in professional boxing. Most successful Japanese boxers are in the lighter divisions, but Japan has hosted world heavyweight championship matches, including those in which George Foreman and Mike Tyson (twice, including his loss to Buster Douglas) have defended their titles.

Other popular sports include professional wrestling (both male and female), kick boxing, Formula One racing, and volleyball. Tennis is very popular, and major Japanese corporations often sponsor WCT tournaments in Japan.

The Japanese men's and women's professional golf tours also have strong viewer support, and there are usually several foreign players competing at each pro event.

Horse racing has an avid following in Japan, and on- and off-track government-supervised betting is legal for people 20 years of age and over. Horse racing has shed its somewhat stodgy image, and weekend and night races attract many young women and their dates. Other forms of legalized gambling in Japan are betting on motorboat, bicycle, and motorcycle races; the ubiquitous *pachinko* (a Japanese version of pinball machine); and *takarakuji* (lotteries) sponsored weekly by city governments and the national government.

Whether you are a spectator or an active participant, many sports and recreational options are available to you in Japan and provide a welcome change of pace from working life.

A mass of neon signs lights up the Tokyo night.

The building housing the Museum of Modern Culture, in Tokyo, is the former home of a prince. (Courtesy of Meguro Ward, Tokyo)

*Ginza's Kabukiza features
kabuki performances year-
round. (Courtesy of
Chuo Ward, Tokyo)*

Bathers relax at a beach on Chiba's Boso Peninsula. (Courtesy of Chiba Prefectural Government)

The Shonan coast, in Kanagawa Prefecture, only about 50 kilometers from Tokyo, is a popular destination in the summer months. (Courtesy of Kanagawa Prefectural Government)

Private clubs and local governments operate sports centers that offer a wide range of facilities, including training gyms, swimming pools, indoor tennis courts, and bowling lanes.

Odawara Castle, about 80 kilometers southwest of Tokyo (Courtesy of Kanagawa Prefectural Government)

A Sunday morning flea market at Nogizaka Shrine, in Tokyo

Akebono, an American from Oahu, Hawaii, became the first non-Japanese to achieve promotion to sumo's highest rank of yokozuna, *in January 1993.*

Hideo Nomo, of Japanese pro baseball's Kintetsu Buffaloes, is widely regarded as the nation's best pitcher. Nomo and other Japanese baseball superstars can now command annual salaries in excess of ¥100 million.

*Spring in the rice paddies
close to the Japan Alps*

*Along with rice, fish is one of
Japan's staple foods. The
Tsukiji wholesale market, in
Tokyo, is one of the nation's
largest suppliers.*

The Daibutsu, or Great Buddha, in Kamakura, was cast in the 13th century, when the city was Japan's capital. The Daibutsu was originally housed in a temple, but this was later swept out to sea by a tsunami (tidal wave), leaving only the statue itself. (Courtesy of Kanagawa Prefectural Government)

The Kushiro Marshes, in eastern Hokkaido, are a beautiful example of the island's natural landscapes. (Courtesy of Hokkaido Prefectural Government)

A snow-capped Mount Fuji rises
above the clouds in winter.

Kyoto's Kinkakuji, covered in gold leaf, is one of the historic city's most famous sights.

The keyhole-shaped mausoleum of Emperor Nintoku, in Osaka, is the largest of its kind in the world. (Courtesy of Osaka Prefectural Government)

The Gion district is Kyoto's traditional geisha *quarters.*

Beyond a welcoming smile.

At ANA, we understand that your comfort depends on our service.
And that the quality of our service depends on the quality of our people.
That is why our staff is selected and trained to be the best in the air.
You will notice their professionalism in the many small details that make your flight
so enjoyable. But beyond their ability and efficiency is their sincere desire to help each traveler
enjoy his or her journey. Because we know each passenger has different needs and tastes,
we go beyond the expected to treat you as a unique individual.
Making extra efforts for our passengers is part of who we are.
And it is also part of the reason why ANA has become Japan's most preferred airline.

All Nippon Airways

· · · · JAPAN'S BEST TO THE WORLD · · · · · ·

Reservations for International Flights: Tokyo (03) 3272-1212 Osaka (06) 372-1212 Nagoya (052) 971-5588 Fukuoka (092) 474-1212

Chapter

19

Traveling in Japan

Japan has many places of scenic, cultural, and historical interest for the traveler, from the ski slopes of Hokkaido in the north to the sandy beaches of subtropical Okinawa. Among the most well-known travel destinations are the former capital Kyoto, with its traditional streets and houses, hundreds of temples and shrines, and priceless artifacts; the Fuji Five Lakes/ Hakone area, offering spectacular vistas of Japan's most famous mountain; Kyushu's Mount Aso, at the center of the largest volcanic crater in the world; and the sacred shrines at Ise. Across the length and breadth of Japan, in fact, there is a wealth of attractions, both natural and man-made, for the traveler. Bookstores carrying English-language books (see Chapter 6) offer a wide selection of travel guides to Japan and will give you all the details you need to plan a trip. Japan National Tourist Organization (JNTO) Tourist Information Centers (TICs, see Telephone Directory) are also very helpful and will provide you with maps, transportation schedules, hotel and inn brochures, and other information.

Compared with other countries, travel in Japan has both advantages and disadvantages. Wherever you go, you are likely to encounter few problems in terms of safety, availability of transportation, or other practical arrangements. However, you should not be surprised at the sheer numbers of fellow visitors to the most popular destinations in peak seasons, and you may be a little disappointed by the extent to which civilization has encroached on most areas. Nevertheless, you will find the time you take to really see Japan, outside the big cities, well spent; traveling around Japan can be a stimulating and richly rewarding experience.

Intercity Rail Lines
Although urban train lines in Japan are usually slow and very crowded, intercity train lines are fast, punctual, and generally far less full. Most intercity lines are run by the JR Group companies, the former Japanese National Railways.

Japan's Shinkansen bullet trains, operated by the JR companies, are among the fastest trains in the world, and some of the newer models can achieve cruising speeds in excess of 270 kilometers (168 miles) per hour. The main Shinkansen route, the Tokaido/Sanyo Shinkansen, runs from Tokyo to Nagoya, Kyoto, Osaka, Kobe, Okayama, Hiroshima, and finally Hakata (Fukuoka), in Kyushu. There are three types of trains on this line: the Nozomi superexpress, the Hikari superexpress, and the Kodama limited express. Hikari trains stop only at major stations, such as Tokyo, Nagoya, Kyoto, and Osaka, and Kodama trains stop at all stations along the line. In 1992, the Nozomi, a slightly faster Shinkansen train, was introduced, cutting the time required to travel the more than 500 kilometers (300 miles) between Tokyo and Osaka from two hours forty-nine minutes (on Hikari trains) to two hours thirty minutes. Nozomi service between Osaka and Hakata is scheduled to commence during 1993.

The Joetsu Shinkansen links Tokyo and Niigata, on the Sea of Japan coast, and has stops close to many of the country's ski resorts. The Tohoku Shinkansen goes north from Tokyo to Sendai and Morioka, in northern Honshu, while the Yamagata Shinkansen is a recently opened offshoot that serves the city of Yamagata.

With regard to train travel, it is worth noting that, for example, although the flying time between Tokyo and Osaka is slightly less than one hour, as opposed to two and a half hours on the fastest Shinkansen train, the time required to reach Tokyo's domestic airport at Haneda, check in, and travel to the center of Osaka from Itami airport makes the actual time required to reach Osaka about the same by plane or by train.

Reservations for Shinkansen trains can be made at the *Midori no Madoguchi* ticket windows at nearly all JR stations, JR travel centers, or travel agencies that book JR tickets. First class is called the Green Car and offers larger, more comfortable seats (although seats in the ordinary cars are not uncomfortable).

Normally, you will have no trouble getting an unreserved seat (*jiyuseki*) on Shinkansen trains. However, during the three major holiday seasons (New Year, Golden Week, and the *O-Bon* summer vacation), you will probably have to stand for the entire journey if you don't have a reserved seat (*shiteiseki*). Reserved seats are only slightly more expensive (approximately ¥500 more) than unreserved seats and can be booked up to a month in advance of the day you want to travel.

The price for a round-trip ticket (reserved seat) to Nagoya is about ¥20,000, to Osaka about ¥26,000, and to Hakata (Fukuoka) about ¥42,000. There is an additional charge of ¥10,000 for using the Green Car (first class) round-trip to Osaka.

JR offers four types of excursion tickets (*shuyuken*) as well as special discounts for travel within designated periods or for people meeting certain age or other requirements; ask for *waribiki-kippu* and you will be quoted the cheapest fare applicable. Anybody using the Shinkansen frequently can obtain a pass, and some travel agencies offer discounted Shinkansen tickets that they have purchased from people who have canceled their reservations.

For visitors to Japan, the Japan Rail Pass is available, which allows economical, unlimited travel on all JR trains, buses, and ferries within a set period. This pass can only be purchased outside Japan. While as a resident you will not be able to benefit from the cheap travel it offers, you might want to recommend it to visiting relatives or friends. A one-week pass costs about the same as a round-trip Shinkansen fare from Tokyo to Kyoto.

Domestic Air Services

The major Japanese airlines that offer domestic flights are All Nippon Airways (ANA), Japan Airlines (JAL), and Japan Air System (JAS). Almost all domestic flights departing from and arriving in Tokyo use Tokyo International Airport at Haneda. There are frequent departures from Tokyo for Osaka, Nagoya, Sapporo, Hiroshima, Fukuoka, and Naha, among other destinations.

As airlines compete with Shinkansen trains on the routes between major cities, airfares are generally only slightly higher than those for superexpress trains. Discounts are available for round-trips and multiple-ticket purchases. Other reductions are available to women passengers and elderly couples. Discount ticket shops, which also sell movie, amusement park, Shinkansen, and other tickets below face value, offer airline tickets below the normal retail price.

In most areas, airports have restrictions on takeoff and landing times. Haneda is open until 11:00 P.M., quite late for a Japanese airport.

Long-Distance Buses

The JR, Keio, Tokyu, and other railway companies operate long-distance buses that make overnight trips between Tokyo and Kansai and other regions. Fares are about half the price of air tickets and 20% to 30% cheaper than the Shinkansen. The buses are comfortable, with reclining seats and blankets, and they also have on-board toilets. However, to reach Osaka, for example, it may take up to eight and a half hours, depending on traffic conditions. Buses depart from Tokyo's major railway stations, such as Shinjuku, Tokyo, Ikebukuro, and Shinagawa.

Ferry Services

Ferry services are available both to domestic destinations, including outlying islands, and to neighboring countries, such as Korea, China, and Russia. The major ports of departure are Yokohama, Kobe, Shimonoseki, Nagasaki, and Hakata. Prices to international destinations are about half the normal airfares, but travel times are of course much longer; the ferry from Yokohama to Shanghai, for instance, takes four days as opposed to a few hours by plane. Ferries, however, are the only way to reach some of the smaller Japanese islands.

Roads

Japan's roads are often congested, and the number of vehicles continues to increase every year. Driving to Hakone, for example— a mountain resort about 100 kilometers (60 miles) from downtown Tokyo—may take several hours, even on a weekday.

The Chuo, Tomei, and other expressways are toll roads but are often even more crowded than ordinary roads. You are advised to leave early in the morning or late at night for road trips out of Tokyo, and, if possible, to schedule your trips for weekdays.

Where to Stay

One of the great pleasures of traveling in Japan is the opportunity to stay in a traditional Japanese inn, or *ryokan,* which will offer you a glimpse of what Japan was like before the expressways and high rises as well as a chance to experience Japanese courtesy at its best. When you arrive, the owner of the *ryokan* will come out and greet you personally. Even if you do not speak a word of Japanese, your wishes will somehow be fulfilled. Your *futon* (bedding) will be laid out on the *tatami* floor. Before your evening meal, often served in the comfort and privacy of your own room, you might want to take a Japanese-style bath, which, although quite hot, will leave you feeling relaxed and refreshed. Rates vary widely but are generally between ¥10,000 and ¥50,000 for one night's stay, and breakfast and dinner are usually included in the bill.

Of course, in such major destinations as Osaka, Nagoya, Kyoto, and Sapporo a wide range of Western-style accommodation is offered, from five-star establishments to no-frills business hotels (see section on accommodation in Chapter 6).

In most destinations, including some of the more out-of-the-way places, there is also the option of staying in a *minshuku,* or private guest house, a less expensive version of a *ryokan.* Rates are usually between ¥8,000 and ¥10,000 for one night's stay, including breakfast and dinner.

A number of other types of accommodation are available, including pensions, temples, *kokumin shukusha* (people's lodgings), and youth hostels, which can be found across the length and breadth of Japan. TICs can provide you with information and also make reservations for your stay.

Destinations

Outside the sprawling urban centers of Tokyo and Osaka, Japan has many beautiful areas and sites of historical and cultural importance, legacies of a unique civilization and many centuries of tradition.

Close to Tokyo are several popular destinations for day trips out of the capital. Kamakura, a seaside town about 60 kilometers (35 miles) south of Tokyo, is famous for its giant, 700-year-old bronze Buddha, the Daibutsu, and its many historic temples and shrines, most of which are within walking distance of the main train station. Tsurugaoka Hachiman Shrine and Kenchoji temple, both dating back to the 13th century, are just two examples. Kamakura can be reached from Tokyo in an hour on the JR Yokosuka Line.

Also popular is the mountain resort of Nikko, which offers outstanding mountain scenery, including streams, lakes, and cascading waterfalls, as well as the ancient Toshogu Shrine, one of the most ornately decorated in all Japan. Nikko can be reached by train in two hours from either Ueno Station or Asakusa Station in Tokyo and is also easily accessible by car.

Further inland is Karuizawa, a well-known summer resort in the mountains northwest of Tokyo. Karuizawa is frequented by many Japanese and foreigners in the summer because of its coolness and accessibility—it is only about two hours from Tokyo by express train departing from Ueno Station.

The area surrounding Mount Fuji is well worth a visit, perhaps overnight or longer. The Fuji Five Lakes area offers beautiful vistas of the mountain, in clear weather. A popular resort spot for city dwellers is nearby Hakone, famous for its clean air and hot springs as well as the ropeway that takes you from the best known of these, Owakudani, to Lake Ashinoko, affording spectacular views of Mount Fuji. You can get to Hakone in about one and a half hours by the Tokaido Shinkansen to Odawara, leaving from Tokyo Station, or by the Odakyu Line Romance Car to Yumoto, which leaves from Tokyo's Shinjuku Station.

Shimoda, on the tip of the Izu Peninsula, a favorite beach and spa area southwest of Tokyo, is well known as the spot where Townsend Harris opened the first American consulate in Japan. Beach houses can be rented at Shimoda for the summer months, and the town can be reached by train from Tokyo in two and a half hours.

Slightly further afield is Ise, another popular sightseeing destination that offers both the Grand Shrines of Ise—the most sacred and venerated of all Shinto shrines in Japan—and magnificent seascapes and coastal scenery. A remarkable feature of the Ise shrines is that they are reconstructed, with elaborate rites, every 20 years. Ancient skills and outstanding craftsmanship are employed in the reconstruction, and no nails or steel are used. In Toba, on the coast close to Ise, pearl cultivation still is a thriving industry, and traditional pearl diving is demonstrated for visitors. Ise can be reached in two hours by train from Nagoya.

The two best-known centers of historical interest in Japan are Kyoto and Nara, both offering enough attractions to warrant at least a few days' stay. These cities are very well preserved as they have not been damaged by major earthquakes for hundreds of years and were not bombed during World War II. Most of Japan's emperors are buried in Kyoto and Nara, and their massive, mound-like mausoleums, some enclosed by moats, dot the landscapes of the two ancient cities.

Kyoto, about a two-and-a-half-hour ride from Tokyo on the Shinkansen (and about 40 minutes by local train from Osaka), was Japan's imperial capital and the center of its culture from 794 to 1868. In addition to the old Imperial Palace and the Katsura Imperial Villa, Kyoto has many Shinto shrines and Buddhist temples of great architectural beauty. Outstanding among these is Kinkakuji, or Golden Pavilion, which was originally built as the villa of a Kyoto nobleman but was converted into a temple upon his death. The exterior is covered with gold foil, hence its name. Unfortunately, the original building was destroyed by fire in 1950, but a replica was constructed in 1955, the building that you see today. Other famous landmarks are Kiyomizudera, Nijo Castle, and Sanjusan Gendo, housing 1,000 golden statues of the goddess Kannon.

Gardens are an integral part of Kyoto, perhaps the most famous of which is the Zen rock garden at Ryoanji. In these gardens, rocks, plants, and streams have been laid out in landscapes designed to evoke a feeling of harmony. The city is also the center of such traditional industries as silk, ceramics, lacquerware, and doll making.

Nara is even older than Kyoto. It was the nation's capital from 710 to 784 and the cradle of Japan's arts, crafts, literature, and industry. Buddhism exerted a strong influence on Nara's architecture, of which two of the most famous examples are Yakushiji and Horyuji temples. Horyuji is more than 1,000 years old and is said to be the world's oldest wooden building. The two temples comprise a total of about 40 wooden buildings, containing some of the most outstanding architectural and sculptural artifacts of Japan. Nara is also the site of the largest wooden structure in the world, the Daibutsuden, which forms part of Todaiji temple and houses a giant Buddha, the biggest bronze statue on earth. Nara is particularly pleasant to visit in April, when the *sakura* (cherry trees) are in full bloom and the city is at its most enchanting. Nara can be reached in 35 minutes by limited express train from either Osaka or Kyoto.

The Tohoku region, in northern Honshu, is much less crowded than the Kanto or Kinki regions and can be reached in a few hours by Shinkansen from Tokyo. The pace of life is slow in Tohoku, and in many areas, traditional crafts still flourish.

Japan's northernmost main island, Hokkaido, is the least crowded, with a population of only 5.6 million. With its beautiful scenery and clean air and some of the best ski resorts in Japan, Hokkaido has much to offer throughout the year. The Seikan Tunnel, the world's longest undersea tunnel, links Hokkaido with Honshu. The tunnel is presently used only by local railway lines, although there has been speculation that the Shinkansen will eventually be routed through the tunnel to Sapporo.

At the other end of the Japanese archipelago is Kyushu, the southernmost main island. From Hakata (Fukuoka), its principal port of entry—which can be reached in about six hours by Shinkansen from Tokyo or an hour and a half by plane—many spots of both scenic and cultural interest are easily accessible. The coastal town of Beppu, to the east, is a famous hot-spring resort with a lively atmosphere. Mount Aso, further inland near the center of Kyushu, is a still-active volcano in the middle of the largest volcanic crater on earth. An hour's train ride away is Kumamoto, worth a visit for its beautiful landscape garden, Suizenji-koen, and castle. Nagasaki, to the west, and Miyazaki, to the south, are other popular destinations.

Still further south, two and a half hours from Tokyo by plane, is Okinawa Prefecture, a string of subtropical islands (also known as the Ryukyus) that stretches over 1,000 kilometers. The southernmost islands are almost within sight of Taiwan. Unlike Japan's main islands, Okinawa does not have rail transportation, so buses, taxis, and automobiles are the main modes of getting around. Okinawa has many excellent beaches and first-class hotels.

There are many other resorts and scenic spots in Japan, and each person has a favorite. Be adventurous; seek out not only the best-known sights but also the lesser-known treasures along the way. You are sure to find traveling in Japan both fascinating and enlightening, a window on one of the most interesting cultures in the world.

ACCJ PUBLICATIONS

Trade and Investment in Japan: The Current Environment

Understand the current business environment for U.S. companies in Japan and find out what it takes for foreign companies to succeed. This study, conducted for the American Chamber of Commerce in Japan by the consulting firm A.T. Kearney, provides statistics, information and in-depth analysis of one of the world's most competitive markets. Includes valuable reports on 31 separate service and manufacturing sectors of industry. 1991, 140 pp.
Price: ¥5,000/$40 for members;
¥7,000/$56 for non-members; air mail $11.

Employment Practices of American Companies in Japan

Learn how U.S. companies treat their employees in Japan from a study prepared by TPF&C and based on the employment practices of 204 ACCJ member firms. Analysis and statistics cover employee relations, development and training, recruitment, personnel policies and local trends. Useful planning tool. 1991, 46 pp.
Price: ¥3,000/$24 for members;
¥5,000/$40 for non-members;
air mail $4.

ACCJ Directory

A complete listing of more than 700 American companies and 2,100 individual members, with address, phone, fax numbers and business description of the firm. Classified section lists firms by sector.
Price: ¥5,000/$40 for members;
¥10,000/$80 for non-members;
air mail $24.

Other Publications and Products

• U.S.–Japan Trade White Paper,1993 (34 Sector Reports)
• Finding a Home in Tokyo, 1991, 18 pp., ¥1,000/$8 for members;
¥1,300/$10 for non-members • Market Japan Seminar Videotape (70 min.) • Audiotaped Speeches • Mailing Lists
• Resident and non-resident membership.
Information upon request.

ACCJ Journal

Monthly business magazine containing timely articles about doing business in Japan; written by experts about those who know what it takes to succeed in Japan.
Price: ¥8,000/$64 per year,
includes sea mail;
air mail $60.

Living in Japan

A popular book intended for families anticipating a move to Japan. Topics include moving and what to bring, getting settled, culture, schools, health care, business and finance, working spouses, typhoons and earthquakes, legal affairs and the Kansai area. 1993. 200+ pp.
Price: ¥3,000/$24 for members;
¥4,900/$39 for non-members;
air mail $13.

Setting up an Office in Japan

How to set up shop in Japan, with detailed sections on real estate in Tokyo, contract negotiations and fees, plus the basics on communications, legal services, taxes, banking, patents, staffing, and dozens of business issues based on advice from ACCJ members and other local sources. Osaka/Kobe, Nagoya and other cities and industrial sites included. Spring 1993.
Price: ¥3,000/$24 for members;
¥4,900/$39 for non-members; air mail $13.

Exporting to Japan

A nuts-and-bolts guide for those interested in exporting to Japan; includes samples of documentation, letters of credit, terminology and shipping information. 1989, 57 pp.
Price: ¥1,300/$10 for members;
¥2,000/$16 for non-members;
air mail $3.

ACCJ ORDER FORM

Please send me the publications circled above.

Name: _____

Address: _____

Tel: _____ Fax: _____

Check enclosed ☐ (No bank transfers; non-members please pay in advance.)

Charge to my ☐ AMEX ☐ VISA ☐ MASTERCARD

Card no:_____ Expiry: _____

Signature: _____

AMERICAN CHAMBER OF COMMERCE IN JAPAN
Fukide Building. No 2, 4-1-21 Toranomon, Minato-ku, Tokyo 105, Japan
Tel: (03) 3433-5381 Fax: (03) 3436-1446
Also available at: U.S. CHAMBER OF COMMERCE, International Division,
1615 H St. NW, Washington D.C. 20062 Tel: (202) 463-5460 Fax: (202) 463-3114

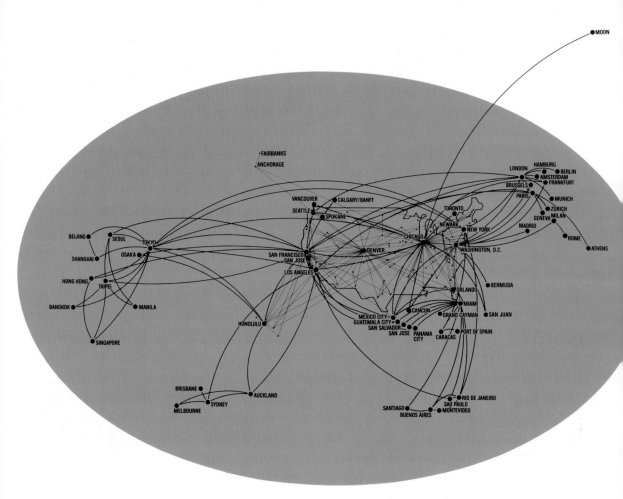

Well, it's conceivable isn't it?

While flying you to the moon isn't currently in our plans, flying you to the ends of the Earth certainly is.

United maintains a worldwide network that provides access to 160 cities throughout the U.S., Asia, Europe, Australia and South America. In addition, our highly regarded First Class and Connoisseur Class[SM] services make United the airline of choice for international business travelers.

Come fly the airline that's uniting the world. Come fly the friendly skies.

● Routes and schedules are subject to ch

In Tokyo, the best kind of service isn't always the most visible.

There are times when nothing is quite
as soothing as the familiar fragrance of potpourri.
Discover the Sheraton Grande.
Just fifteen minutes from Tokyo Station.
And really a world apart.

**Sheraton Grande
Tokyo Bay**
HOTEL & TOWERS

ITT Sheraton
WORLDWIDE HOTELS, INNS, RESORTS & ALL-SUITES

For more information or reservations, please call:
Hotel: 0473-55-5555
Ginza Sales Office: 03-3562-6131
Osaka Sales Office: 06-314-1019
Nagoya Sales Office: 052-972-6331

Chapter

20

The Kansai Region

Most of the chapters in this book contain information that is relevant wherever you are in Japan; however, many of the details apply specifically to the Tokyo/Yokohama area. If you are moving to the Osaka/Kobe/Kyoto region, known as Kansai, you will need additional information about your new home, which this chapter provides.

As most foreign businesspeople in Kansai live in either the Kobe area or neighboring Ashiya or Nishinomiya, much of this information relates to those areas.

Introduction

Kansai, which extends from Kyoto to Himeji, lies approximately 500 kilometers (300 miles) southwest of Tokyo and is the second largest commercial and industrial region in Japan, after Kanto. This area, because of its historical, political, and economic importance, has long attracted large numbers of tourists as well as foreign businesspeople and their families. In general, most foreigners feel that life is less hectic in Kansai than in Tokyo. Rents are somewhat lower, and it is easier to get around. The foreign community is perhaps more closely knit than that in Tokyo, and the atmosphere seems to be less formal.

The city of Kobe dates back to the fourth century, when it was established as a village called Mukonominato. In 1868, in the closing months of the Tokugawa shogunate, Kobe was one of the first ports opened to the outside world. It was then no more than a small fishing village near the Ikuta Shrine, but an excellent harbor to the south made the village attractive to foreign traders. Early descriptions and pictures of Kobe show it situated between a narrow, sandy shore of the Inland Sea and steep, pine-covered mountains to the north. With no other facilities available, early foreign residents set up their businesses and residences in rented *sake* warehouses; others lived in temples. Despite periodic typhoons and the spread of disease, trade prospered. A foreign settlement evolved in the area between what is now the Daimaru department store and the New Port Hotel, establishing its own athletic and social club, fire brigade, cemetery, and churches.

Today's Kobe, a sister city of Seattle, Marseilles, and Tientsin, is an industrial port city with a population of 1.5 million. Manufacturing is centered on shipbuilding, iron and steel, industrial vehicles, textiles, and electronics. The Kobe area is also famous for its high-quality beef and seafood as well as its *sake*.

Many of Kobe's residents, including foreigners, work in nearby Osaka, a dynamic city of over 3 million residents. Osaka is sometimes compared to Chicago because the two share a "second city" status. Osaka's diverse economic activities include both light and heavy manufacturing, pharmaceuticals, wholesaling, foreign trade, and finance.

Both Kyoto and Nara, Japan's most famous historic cities, are easily accessible from either Osaka or Kobe. The centuries-old temples and numerous festivals in these cities entice visitors to return again and again.

Kansai, with its shorelines, mountains, temples and shrines, and long, fascinating history, has much to offer the person looking for a comfortable lifestyle, pleasant surroundings, and a wealth of opportunities to enjoy a rich and varied culture. If you have a special interest in a certain aspect of this culture, all you need to do is mention it to someone; your interest will most likely be accommodated. Kansai's warmhearted and generous people are one of its greatest assets.

Many organizations are also available to provide you with various types of assistance. We strongly urge you to contact the Kansai Chapter of the ACCJ if you are considering a move to the Kansai region. It can be reached at the following address:

The American Chamber of Commerce in Japan Kansai Chapter
Business Center 301, East Court Two,
1-14, Koyocho Naka, Higashi Nada-ku, Kobe 658
Tel: (078) 857-9745   Fax: (078) 857-6714

Accommodation

The housing situation in Kansai is similar to that elsewhere in Japan; please refer to the general section on accommodation in Chapter 6 for information on finding a suitable house or apartment, rents, and practical arrangements.

Housing tends to be more expensive in Kobe than in Osaka and the surrounding area. Most Western-style housing is found to the north of the Hankyu Railway Line, on the mountainside. In Kobe, there are a number of recently built Western-style apartments with relatively large rooms, two or more bathrooms, and heating and air-conditioning systems. There are also detached houses in the outlying areas.

Rents in Kansai vary from ¥100,000 for a small Japanese-style apartment to up to ¥1.3 million for a luxury Western-style apartment.

Utilities

When you move to a new house or apartment, the landlord or real estate agent will usually take care of connecting the utilities, but the following should be noted. For the payment of bills, see the general section on utilities in Chapter 6.

Electricity

Electrical currents in Japan are not uniform. Generally speaking, western Japan, including Osaka and Kobe, uses 60 cycles and 100 volts. Some apartments in Kobe use 200 volts or 220 volts, like certain European systems. Such apartments may add an extra fee to your monthly electricity bill.

Before using any appliance, you should check whether it was made for the local current. If not, a transformer can be used to alter the current. It is inadvisable to use certain appliances, for example, a refrigerator or a computer, on the incorrect current without a transformer, as doing so may damage the motor.

The Kansai Denki Company is responsible for all electric power in the Kansai region and offers services that include checking all house wiring, fixing short circuits, and extending special wiring, among others. You can call the service telephone numbers day or night. You will need to give your code number, which is written at the top of your monthly meter slip. The telephone number of the main office is (06) 441-8821. The substations are the Sannomiya Service Station (Tel: (078) 391-6041, serving Higashi Nada, Nada, and Chuo wards) and the Hyogo Service Station (Tel: (078) 681-3151, serving Nagata, Suma, Hyogo, Tarumi, and Kita wards).

Gas

Gas equipment manufactured for use in the Kansai region differs from that manufactured for the Kanto region. It can be dangerous to use equipment designed for Tokyo in Kansai, as this may result in gas poisoning. Again, be sure to check the specifications of any appliances before buying or installing them.

The Osaka Gas Company (OGC, Emer. Tel: (06) 583-0233) has agents in every ward whom you can call to check possible defects in OGC-made stoves, heaters, and other appliances. The Shinkaichi Gas Building Service Station (Tel: (078) 576-5231) can provide the telephone number of each ward's service station.

Water

The water company (*suidokyoku*) has branch offices in every ward. When you call, be prepared to give the meter number as it appears on your bill.

Refuse Disposal

Kansai follows the same refuse disposal system as described in Chapter 6, with refuse being separated into burnable and nonburnable waste. The Kobe City authorities will not collect waste that falls outside the normal categories—such as industrial waste, inflammables, and explosives—with regular garbage. If you have to dispose of such materials, contact the Kobe Municipal Office (*shiyakusho,* Tel: (078) 331-8181) or a junkyard. Failure to comply with regulations may result in a fine of up to ¥200,000.

Postal Services

Information on foreign and domestic mail, including packages, is given in the *English Telephone Directory* —the primary reference for postal, telephone, and other services.

The main post office in Kobe is the Kobe Chuo Post Office (south of the west end of Motomachi Shopping Street), open from 8:00 A.M. to 8:00 P.M. on weekdays and from 8:00 A.M. to noon on Saturdays. Another central post office is Kobe Minato (usually referred to as the Kobe Port Post Office), behind and to the south of city hall and northwest of the U.S. consulate general. In addition to keeping the same hours as the Kobe Chuo Post Office, the Kobe Minato office is open on Sunday mornings. Both of these post offices can handle overseas packages.

Domestic Help

It may be difficult, but it is possible to find domestic help in Kansai. Many families have cleaning women who work one or two days a week, and some have live-in cooks or maids. Other families have found university students who live in and earn their room and board by helping with housework. Domestic help can be particularly valuable in dealing with tradespeople, arranging for the delivery of milk, newspapers, and heating oil, and paying monthly bills.

Daily helpers receive wages of about ¥7,000 to ¥8,000 a day plus transportation and bonuses of one month's wage in June and December. If you hire domestic help, you should consider purchasing liability insurance.

Help with home catering is also available through various foreigners' clubs and associations (see later in this chapter).

Schooling

Good educational facilities are available in the Kansai region. There are a number of international schools in Kobe (and one in Osaka) that offer educational programs in English. In Kobe, there are also German and Norwegian schools. Japanese public schools accept foreign students, but at the intermediate and upper levels language is often a problem. Because of this, virtually all foreigners enroll their children in international or foreign schools. The curriculum at the secondary level is college preparatory; however, only a limited number of programs exist for students who want a commercial or technical education. As in the Tokyo area, there are few English-speaking schools or community resources for students with major learning disabilities, emotional disturbances, or handicaps. Parents contemplating an assignment in Japan should be aware of this prior to accepting a post. See Chapter 12 for general details concerning education in Japan and for a listing of international schools, kindergartens, and nursery schools.

Medical Care and Facilities

Medical facilities in the Kobe region are listed in the Telephone Directory at the end of this book.

Reporting a Death

Procedures to be followed upon the death of a U.S. citizen are given in Chapter 15. When reporting a death in the Kansai region, the following information should be noted:

•Outside Kobe, call the police station that has jurisdiction over the area where the death occurred.

•In Kobe, call the Kobe Kaisei Hospital (Tel: (078) 871-5201). Tell the operator the name of the person who died and ask to have a doctor come to the place where the body is.

•In an emergency, when a person has been taken to another hospital and passes away there, it is still best to call the Kobe Kaisei Hospital.

Shopping
Food

There are three different types of stores for food shopping in the Kansai region: local neighborhood markets and cooperative stores, which carry a comprehensive array of daily goods but generally stock few imported goods; supermarkets, usually in the larger neighborhoods, which sell some imported commodities; and supermarkets and stores oriented specifically toward foreigners. And Kansai, like elsewhere, is not without its convenience stores every few blocks.

In the Kobe area, you will find a wide selection of food. Fresh fruit and vegetables are plentiful and of excellent quality. Some cuts of meat are not readily available; however, most butcher shops and the larger supermarkets will cut to your specification on request.

Supermarkets, such as Daiei, Japan's largest chain of supermarkets, can be found in most neighborhoods. Daiei's prices are among the cheapest, but there is no delivery, unlike with local neighborhood stores.

In addition, there are cooperative stores in almost all districts; their symbol is two standing figures in a blue circle. These offer a wide selection of reasonably priced food and other items as well as delivery services.

U.S. and European food products can be found at Hinomaru, Kobe Grocers, and Kobe Food Liner in Kobe, Ashiya, Shukugawa, Rokko, and elsewhere. These stores all offer delivery service for orders placed either by phone or in person, and English is spoken.

As in Tokyo, the basements of department stores in Kansai (Daimaru, Hankyu-Sannomiya, Rokko-Oasis, Sogo) carry an extensive selection of food—cooked, canned, fresh, and imported—but prices are slightly higher than at supermarkets.

Chinese food products are sold in the Motomachi area of Kobe, behind the Maruzen bookstore, and Indian foods and spices are also available at specialty shops.

Drugs

Although prescriptions for specific drugs are usually filled at the doctor's office, there are two discount drugstores in Kansai: Shinyakudo, which is in Santica Town, Sannomiya, off Center Gai, and the one in the basement of the Ladies' Daiei in Sannomiya.

Books, Magazines, and Newspapers

Books, periodicals, and newspapers from foreign countries can be purchased in Kansai at leading hotels and outlets of the Kinokuniya and Maruzen chains of bookstores.

English-language daily newspapers—the *Japan Times,* the *Mainichi Daily News,* the *Daily Yomiuri,* and the *Asahi Evening News*—are readily available in the Kobe area at larger newsstands and train stations. Daily delivery can also be arranged. Most are printed in a regional Osaka edition and thus contain features specific to the Kansai region in addition to the latest news.

Transportation

Getting around by train in the Kansai region can be very easy if you take the time to familiarize yourself with the signs and schedules. The Osaka/Kobe corridor is served by the Hankyu and Hanshin railway lines as well as by West Japan Railway Company (JR West). Outside that well-traveled path, several other private lines, including those operated by JR West, provide quick, convenient service to all parts of the region.

Osaka International Airport at Itami, about 40 minutes by car from Kobe or 20 minutes from downtown Osaka, serves all Kansai residents and is the region's gateway to all parts of the world. Construction of Kansai International Airport is now in progress, scheduled for completion in the summer of 1994. The new airport will be the first in Japan to operate around-the-clock.

Driving in Kansai

Driving in Kansai is basically the same as in the rest of Japan. The roads are often narrow and crowded, and everyone seems to be in a hurry. The main difference in Kobe is that almost all roads go up and down steep hills.

For details concerning licensing requirements, procedures for obtaining and maintaining a car, and traffic and parking regulations, refer to Chapter 9.

In the Osaka/Kobe area, your nearest licensing office is the Hyogo Prefectural Examination Office in Akashi.

Clubs and Associations

The three main foreigners' clubs in Kobe are the Kobe Club, Kobe Regatta and Athletic Club, and the Shioya Country Club. Each offers a wide variety of social and sports events, has recreational facilities, and features reciprocal arrangements with various affiliated clubs elsewhere in Japan, including the Tokyo American Club and the Yokohama Country and Athletic Club.

Learning about Japan

To better understand Japan, a newcomer should try to learn some of the language—at least enough to get around. There are a number of language schools in the Kansai region. These schools use different methods of instruction and vary in the intensiveness of the programs they offer. It is best to do some research and visit a few different schools before deciding which best suits you.

Many other cultural opportunities are also available for you while living in the Kansai region, for example, studying the traditional arts of *ikebana* and *shodo* or the martial arts of *aikido* and *karate*. Becoming involved in the local culture by taking advantage of some of these opportunities is sure to make your stay more rewarding and fulfilling.

Chapter

21

Sayonara

When you leave Japan, you will find that a little planning for your departure will ease the pressure associated with relocation. This final chapter of *Living in Japan* is a guide to help you say *"sayonara."*

Exit Procedures

The only government requirement for persons leaving Japan is the return of the Certificate of Alien Registration at the port of departure. If your departure is not permanent, and you plan to return to Japan on your present visa status, you must obtain a reentry permit (see Chapter 4); in this case, you will not be required to give up your alien registration card.

Health Regulations

As of this writing, the U.S. government does not require that people entering directly from Japan provide proof of vaccination against disease. However, these regulations are subject to change without notice, and you would be wise to check with the U.S. Embassy or the nearest consulate before your return. If you have recently visited other countries or plan on doing so on your way home, inoculation against smallpox, cholera, or other diseases may be necessary.

Those leaving Japan on temporary or permanent assignment to a third country should be sure to get in touch with that country's embassy or consulate to establish required health procedures.

Planning Checklist

If you are intending to leave Japan, making sure you have done the following will make your departure that much easier:

•Give your landlord as much notice as possible. Often rental agreements stipulate a certain period of notice, perhaps a month or more, and failure to comply may result in total or partial forfeiture of your deposit money.

- Arrange for utility services to be discontinued if this is necessary, but it is advisable to retain telephone service through moving day.
- Arrange for club memberships to be transferred or discontinued. If this is not possible, give notice of your intended move and request that the final bill be sent to you one week before departure. If you will be returning to Japan from time to time, you may wish to maintain your member status; some clubs do offer life memberships, and usually no dues are assessed while you are resident outside Japan.
- Go to the post office and complete a change-of-address card. The post office will not forward mail internationally, so arrange to have mail sent to your company or friends in Japan and have them forward it to you.
- Inquire about schools at your new location and the procedures for transferring children's school records. Obtain letters of introduction from their present school.
- Arrange to have medical and dental records transferred.
- Arrange shipment of your pets and their immunization records. Remember, not all countries allow importation of pets.
- Notify tax authorities and pay any unpaid tax bills.
- Arrange for the printing of change-of-address notification cards.
- Check the validity of travel documents and inoculation or vaccination certificates.
- Arrange the transfer of all your valuables, such as jewelry, coin collections, or stocks and bonds, if you are not carrying them with you on the flight.
- Find out whether your TV and other electrical appliances can be used at your new location.
- Call the city sanitation department to arrange for disposal of waste that cannot be collected as garbage. Moving companies can also dispose of unwanted furniture and other items but will likely charge more for the transportation involved than the city sanitation department does.
- Update insurance records.
- Obtain visas for your new location, if necessary.
- Obtain the necessary documentation for the importation of your household goods to your new location.
- Refill all medical prescriptions and check to see that they are refillable at your destination.

- Transfer or close bank accounts and close safe deposit boxes.
- Determine whether an import license will be needed at your new destination for the importation of alcoholic beverages. If a license is required and cannot be readily obtained, dispose of all liquor.
- Notify newspaper delivery agents and grocery stores of your move and arrange for bills to be settled before your departure.
- Arrange for the pickup of items that are to remain in storage.

The day before your move, set aside all important papers, passports, documents, valuables, money, and clothing that will be on your person. These items should be kept in a safe place where they will not be inadvertently packed with your furnishings.

Insurance coverage for your move is advisable. Prepare an inventory well in advance and obtain written appraisals for your valuables. Policy arrangements can be made through your mover or directly with your insurance agent.

If you are moving to another foreign country, research that country prior to your move. The embassy of the country can provide you with details of import regulations and general information that may save you time and expense.

Household Goods and Personal Effects

Disposing of the unwanted goods and effects that you have accumulated during your tenure in Japan can prove to be a bit of a headache, but you have several options:

- Charitable donations. Charity is a Western concept that has not really caught on in Japan; there are relatively few private organizations dedicated to the support of the needy. Japan is an affluent country, and the government welfare system is generally considered to be more than adequate, although as in any other developed country, there are some homeless people and vagrants who may not be eligible for welfare benefits. Churches and international schools often hold white elephant sales, the proceeds from which are put toward worthy causes. The Salvation Army is also quite active, and they can arrange to pick up unwanted clothes or furnishings. In Tokyo, the Salvation Army's headquarters is located at 2-27, Kanda Jimbocho, Chiyoda-ku, Tokyo 101 (Tel: (03) 3237-0881).
- "*Sayonara* sales." International supermarkets, such as the National Azabu Supermarket, and some clubs often have bulletin boards on which you can post a notice listing items that you want to sell or give away. English-language newspapers and magazines

also have columns advising readers of *sayonara* sales. Many of the secondhand bookstores in the Jimbocho area of Tokyo buy used English-language books in either paperback or hardcover, although they don't pay much.

Moving

The easiest and most efficient way to move your household goods and personal effects is with a professional moving company; however, this is expensive. Many departing expats have all or part of their moving expenses paid by their employer. In some cases, the employer makes all arrangements with a moving company; in other cases, the employee must make arrangements privately. When selecting a moving company, be sure to choose one that has overseas offices.

Air deliveries are fast. Since they are much more expensive than surface shipments, it is best to include only things you will absolutely need upon arrival at your destination. Important papers and clothing, for example, are items that you might well want to send by air. Surface shipments can be arranged in a number of ways to suit your needs. It is best to consult your mover for details.

The cost of small shipments is often more than the value of the goods they contain. This is especially true if you ship only a few boxes of used clothing, books, and mementos of Japan. In this case, it is often cheaper to use surface mail. Check with the nearest large post office as to the size and weight limitations for each box. Mark your goods "used clothing and personal effects" to avoid delays at customs and possible duty assessments at the port of entry to the United States.

U.S. Customs and Import Regulations

The regulations covering the importation of goods into the United States are comprehensive. U.S. customs inspectors enforce not only customs regulations but also many of the laws and requirements of other government agencies. Listed here are a few general guidelines. Specific details on other points may be obtained from the U.S. Embassy in Tokyo or from the nearest U.S. consular offices in other areas of Japan.

Used household effects, including housekeeping equipment, books, standard furniture, and linen, can generally be brought into the United States duty free, if the goods were actually used abroad by the family for a period of not less than one year and are not intended for any other persons nor for resale.

Some items, however, such as jewelry, photographic equipment, stereo components, motor vehicles, boats, and consumable items, cannot be passed free of duty as household goods. The U.S. Customs Service considers these items to be personal effects. Any item that appears to be new may be questioned. Keep the bill of sale for all such items in case you are required to show evidence.

Prohibited Items

- Most agricultural products, such as fruit, vegetables, plants, poultry, and meat or meat products
- Endangered species or their by-products
- Organic materials harmful to public health or agriculture
- Birds, monkeys and other primates, and turtles
- Hazardous articles and substances, such as narcotics and dangerous drugs, absinthe, toxic and poisonous substances, switchblade knives, fireworks, and dangerous toys
- Seditious and treasonable materials
- Obscene articles and publications
- Products made by forced labor or in prisons
- Books, records, software, or other items that violate copyright laws

Restricted Items

- Agricultural Items. Food, plants, and animals and their by-products are subject to restrictions and inspection and require export permits from the country of origin and import permits. (For further information, contact APHIS, Department of Agriculture, Hyattsville, Maryland.)
- Currency. More than $10,000 or the equivalent in U.S. or foreign currency, traveler's checks, money orders, and negotiable instruments or investment securities in bearer form must be reported to customs. It is not illegal to transport or to cause to be transported any amount into or out of the United States, but amounts over $10,000 must be reported on Customs Form 4790, available at all U.S. ports of entry.
- Automobiles. Unless you have diplomatic status in Japan, you cannot purchase an export model of a Japanese car in Japan. To ship home a Japanese domestic-model car will require extensive and expensive modification of the vehicle. (For further information, contact the Environmental Protection Agency, Washington, D.C.; and the Department of Transportation, Washington, D.C.)

• Research Materials. Disease organisms and vectors for research or educational purposes require import permits. (For further information, contact Foreign Quarantine Program, U.S. Public Health Service, Center for Disease Control, Atlanta, Georgia; and APHIS, Department of Agriculture, Hyattsville, Maryland.)

• Cultural Treasures, Art, or Artifacts. Especially pre-Columbian. Check with U.S. customs and the country of export for special requirements.

• Firearms and Ammunition. Subject to restrictions and import permits. (For further information, contact the Bureau of Alcohol, Tobacco and Firearms, Department of the Treasury, Washington, D.C.)

• Medicines Containing Narcotics. Strictly controlled with severe penalties. If you require medicines containing habit-forming drugs or narcotics (for example, cough medicines, diuretics, heart drugs, tranquilizers, sleeping pills, depressants, stimulants), you should have a prescription or written statement from your physician that the medicine is being used under a doctor's direction and that it is necessary for your physical well-being while traveling, and you must carry drugs in their original containers.

• Merchandise Originating in North Korea, Iran, Iraq, Vietnam, Cambodia, or Cuba (and all goods containing Cuban components). Subject to restriction and require import licenses. (For further information, contact the Office of Foreign Assets Control, Department of the Treasury, Washington, D.C. Request FAC Regulations and Cuban Assets Control regulations.)

• Foreign-Made Items. Some articles may be restricted by trademark owner. (Obtain the Customs Service's leaflet *Trademark Information for Travelers* from the U.S. Embassy or the nearest consulate.)

Special Notes about U.S. Customs

You are unlikely to have any problems with U.S. customs when you ship your effects back home, provided your shipment consists of standard household effects in normal and usual quantities. There are a few special items, however, that may require special attention.

• Ivory. African and Asian ivory is obtained from endangered species of elephants. If you possess large amounts of either African or Asian ivory, you will need to check with U.S. customs authorities. The importation of ivory may be restricted or prohibited, depending upon the type of ivory and the year you acquired it.

• Computers. Personal computers used at home by you and your family can easily be included in your shipment. There are no special restrictions on taking computers or software into the United States, provided the software is not pirated. Pirated versions are subject to confiscation.

• *Tatami* Mats and Stone Lanterns. *Tatami* mats must be fumigated for entry into the United States. A certificate of fumigation should be attached to your packing list. Brand new stone lanterns are no problem, but if you take one that has moss growing on it, the lantern should be steamed, cleaned, and fumigated.

• Pets. All pets and animals are subject to quarantine. The length of quarantine varies from state to state, Hawaii having the longest (120 days for dogs and cats). Proof of rabies vaccination and a certificate of good health are required.

By carefully following the steps outlined in this chapter, you should have no trouble upon your return to the United States.

YOUR MOVE DESERVES THE BEST

The
ODEK
team

ODAWARA UNYU MOVING CO., LTD.
INTERNATIONAL ACCOUNT SERVICES DEPARTMENT

(03) 3763-6141

Telephone Directory

Emergencies

Police   110
Fire & Ambulance   119
Hospital Information (Tokyo)   (03) 3212-2323

Other Telephone Services and Information

Japan Helpline   (0120) 46-1997 (24-hour, toll-free)
NTT Information (domestic
  telephone inquiries)   104
                                    (03) 3277-1010 (Tokyo)
                                    (045) 322-1010 (Yokohama)
Police (general information)   (03) 3501-0110 (Tokyo)
Time   117
Tokyo Alcoholics Anonymous   (03) 3971-1471
Tokyo English Life Line (TELL)   (03) 5481-4347
Weather   177
                                    (03) 3755-7111
                                       (Yokota Air Base)

Immigration and Other Government Offices

Tokyo Regional Immigration
  Office (Otemachi)   (03) 3213-8111
      Hakozaki Branch Office   (03) 3664-3046
      Visa Information   (03) 3213-8523~7
Yokohama Immigration Bureau   (045) 681-6801

Embassies

Afghanistan   (03) 3407-7900
Algeria   (03) 3711-2661
Argentina   (03) 5420-7101
Australia   (03) 5232-4111
Austria   (03) 3451-8281~3
Bangladesh   (03) 3442-1501
Belgium   (03) 3262-0191~5
Belize   (03) 3443-0338
Bolivia   (03) 3499-5441/2
Brazil   (03) 3404-5211~8
Brunei Darussalam   (03) 3447-7997
Bulgaria   (03) 3465-1021~4
Canada   (03) 3408-2101
Central Africa   (03) 3485-7591
Chile   (03) 3452-7561/2
China   (03) 3403-3380
Colombia   (03) 3440-6451, 6491
Costa Rica   (03) 3486-1812
Côte d'Ivoire   (03) 3499-7021~3
Cuba   (03) 3716-3112
Cyprus   (03) 3347-2247

Czech Republic	(03) 3400-8122, 8123, 8125
Denmark	(03) 3496-3001
Dominican Republic	(03) 3499-6020
Ecuador	(03) 3499-2800, 2866
Egypt	(03) 3770-8021~3
El Salvador	(03) 3499-4461
Ethiopia	(03) 3718-1003~5
Fiji	(03) 3587-2038
Finland	(03) 3442-2231
France	(03) 5420-8800
Gabon	(03) 3448-9540
Gambia	(03) 3444-7806
Germany	(03) 3473-0151~7
Ghana	(03) 3710-8831~3
Greece	(03) 3403-0871
Guatemala	(03) 3400-1830, 1820
Guinea	(03) 3769-0451
Guyana	(03) 3588-2222
Haiti	(03) 3486-7070, 7096
Holy See (Vatican City)	(03) 3263-6851~3
Honduras	(03) 3409-1150
Hong Kong (tourist information)	(03) 3503-0731
Hungary	(03) 3798-8801~4
Iceland (consulate)	(03) 5493-8776
India	(03) 3262-2391~7
Indonesia	(03) 3441-4201
Iran	(03) 3446-8011
Iraq	(03) 3423-1727
Ireland	(03) 3263-0695
Israel	(03) 3264-0911~5
Italy	(03) 3453-5291~6
Jamaica	(03) 5466-4120
Jordan	(03) 3580-5856~8
Kenya	(03) 3723-4006
Kiribati (consulate)	(03) 3201-3487
Korea, South	(03) 3452-7611~9
Kuwait	(03) 3455-0361/2
Laos	(03) 5411-2291
Lebanon	(03) 3580-1227, 1206
Liberia	(03) 3441-7138, 7169
Libya	(03) 3477-0701~4
Luxembourg	(03) 3265-9621~3
Macao (tourist information)	(03) 3501-5022
Madagascar	(03) 3446-7252/3
Malaysia	(03) 3476-3840
Malta (consulate)	(03) 3917-1161
Mariana Islands (tourist information)	(03) 3582-5781
Mauritania	(03) 3449-3810
Mauritius (consulate)	(03) 3211-8569
Mexico	(03) 3581-1131~5
Monaco (consulate)	(03) 3211-4994
Mongolia	(03) 3469-2088

Morocco	(03) 3478-3271~4
Myanmar	(03) 3441-9291~5
Nepal	(03) 3705-5558/9
Netherlands	(03) 5401-0411~5
New Zealand	(03) 3467-2271
Nicaragua	(03) 3499-0400
Niger	(03) 3505-6371
Nigeria	(03) 5721-5391
Norway	(03) 3440-2611
Oman	(03) 3402-0877, 0749
Pakistan	(03) 3454-4861~4
Panama	(03) 3499-3741/2
Papua New Guinea	(03) 3454-7801~4
Paraguay	(03) 5570-4307
Peru	(03) 3406-4240~3
Philippines	(03) 3496-2731~6
Poland	(03) 3711-5224~6
Portugal	(03) 3400-7907/8
Puerto Rico (tourist information)	(03) 3213-5206
Qatar	(03) 3446-7561/2
Romania	(03) 3479-0311~3
Russian Federation	(03) 3583-4224
Rwanda	(03) 3486-7800/1
St. Lucia (consulate)	(03) 3587-1011
St. Vincent (consulate)	(03) 3587-1011
San Marino	(03) 3498-8427
Saudi Arabia	(03) 3589-5241
Senegal	(03) 3464-8451
Seychelles (consulate)	(03) 3379-2255
Singapore	(03) 3586-9111
Slovak Republic	(03) 3400-8122, 8123, 8125
Solomon Islands	(03) 3562-2331
South Africa	(03) 3265-3366~9
Spain	(03) 3583-8531~3
Sri Lanka	(03) 3585-7431
Sudan	(03) 3476-0811
Swaziland	(03) 3864-2075
Sweden	(03) 5562-5050
Switzerland	(03) 3473-0121
Syria	(03) 3586-8977
Tahiti	(03) 3265-0468
Taiwan (de facto embassy)	(03) 3280-7811
Tanzania	(03) 3425-4531~3
Thailand	(03) 3441-7352
Tonga (consulate)	(03) 3502-2371
Tunisia	(03) 3353-4111~3
Turkey	(03) 3470-5131, 6380
Tuvalu (consulate)	(03) 3201-0884
Uganda	(03) 5493-5690
United Arab Emirates	(03) 5489-0804
United Kingdom	(03) 3265-5511
United States	(03) 3224-5000

Uruguay	(03) 3486-1750, 1888
Venezuela	(03) 3409-1501/2
Vietnam	(03) 3466-3311
Western Samoa (consulate)	(03) 3211-7604
Yemen	(03) 3499-7151/2
Yugoslavia	(03) 3447-3571~3
Zaire	(03) 3423-3981~3
Zambia	(03) 3445-1041, 1043
Zimbabwe	(03) 3280-0331/2

Tokyo Ward Offices

Tokyo Metropolitan Government	(03) 5321-1111
Adachi	(03) 3882-1111
Arakawa	(03) 3802-3111
Bunkyo	(03) 3812-7111
Chiyoda	(03) 3264-0151
Chuo	(03) 3543-0211
Edogawa	(03) 3652-1151
Itabashi	(03) 3964-1111
Katsushika	(03) 3695-1111
Kita	(03) 3908-1111
Koto	(03) 3647-9111
Meguro	(03) 3715-1111
Minato	(03) 3578-2111
Nakano	(03) 3389-1111
Nerima	(03) 3993-1111
Ota	(03) 3773-5111
Setagaya	(03) 3412-1111
Shibuya	(03) 3463-1211
Shinagawa	(03) 3777-1111
Shinjuku	(03) 3209-1111
Suginami	(03) 3312-2111
Sumida	(03) 5608-1111
Taito	(03) 5246-1111
Toshima	(03) 3981-1111

Tokyo City Offices

Akikawa	(0425) 58-1111
Akishima	(0425) 44-5111
Chofu	(0424) 81-7111
Fuchu	(0423) 64-4111
Fussa	(0425) 51-1511
Hachioji	(0426) 26-3111
Higashi-Kurume	(0424) 73-5111
Higashi-Murayama	(0423) 93-5111
Higashi-Yamato	(0425) 63-2111
Hino	(0425) 85-1111
Hoya	(0424) 21-2525
Inagi	(0423) 78-2111

Itsukaichi	(0425) 96-1511
Kiyose	(0424) 92-5111
Kodaira	(0423) 41-1211
Koganei	(0423) 83-1111
Kokubunji	(0423) 25-0111
Komae	(03) 3430-1111
Kunitachi	(0425) 76-2111
Machida	(0427) 22-3111
Mitaka	(0422) 45-1151
Musashi-Murayama	(0425) 65-1111
Musashino	(0422) 51-5131
Ome	(0428) 22-1111
Tachikawa	(0425) 23-2111
Tama	(0423) 75-8111
Tanashi	(0424) 64-1311

Medical Services (Tokyo)

AIDS Hotline	(03) 3359-2477
American Pharmacy	(03) 3271-4034
Central Clinic	(03) 3571-2841
International Catholic Hospital (Seibo Byoin)	(03) 3951-1111
International Clinic	(03) 3583-7831
International Medical Information Center	(03) 3706-4243
Japanese Red Cross Medical Center	(03) 3400-1311
Jikei University Hospital	(03) 3433-1111
Juntendo University Hospital	(03) 3813-3111
Keio University Hospital	(03) 3353-1211 (day)
	(03) 3353-1208 (night)
Kyorin University Hospital	(0422) 47-5511
Medical Dispensary	(03) 3434-5817
Musashino Red Cross Hospital	(0422) 32-3111
National Azabu Pharmacy	(03) 3442-3181
National Cancer Center	(03) 3542-2511
National Medical Clinic	(03) 3473-2057
Roppongi Pharmacy	(03) 3403-8880
St. Luke's International Hospital (Seiroka Byoin)	(03) 3541-5151
Saiseikai Central Hospital	(03) 3451-8211
Sanno Clinic	(03) 3402-3151
The Second National Tokyo Hospital	(03) 3411-0111
Tokyo British Clinic	(03) 5458-6099
Tokyo Clinic Dental Office	(03) 3431-4225
Tokyo Maternity Clinic	(03) 3403-1861

Tokyo Medical and
Surgical Clinic   (03) 3436-3028
Tokyo Metropolitan Hiroo
General Hospital   (03) 3444-1181
Tokyo Metropolitan Police
Hospital   (03) 3263-1371
Tokyo Sanitarium Hospital
(Tokyo Eisei Byoin)   (03) 3392-6151
Tokyo University Hospital   (03) 3815-5411
Tokyo Women's Medical
College Hospital   (03) 3353-8111

Medical Services (Yokohama)

Altinbay Clinic   (045) 681-2113
Bluff Clinic   (045) 641-6961 (day)
                                  (045) 641-6964 (night)
Seishindo Pharmacy   (045) 314-9009
Yokohama City University
Hospital   (045) 261-5656

Medical Services (Kobe)

Kobe Adventist Hospital   (078) 981-0161
Kobe Central Municipal Hospital   (078) 302-4321
Kobe Kaisei Hospital   (078) 871-5201
Kobe University Hospital   (078) 341-7451
Konan Hospital   (078) 851-2161
Miyaji Hospital   (078) 451-1221
Rokko Island Hospital   (078) 858-1111

Religious Organizations (Tokyo)

Ahmadiyya Moslem Center   (03) 3849-7899
Arabic Islamic Institute   (03) 3370-5995
Assemblies of God   (0425) 51-0966
Atonement Evangelical
Lutheran Church   (0424) 71-1855
Bahai Faith   (03) 3209-7521
Calvary Conservative
Baptist Church   (0425) 57-0654
Church of Christ   (03) 3291-0478
Church of Jesus Christ
of Latter-Day Saints   (03) 3496-6337
Church of St. Mary's   (03) 3396-0305
Denenchofu Lutheran Church   (03) 3721-4716
First Church of Christ
Scientist   (03) 3499-3951
Franciscan Chapel Center   (03) 3401-2141
Friends Jido Center   (03) 3203-7245
Full Gospel Tokyo Church   (03) 3357-2106

International Christian Assembly	(03) 3940-6691
International Christian University Church	(0422) 33-3323
Islamic Center Japan	(03) 3460-6169
Japan Buddhist Federation	(03) 3437-9275
Japan Islamic Congress Majid	(03) 3205-1313
Japan Lutheran Church	(03) 3261-5266
Japan Muslim Association	(03) 3370-3476
Jewish Community of Japan	(03) 3400-2559
Jinja Honcho (United Shinto Shrines Association)	(03) 3379-8011
Kanto Plains Baptist Church	(0425) 51-1915
Kurume Bible Fellowship	(0424) 73-9259
New Otani Garden Chapel	(03) 3265-1111
Ochanomizu Christian Center	(03) 3296-1001
Orthodox Church	(03) 3295-6879
Religious Society of Friends	(03) 3451-7002
Russian Orthodox Church	(03) 3341-2281
St. Alban's Anglican Episcopal Church	(03) 3431-8534
St. Andrew's Church	(03) 3431-2822
St. Anselm's Priory	(03) 3491-5461
St. Ignatius Church	(03) 3263-4584
St. Luke's Chapel	(03) 3541-5151
St. Paul Evangelical Lutheran Church	(03) 3261-3740
Salvation Army	(03) 3237-0881
Shalom Church Shinjuku	(03) 3371-7558
Shibuya Catholic Church	(03) 3463-5881
Sri Sathya Shi Center	(03) 3447-0408
Tokyo Baptist Church	(03) 3461-8425
Tokyo International Church	(03) 3464-4512
Tokyo Lutheran Church	(0422) 55-1682
Tokyo Mosque	(03) 3469-0284
Tokyo Union Church	(03) 3400-0047
Tokyo Unitarian Fellowship	(03) 3392-2227
Tsukiji Honganji	(03) 3843-9511
Watch Tower Bible & Tract Society	(03) 3453-0404
West Tokyo Union Church	(0422) 33-0993
Yokota Baptist Church	(0425) 53-2577
Yokota Church of Christ	(0425) 52-7964

Tourist Information

Asakusa Tourist Information Center	(03) 3842-5566 (Tokyo)
Atami City Tourist Information Association—Izu	(0557) 85-2222
Fuji Visitor's Center	(0555) 72-0259
Ito Tourist Association (Izu)	(0555) 37-6105

JNTO Tourist Information Centers (TICs):

Tokyo	(03) 3502-1461
Kyoto	(075) 371-5649
Narita	(0476) 32-8711

Japan Travel Phone—Toll Free
  Tourist & Travel Information:

Eastern Japan	(0120) 222-800
Western Japan	(0120) 444-800
Kamakura Tourist Association	(0467) 22-3350
Kanagawa Prefectural Tourist Assocation	(045) 681-0007
Shimoda City Tourist Association	(0558) 22-1531
Teletourist (current local events)	(03) 3503-2911 (Tokyo)
Yokohama International Tourist Association	(045) 641-5824

Transportation Information (Tokyo)

Flight Information:

Haneda	(03) 3747-8010
Narita	(0476) 32-2800
Tokyo City Air Terminal (TCAT)	(03) 3665-7156
JR East Infoline	(03) 3423-0111

Lost & Found:

Eidan (Teito) Subways	(03) 3834-5577
JR	(03) 3231-1880
Taxi	(03) 3648-0300
Toei bus/subway	(03) 3818-5760

Road Traffic Information:

Tokyo	(03) 3581-7611
Highway	(03) 3264-1331
Subway Information Service	(03) 3837-7111

International Airlines (Tokyo)

Aeroflot	(03) 3434-9671
Air France	(03) 3475-1511
Air India	(03) 3214-7631
Airlanka	(03) 3573-4261
Air New Zealand	(03) 3287-1641
Alitalia Air Lines	(03) 3580-2181
All Nippon Airways	(03) 3272-1212
American Airlines	(03) 3248-2011
British Airways	(03) 3593-8811
CAAC	(03) 3505-2021
Canadian Airlines International	(03) 3281-7426
Cathay Pacific Airways	(03) 3504-1531
China Airlines	(03) 3436-1661
Continental Airlines	(03) 3592-1631
Delta Air Lines	(03) 5275-7000
Egypt Air	(03) 3211-4521
Finnair	(03) 3222-6801

Garuda Indonesian Airways	(03) 3593-1181
Iberia Airlines of Spain	(03) 3582-3631
Iran Air	(03) 3586-2101
Iraqi Airways	(03) 3264-5503
Japan Airlines	(03) 5489-1111
Japan Air System	(03) 3438-1155
Japan Asia Airways	(03) 3455-7511
KLM Royal Dutch Airlines	(03) 3216-0771
Korean Air	(03) 5443-3311
Lufthansa German Airlines	(03) 3580-2111
Malaysia Airlines	(03) 3503-5961
Northwest Airlines	(03) 3533-6000
Pakistan International Airlines	(03) 3216-6511
Qantas Airways	(03) 3503-7000
Sabena Belgian World Airlines	(03) 3585-6151
Scandinavian Airlines System	(03) 3503-8101
Singapore Airlines	(03) 3213-3431
Swiss Air	(03) 3212-1016
Thai Airways International	(03) 3503-3311
United Airlines	(03) 3817-4411
Varig Brazilian Airlines	(03) 3211-6751
Virgin Atlantic Airways	(03) 5269-2680

Domestic Airlines (Tokyo)

All Nippon Airways	(03) 5489-8800
Japan Airlines	(03) 5489-2111
Japan Air System	(03) 3432-6111

Hotels in Tokyo

Akasaka Prince Hotel	(03) 3234-1111
Akasaka Tokyu Hotel	(03) 3580-2311
Akihabara Washington Hotel	(03) 3255-3311
ANA Hotel Tokyo	(03) 3505-1111
Asakusa View Hotel	(03) 3847-1111
Atagoyama Tokyu Inn	(03) 3431-0109
Azabu City Hotel	(03) 3453-4311
Belmonte Hotel	(03) 3864-7733
Capitol Tokyu Hotel	(03) 3581-4511
Century Hyatt Tokyo	(03) 3349-0111
Dai-ichi Hotel Annex	(03) 3503-5611
Dai-ichi Inn Ikebukuro	(03) 3986-1221
Dai-ichi Inn Omori	(03) 3768-3111
Fairmont Hotel	(03) 3262-1151
Four Seasons Hotel Chinzan-so	(03) 3943-2222
Gajoen Kanko Hotel	(03) 3491-0111
Ginza Capital Hotel	(03) 3543-8211
Ginza Dai-ichi Hotel	(03) 3542-5311
Ginza Marunouchi Hotel	(03) 3543-5431
Ginza Nikko Hotel	(03) 3571-4911
Ginza Tobu Ramada Renaissance Hotel	(03) 3546-0111

Ginza Tokyu Hotel	(03) 3541-2411
Haneda Tokyu Hotel	(03) 3747-0311
Harumi Grand Hotel	(03) 3533-7111
Hibiya Park Hotel	(03) 3503-0111
Hill-Top Hotel	(03) 3293-2311
Holiday Inn Tokyo	(03) 3553-6161
Hotel Edmont	(03) 3237-1111
Hotel Grand Business	(03) 3984-5121
Hotel Grand-Palace	(03) 3264-1111
Hotel IBIS	(03) 3403-4411
Hotel Kayu Kaikan	(03) 3230-1111
Hotel Laforet Tokyo	(03) 5488-3911
Hotel Lungwood	(03) 3803-1234
Hotel Metropolitan	(03) 3980-1111
Hotel New Otani	(03) 3265-1111
Hotel Nikko Narita	(0476) 32-0032
Hotel Okura	(03) 3582-0111
Hotel Pacific Meridien Tokyo	(03) 3445-6711
Hotel Sunlite	(03) 3356-0391
Hotel Takanawa	(03) 5488-1000
Hotel Toshi Center	(03) 3265-8211
Imperial Hotel	(03) 3504-1111
Keio Plaza Intercontinental Hotel	(03) 3344-0111
Kichijoji Tokyu Inn	(0422) 47-0109
Makuhari Prince Hotel	(0472) 96-1111
Marunouchi Hotel	(03) 3543-5431
Meguro Gajoen	(03) 3491-4111
Mitsui Urban Hotel Ginza	(03) 3572-4131
Miyako Hotel Tokyo	(03) 3447-3111
Miyako Inn Tokyo	(03) 3454-3111
Narita Tokyu	(0476) 33-0109
Narita View Hotel	(0476) 32-1111
New Sanno U.S. Forces Center	(03) 3440-7871
New Takanawa Prince Hotel	(03) 3442-1111
Omori Tokyu Inn	(03) 3768-0109
Palace Hotel	(03) 3211-5211
President Hotel	(03) 3497-0111
Roppongi Prince Hotel	(03) 3587-1111
Royal Park Hotel	(03) 3667-1111
Ryogoku Pearl Hotel	(03) 3626-3211
Sheraton Grande Tokyo Bay	(0473) 55-5555
Shiba Park Hotel	(03) 3433-4141
Shibuya Tobu Hotel	(03) 3476-0111
Shimbashi Dai-ichi Hotel	(03) 3501-4411
Shinagawa Prince Hotel	(03) 3440-1111
Shinjuku Prince Hotel	(03) 3205-1111
Shinjuku Washington Hotel	(03) 3343-3111
Sunplaza Hotel	(03) 3388-1151
Sunshine City Prince Hotel	(03) 3988-1111
Takanawa Prince Hotel	(03) 3447-1111
Tokyo Bay Hilton Hotel	(0473) 55-5000
Tokyo Hilton Hotel	(03) 3344-5111

Tokyo Hotel Urashima	(03) 3533-3111
Tokyo Prince Hotel	(03) 3432-1111
Tokyo Station Hotel	(03) 3231-2511
Yaesu Fujiya Hotel	(03) 3273-2111
Yaesu Terminal Hotel	(03) 3281-3771

Hotels in Yokohama

Shin Yokohama Prince Hotel	(045) 471-1111
Yokohama Isezakicho Washington Hotel	(045) 243-7111
Yokohama Prince Hotel	(045) 751-1111

Hotels in Kobe

Arima Grand Hotel	(078) 904-0181
Business Hotel Koshien	(0798) 48-0333
Chisan Hotel Kobe	(078) 341-8111
Dai-ichi Grand Hotel	(078) 331-5550
Hotel Kobe	(078) 221-5431
Hotel Okura Kobe	(078) 333-0111
Kobe Gajoen Hotel	(078) 341-0301
Kobe Hana Hotel	(078) 221-1087
Kobe Tokyu Inn	(078) 291-0109
Kobe Towerside Hotel	(078) 351-2151
Kobe Union Hotel	(078) 222-6500
Kobe Washington Hotel	(078) 331-6111
Oriental Hotel	(078) 331-8111
Rokko Oriental Hotel	(078) 891-0333
Rokkosan Hotel	(078) 891-0301
Sannomiya Terminal Hotel	(078) 291-0001

Hotels in Osaka

Airport Prince Hotel	(0724) 63-2235
ANA-Sheraton Hotel Osaka	(06) 347-1112
Ark Hotel	(06) 252-5111
Business Hotel Precontract Center	(06) 311-0909
Business Hotel Princess	(0724) 38-7810
Chisan Hotel Shinsaibashi	(06) 263-1511
City Route Hotel	(06) 448-1000
East Hotel	(06) 364-1151
Esaka Central Hotel	(06) 339-0088
Esaka Tokyu Inn	(06) 338-0109
Holiday Inn Nankai Osaka	(06) 213-8281
Hotel Airport Fuji	(06) 843-8811
Hotel Echo Osaka	(06) 633-1141
Hotel Hanshin	(06) 344-1661
Hotel Kansai	(06) 312-7971
Hotel Keihan Osaka	(06) 945-0321
Hotel New Hankyu	(06) 372-5101
Hotel New Hankyu Annex	(06) 372-5101

Hotel New Otani Osaka	(06) 941-1111
Hotel Parkside	(06) 386-9191
Hotel Sun Route Sakai	(0722) 32-0303
Hotel Sun Route Umeda	(06) 373-1111
Hotel Sun White	(06) 942-3711
Hotel The Lutheran	(06) 942-2281
International Hotel Osaka	(06) 941-2661
Mitsui Garden Hotel	(06) 223-1131
Mitsui Urban Hotel Osaka	(06) 374-1111
Miyako Hotel Osaka	(06) 773-1111
New Oriental Hotel	(06) 538-7141
New Osaka Hotel	(06) 305-2345
Osaka Airport Hotel	(06) 885-4621
Osaka Castle Hotel	(06) 942-2401
Osaka Dai-ichi Hotel	(06) 341-4411
Osaka Fujiya Hotel	(06) 211-5522
Osaka Garden Palace	(06) 396-6211
Osaka Grand Hotel	(06) 202-1212
Osaka Green Hotel	(06) 532-1091
Osaka Hilton International	(06) 347-7111
Osaka Riverside Hotel	(06) 928-3251
Osaka Teikoku Hotel	(06) 211-8151
Osaka Terminal Hotel	(06) 344-1235
Osaka Tokyu Hotel	(06) 373-2411
Osaka Tokyu Inn	(06) 315-0109
Plaza Osaka	(06) 303-1000
Royal Hotel	(06) 448-1121
Senri Hankyu Hotel	(06) 872-2211
Tennoji Miyako Hotel	(06) 779-1501

Japanese National Holidays

There are 13 national holidays in Japan. If a national holiday falls on a Sunday, the following Monday is a compensatory day off. May 4, which falls between Constitution Day and Children's Day, is also a national holiday, although it has no specific title; the week commencing April 29, with its four national holidays, is known as Golden Week, and many private companies are closed for the whole period.

There is only one official national holiday for New Year (January 1), but most government offices and private companies are closed for at least four or five days.

The current national holidays are as follows:

January 1   *Gantan,* or New Year's Day.

January 15   *Seijin no Hi,* or Coming of Age Day.
Young people who have turned 20, the legal age of majority, in the preceding year dress in *kimono* and attend ceremonies at local government offices, shrines, and other locations.

February 11   *Kenkoku Kinenbi,* or National Foundation Day.
A prewar holiday reinstituted in 1966, this day commemorates the foundation of Japan as a nation (according to legend, in 560 B.C.).

March 21   *Shunbun no Hi,* or the Vernal Equinox.
Traditionally, Japanese people visit and attend to the graves of their ancestors on this day.

April 29   *Midori no Hi,* or Greenery Day.
This day was originally celebrated to mark the birthday of the Showa emperor, who died in 1989. The late emperor was a respected amateur botanist, and the day is now equivalent to the American Arbor Day, with tree-planting ceremonies being held across the nation.

May 3	*Kenpo Kinenbi,* or Constitution Day. This holiday commemorates the promulgation of the new constitution, in 1947.
May 4	Special national holiday linking the holidays on May 3 and May 5.
May 5	*Kodomo no Hi,* or Children's Day.
September 15	*Keiro no Hi,* or Respect for the Aged Day. This holiday honors all citizens over 65 years of age, and special events and parties are held for centenarians.
September 23	*Shubun no Hi,* or the Autumnal Equinox. As on the Vernal Equinox, people visit and attend to the graves of their ancestors.
October 10	*Taiiku no Hi,* or Sports and Physical Fitness Day. This holiday commemorates the opening of the 1964 Tokyo Olympics. Sports festivals and athletic meets are held all over the country.
November 3	*Bunka no Hi,* or Culture Day. This is one of the oldest national holidays; it is also the anniversary of the birth, in 1852, of the Meiji emperor. Oustanding performers and artists are honored on this day.
November 23	*Kinro Kansha no Hi,* or Labor Thanksgiving Day.
December 23	*Tenno Tanjobi,* or the Emperor's Birthday.

Bibliography

Accessible Medical Services for Foreign Residents of Tokyo,
The Metropolitan Tokyo Research Team to Study The Medical System
for The Foreign Community (Dai-Ichi-Hokai Shuppan)

The American Medical Association Family Medical Guide,
The American Medical Association (Random House)

The Anatomy of Dependence, Takeo Doi (Kodansha International)

Business Practices & Taxation in Japan, Takashi Kuboi
(The Japan Times)

Day Walks Near Tokyo, Gary D'A. Walters (Kodansha)

Discover Shitamachi: The Walking Guide to the Other Tokyo,
Sumiko Enbutsu (The Shitamachi Times)

Employment Practices of American Companies in Japan,
Towers, Perrin, Forster & Crosby and the American Chamber of
Commerce in Japan (The American Chamber of Commerce in Japan,
Gakken)

Exporting to Japan, Richard A. Bush (The American Chamber
of Commerce in Japan)

A Guide to Food Buying in Japan, Carolyn R. Krouse (Tuttle)

How to Do Business with the Japanese: A Strategy for Success,
Mark Zimmerman (Tuttle)

Japan as It Is (Gakken)

Japan Cheap and Easy, J. Robert Magee (Yohan)

***Japanese Business Etiquette: A Practical Guide to Business &
Social Success with the Japanese,*** Diana Rowland (Warner Books)

The Japanese Century, Thomas R. Zengage and C. Tait Ratcliffe
(Longman Group (Far East Ltd.))

The Japanese Inn, Oliver Statler (Tuttle)

The Japan Experience: Coping and Beyond, Tazuko Shibusawa and Joy Norton (The Japan Times)

Japan for Kids: The Ultimate Guide for Parents and Their Children, Diane Wiltshire Kanagawa and Jeanne Huey Erickson (Kodansha)

Japan Inside Out, Jay & Sumi & Garet Gluck (Personally Oriented)

Japan Posting (The British Chamber of Commerce)

Kaizen: The Key to Japan's Competitive Success, Masaaki Imai (McGraw-Hill International Editions)

Labor Pains and the Gaijin Boss: Hiring, Managing and Firing the Japanese, Thomas J. Nevins (The Japan Times)

Living for Less in Tokyo and Liking It!, Dial Service Co., Ltd. (ASK Kodansha)

Living in Kobe (CHIC)

Living in Tokyo (Tokyo Metropolitan Government)

More Footloose in Tokyo, Jean Pearce (Weatherhill)

Never Take Yes for an Answer, Masaaki Imai (Simul Press)

A Parents' Guide to Tokyo, Nancy Hartzenbusch and Alice Shabecoff (Shufunotomo)

The Shimoda Story, Oliver Statler (Tuttle)

16 Ways to Avoid Saying No, Masaaki Imai (Nihon Keizai)

TELL International Community Calendar (TELL)

Subways in Tokyo

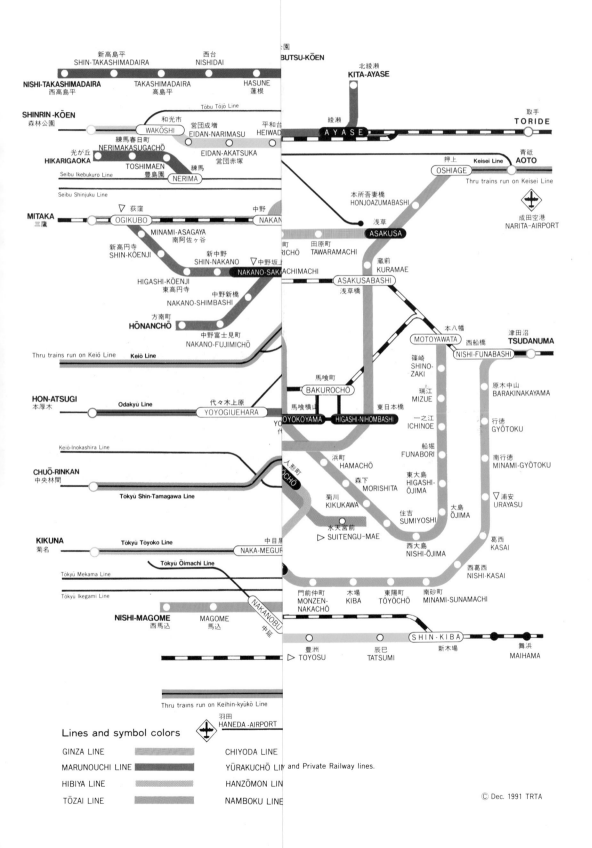

© Dec. 1991 TRTA

NOT ALL OF OUR IDEAS COME FROM THE LAB.

In the search for new and more effective medicines we discovered that it helps to get out of the lab once in a while.
Not only to stay in touch with the outside world, but because nature is a great source of inspiration.
Oceans, trees, bushes and even the soil itself provide invaluable research opportunities.
And all that knowledge goes into developing drugs such as our latest breakthrough,
a compound which controls cholesterol levels in the bloodstream
by striking a balance between the cholesterol you do need, and getting rid of what you don't.
It's the product of sixteen years of research and now it's ready for the world.
From biotechnology to gene research to the pursuit of a healthier world, Sankyo is working toward a better quality of life.

**PHARMACEUTICALS
FOR A WORLD OF PEOPLE.**

SANKYO CO., LTD.